TO ALL WHO HAVE FACED ADVERSITY, BOTH ON THE MAT AND IN LIFE. MAY YOUR DETERMINATION BE A DRIVING FORCE WITH EVERY CHALLENGE YOU ENCOUNTER.

DON'T CRY IN AMERICA

A Memoir of Unexpected Journeys, Family Love, and the Sport of Wrestling

ANTONIO RUSSO &
TONYA RUSSO HAMILTON

Published by Figs & Famiglia
Portland, Oregon

Cover design and typesetting by Bookery

ISBN Hardcover: 979-8-9924446-0-5
ISBN Paperback: 979-8-9924446-1-2
ISBN ebook: 979-8-9924446-2-9

Library of Congress Control Number: 2025904283
For more information, please visit: www.figsandfamiglia.com

CONTENTS

FOREWORD

By Dr. Ilaria Serra

Professor of Italian and Comparative Studies,
Florida Atlantic University

In my book *The Value of Worthless Lives: Writing Italian American Immigrant Autobiographies* (2010), I attempted to theorize the dual nature of autobiographies written by Italian immigrants of the past century, people who were not accustomed or taught to think of themselves as individuals. They were born in a country that emphasized close-knit, sometimes suffocating relationships, where those who stood out were destined to fail, much like oysters leaving the safety of their rock. In that world, *"la via vecchia"* (the old road) is always better than *"la via nuova"* (the new road). This immobile thinking prevailed in Italy, especially in the past century. Yet, these writers have become Americans: they left their homeland, have lived the life of the self-made man, and experienced new possibilities. They stood out, and they were rewarded for it in the land that honors those who risk, those who dare to take the road less traveled. The *earthquake* of migration shook the old wisdom. Antonio Russo is one of these immigrants whose life has become extraordinary, and his story is worth telling.

When Antonio Russo says that wrestling is "a team sport, yet an individual sport," he exemplifies this perfect balance between American individuality and the Italian spirit of community. He wrestled his way through life and his immigration. Not only literally, by becoming a competitive wrestler and a successful coach, but also metaphorically: fighting his way to find his place in the world, from the early skirmishes with his schoolmates to finally landing a coaching job (more than a job, a vocation). Russo embraces his individuality, fighting with fists and kicks, breaking his own shoulder. His desire for self-realization is spelled out: "'*Voglio vincere,*' I said. I want to win." Wrestling becomes his way of coping with a new existence as he explains: "The combative nature of wrestling fit me like a glove; I couldn't get enough. It was the first time my intensity had been met head-on. I could pour out my aggressions on the mat, pushing away all thoughts of missing my family, struggling with the language, and getting along in school."

On the other hand, Antonio never stops yearning for a community from the very moment he is sent to the United States, all alone, as a boy of ten—a trauma never completely healed ("I still don't understand it."). He tells us that his biggest dream was reuniting his family: he first rejoined his parents and siblings in New York and then convinced them to move to Oregon to live by his extended new family. "It was unbelievable, and I was overwhelmed over the purchase of our new home, only three streets down from Aunt Gladys and Uncle Tony. I had accomplished my goal. I would have the best of both worlds—my two families together in Portland, Oregon," he declares. Russo's biggest pride is his belonging to a town, a neighborhood, a group of friends who help each other. He values the generosity of his family: "They didn't think twice about it; my parents were always willing to help those in need." This sense of community is also what makes his mother find peace with her own move: "These new Italian friends helped my mother decide that it was okay for her to call Portland her new permanent home."

Autobiographies of ordinary people are tales of both sorrow and victory. Their hard-earned lesson is one of self-sufficiency and relentless hard work. They may not have glamorous careers, overflowing bank accounts, or palaces to boast about. Instead, they are people who made it by trusting in the simple, honest labor of their hands. Antonio's father "wanted to do something with his hands," and his mother often repeated, "If you work hard, good things will happen." One of the most powerful scenes in the book features this immigrant mother responding to the mockery of a passport officer who notices she cannot write. "Holding up both of her hands, my mother replied, 'Do you see these hands? These hands work hard! These hands can do anything!'" (They can even break a wooden spoon over her children's heads!)

Antonio's final reflections echo this philosophy and impart the humble wisdom of ordinary immigrants: "I've learned that, back when I was barefoot, working on our leased farmland and dirty from head to toe in my beloved countryside, or wracking my brain to learn something in school, my mother's words rang true: "You have to work hard. And if you do, good things will happen." Good things that filled many conversations with his daughter, and have now become the pages in this precious book.

CHAPTER ONE

Italy, 1940

Like most celebrated occasions in a large Italian family—weddings, holidays, the after-Mass Sunday meal—my arrival into this world on October 8, 1940, was nothing short of loud and uproarious. The gathering was complete with thick, hard-crusted bread, salad made from tomato and onion fresh from the earth, and my family's drink of choice, red wine.

Roccarainola, Italy, affectionately known as "Rocca," is a small, poverty-stricken town in the heart of the Campania region. It is also the place of my birth. Rocca is in the province of Naples—my home sits at Via Marco Taliento Provincia di Napoli, about twenty miles to the northeast of the city, and its citizens are proudly Old-World Neapolitans. My father's family, the Russos, were hardly able to contain their excitement about the arrival of their first grandchild—my grandfather especially, knowing that in the Italian tradition, if it were a boy, this would be his namesake. The Russos were reserved in personality and tall in stature, both atypical by southern Italian standards. My father, Aniello, was nearly six feet tall, and unless under the spell of his beloved red wine or relentlessly provoked, he was quite reserved.

Joining the Russos on the day of my birth were the Casorias, my mother's prodigious family. Teresa, my mother, had eleven siblings, and births were commonplace up and down the Casoria side. They were effervescent, joyful and loud, near brilliant in their ability to eat and talk simultaneously, and inordinately passionate. They could be conversing about anything, but it all sounded the same: like an argument.

The Casorias were compact and voluptuous in shape, and their trademark was their thick, dark, wavy hair. My mother's was especially striking with a one-inch albino strip that framed the right side of her face and set off the rest of her jet-black hair.

Stories abound of my multitude of bustling cousins running around our small *piazza* chasing one another, playing soccer, and stirring up dirt while the local midwife assisted in my debut. My father drank wine and nervously climbed up and down the steep staircase that lined the archaic mortar building that was our home.

Several times, he knocked on the door to check on the birth in progress, and each time the midwife called out, "*Il bambino non è arrivato ancora!*" to let him know I had not yet arrived. When she finally stepped outside and told my father he had a son, my father, his face as red as the wine he'd been drinking, raised both arms to the sky and announced to all in the courtyard, "*Mio figlio è arrivato!*" My son is here!

*A recent photo of the stairs my father climbed to check on my birth.
I was born behind the door at the top. Aside from a few minor
changes, they are essentially the same as they were in 1940.*

Being the firstborn son of my parents and the firstborn grandchild on the Russo side, I was named after my father's father, Antonio—from Sant'Antonio (Saint Anthony), the Catholic patron saint of miracles. This was a common name in our region of Italy, and our small town had an especially large collection of Antonios. Russo, my surname, is the southern Italian version of the name Rossi, which comes from the word *rosso*, meaning red.

I spent my earliest years living in the same home as my paternal grandparents, our piazza bursting with aunts, uncles, and their children. My mother returned to work nearly the day after I was born, handing me off to her sister Lucia for feedings.

Aunt Lucia added me to her brood while my mother and father worked during the days, bringing in what little income they could—my father farming the fields or delivering goods, my mother a laborer in a cherry cannery, where, as the story goes, she begged for employment at the age of ten.

My grandparents, especially Grandma Nappi-Russo, played a primary role in the early years of my upbringing. Grandma Nappi, olive-skinned and tiny, without an ounce of fat, had endless energy and for her size was amazingly strong. I used to trek into the hills by her side to help her gather hazelnut and olive tree limbs for the oven and fireplace. When she picked up the branches, I could see the muscle definition in her biceps and forearms, and her strength astounded me as she carried the branches tied into bundles on top of her head.

I was enamored with my Grandma Nappi, and it was a special treat for me to stay up late in the evening and sit by her side in front of the fire, roasting chestnuts and hazelnuts. Her head was always wrapped with a vibrant scarf; the glow of the fire set off her white hair along its edge and highlighted the deep lines set like sideways smiles on each side of her tanned face. When I wasn't hanging on Grandma Nappi's skirt, I spent most of my time playing and running barefoot around our piazza and in the countryside with my cousins.

Years later, I realized I had arrived in this world during the deadliest conflict in human history, World War II, and right in the backyard of Naples, the most heavily bombed Italian city in those years. Although I was young, the war left deep impressions on my psyche.

During the quiet times, when the air raids had mostly ended, we walked to and from our leased farmland, passing American soldiers who had set up posts at the local silos. They handed chocolate bars to my cousins and me, yelling out, "*Ciao ragazzi! La mia famiglia viene da Napoli.*" Their families had come from Naples, and now they were fighting in the war as American soldiers. We could not get enough of that chocolate, all of us laughing and running around, loving the attention and the delectable treat.

The bomb-tattered hillsides full of scrap metal and shrapnel piqued our curiosity; fragmented weapons were unearthed treasures just waiting to be found. There was a large culvert used to carry rainwater to the orchards that went under the street and up into the hills surrounding our neighborhood. One day, my friend Michele and I spent hours exploring and scavenger-hunting inside the culvert. Our parents had warned us that this wasn't safe by telling us stories about children who had been killed or maimed by leftover grenades that had detonated unexpectedly. Our curiosity far outweighed our fear and common sense, though, and before we knew it, our feet were scraped up from the metal fragments lying about. After one misstep on a jagged piece of metal, I had a deep slice on the inside of my left foot from my heel up to my ankle. I bled profusely and paid twice for my foolery that day: once while walking home, each step delivering excruciating pain, and then later, receiving a tetanus shot and stitches.

During the dark times, my family ran for our lives, Grandma Nappi dragging me along. *"Fa presto!"* she'd yell, squeezing my hand so tight it hurt. The bombers hummed loudly overhead, and the sight of hundreds of them cast like black shadows against the sky terrified me. My racing heart nearly pounded out of my chest as we ran for cover, my grandfather holding the large wooden door open as we climbed deep into the dank earth, down a winding staircase into our shared wine cellar below.

I had been down there before when Grandma Nappi towed me along to fill the family wine jugs. This fascinating and mysterious place under the earth, *sottoterra*, scared but also intrigued me. The wine barrels, enormously round and stacked on their sides halfway to the ceiling, towered over Grandma Nappi's tiny frame, and the potent aroma of red wine was dizzying.

During the bombings, with my entire family gathered in the cellar, I would crouch down, close my eyes, and cover my ears. My own heartbeat pounded through anyway, except when the deafening explosions came, the noise freely piercing my improvised attempt to shut it out.

Time passed in this fashion for months on end, and the jubilant days that finally marked the end of the war became a grand celebration with crowds gathering in the streets chanting and singing, *"Mussolini è morto, Mussolini è morto!"* Mussolini is dead!

Casoria–Russo Family circa 1942. I'm the smallest one in front, my shoulders being held by Grandma Nappi.

CHAPTER TWO

Horse And Cart

The war was over, I was growing up, and I started spending considerable time alone, unencumbered and free, on the few acres of farmland leased by my family. I had specified duties, and one of them was to tend to the animals, especially our hens, from which I would occasionally crack a raw egg directly into my mouth and let it slide down my throat to fill my stomach when I was hungry. We also had delivery horses, an occasional cow, and a couple of donkeys.

Another of my chores was making sure the crops were watered. We irrigated our fields with well water, so I had to harness one of our donkeys to a pole that rotated in a circle to draw the water from the well into the aqueducts. As the water flowed to our crops, I loved to race the stream down the small aqueduct, running as fast as I could and using a large hoe to turn the water down each row.

Among our crops were rotund, deep red tomatoes that weighed nearly a pound each and shiny purple eggplants, full and ready to split at the slightest touch of a knife. Our corn, potatoes, onions, zucchini, and peppers were favorites of the merchants; all disappeared quickly at market. Cantaloupe, watermelon, and fig, cherry, and plum trees were also no strangers to our land. The grapes we grew didn't go to market; instead, our small community vineyard provided just enough for the family to make our precious red wine.

Picking the plump clusters of crimson grapes during the fall harvest was a favorite time of year for everyone. The children were most excited for the crush, the grapes bursting beneath our stomping feet in the huge vat. As the adults siphoned the juice into barrels for fermentation, we dipped our small tin cups in and drank the sweet nectar straight from the barrel, the whole lot of us purple from head to toe.

Those boisterous times with family contrasted sharply with the times I was in the fields alone. There, I was easily distracted from my chores, often deciding to climb a tree to check out an interesting bird or chase a rabbit down alongside the hedgerows. Limits did not exist for me. If I had my mind set on something, I did it. My hardheadedness and thirst for adventure had earned me a reputation with the adults, that of being impulsive and a risk-taker. As much as I wanted the adults in my life to be pleased with me, I had a nearly uncontrollable yearning to live life to the fullest every day, running and playing hard and exploring my land. This became the crux from which most of my decisions were made.

My mother protested whenever I wanted to accompany my father on his routes to deliver our produce to the markets and convents, as she always protested anything that was, in her mind, frivolous or a possible danger to her children. She thought I was better left to work in the fields and tend the farm. But when I was around seven years old, I was finally big enough to be of help, and my father wanted me with him, especially on one particular trip. After his deliveries, my father would be continuing on to a festa to honor the Holy Mother, and it was important to him that I be a part of this religious celebration. A couple of my uncles would be coming along to help as well, and my dad had promised to take anyone from our piazza who wanted to make the holy journey.

Uncle Aniello driving one of our farm carts on the streets of Cicciano.

After helping load the wagon with our goods, my mother grabbed my face and kissed me goodbye. She glared at my father, who was just beginning to hoist himself into the driver's seat, and her shrill voice called sharply, long and drawn out, "Anieeeeeeeel!" My mother always yelled, and she always shortened my father's name from Aniello to Aniel.

"*Stai attento con lui!*" she spat, warning my father to be careful with me.

"*Non ti preoccupare!*" he yelled back sharply and then mumbled under his breath about how all my mother did was worry.

"*Madonna mia!*" my mother sang out as she walked away.

The wagon was full of people and goods: our produce and grain and my aunts and uncles. As we began our deliveries, I enjoyed our stops at the markets and the jerky back-and-forth rhythm of the wagon. At one stop, my father accepted some provolone cheese and olive oil in exchange for our produce. He pulled out a small, sharp blade from its home in his breast pocket and cut me a hunk of the dry, salty cheese. It was a special treat, and I savored every bite as we bounced along—until we arrived at the convent.

I froze when the nuns in their long black robes and covered heads came to greet my father. Sitting upright, looking straight ahead, and staying as still as possible, I thought, *Se non mi muovo, non mi vedono.* If I don't move, they can't see me.

I tried as hard as possible to avoid eye contact, as I was sure their mystic nun powers could bore through my skull and into my brain to view all of my sins and devilish antics—times like when my friend Michele and I were chasing birds up and down the gravel road near our piazza. We were trying to sneak up on the shiny black creatures and catch them by their tail feathers. Neither of us had quick enough feet or hands, though. I don't know what made me do it, but in a flash, I reached down, grabbed a rock, and threw it fast and hard at one of the large blackbirds. To my thrill and horror, it struck the bird dead, hitting him in the back of the skull right at the nape of his neck.

"*L'hai ucciso!*" my friend Michele screeched. You killed him! I was shocked and, although impressed with my marksmanship, was immediately flooded with feelings of guilt. I sprinted to the dead bird and stared down at him in awe. I picked him up and ran home to my mother and father, confident that my father, an excellent hunter himself, would be impressed. I ran into our courtyard where my mother and aunts were baking bread in the outdoor brick oven.

"*Mamma, ho ucciso un uccello!*" I blurted, out of breath, holding the bird up for them to see. I killed a bird! The ladies laughed at me, finding my excitement over the bird amusing. I then showed my father, and he was proud of my conquest, but I was immediately conflicted when I heard him yell over his shoulder, "*Teresa, metti l'uccello nella salsa!*" He wanted my mother to add it to our sauce for dinner.

I was not going to have it. I cried to my father, "*Io non mangio quel uccello!*" I will not eat that bird! At least, I did not intend to. I chewed slowly that evening, knowing deep down that each chunky bite was my unsuspecting, helpless victim.

I stayed still in the wagon, my stomach churning as memories of wrongdoing continued to rise to the surface for the viewing pleasure of the nuns.

There was also the time I had been tending to my chores by myself out on the farm, picking suckers from the bottom of the tomato plants. I was hot and thirsty, not to mention famished, having been out there since sunup. Our neighbor's watermelon patch in the next field over had been teasing me all day long with rows of perfectly round green melons filled with what I knew to be pure, sweet, thirst-quenching satisfaction. I pushed the thought to the back of my mind, knowing it wouldn't be right to steal a melon, but my stomach got the best of me, and I finally broke, deciding to shirk my duties and help myself to one of my favorite delectable treats. I cut plugs into three large melons only to find they were pink and not quite ripe enough. I replaced the plugs, hoping they would go unnoticed.

On the fourth one, I cut into juicy, sweet red flesh and ate to my heart's content. I finished off the entire melon, ran back to my father's cornfield to bury the rinds, and, before I knew it, my stomach had bloated and swelled, hard and round like the melon I had just devoured. Hunched over, I headed for our *il pagliaro*—a small barn-like structure made out of sticks, straw, and cornstalks used for shelter on the farm—holding my belly with sticky hands as the pain increased. When I arrived, if my swollen belly wasn't enough to incriminate me, the fact that I had tried to bury the evidence between the rows in my father's cornfield sealed my fate. My father was angry, but the punishment from my gut was worse than anything I would incur from him.

As my father finished the nuns' delivery, I began getting drowsy, more than ready to be free from their mind-lock. I sighed in relief when my father and uncles came back to the cart and we continued on our way. Although I was leaving the nuns behind for now, I knew I would see them again on Sunday. *Farò il bravo fino a domenica,* I promised myself. I will be good until Sunday.

We continued from the convent to the grotto where we would spend the day paying tribute to the Holy Mother, and I enjoyed the outdoor cathedral, the array of delicious foods, and the masses of people. We ate and celebrated all day, my belly was full, and the adults were rejoicing and excessively chatty. As the sun began to set, we loaded ourselves back into the wagon and headed for home.

The sounds of the horses' hooves and the wagon rolling along took on a numbing vibration, and at some point everyone got out of the wagon to stretch and eat, but I stayed put because I was too tired to move. The horses had their heads down, grazing on some grass in front of them, and they decided to suddenly lurch forward to a new patch of grass. As they did, I was thrown out of the wagon and pinned between the wheel and the side of the cart as it continued to move.

Generally, my father was a quiet man of few words in a family of verbose people, but as I faded in and out, I can still hear him threatening to kill anyone and everyone around if I lost my life. *"Mio Dio! Ucciderò tutti se muore mio figlio!"* he shouted and then covered me with his shirt, picked me up, and carried me limp in his arms back into the wagon.

Waking again to my screaming mother, it was hard to breathe, and my head hurt; I could tell it had been cut open across the back, and I knew I was bathed in my own blood. My mother had wrapped my wounds in dry towels and laid me on the sleeping cot I shared with my brother.

"Perché hai portato mio figlio?" Why did you take my son, I heard her scream as I drifted away again. She kept asking my father why he had taken me, and I felt sorry for him. It wasn't his

fault; it was mine. I was the one who had fallen asleep.

The next time I woke, the sun was beaming in through the dirty window across the room. Morning. Dust particles floated through the air above my head, and then, changing my line of vision, something obstructed my view. I strained to gain focus, and as my eyes adjusted, I realized my little brother's nose was almost touching mine. He was staring intently into my eyes with a questioning look. I concentrated on his curly black hair and brooding eyes.

Too young to understand, he asked, "*Sei vivo?*" Are you alive? "*La mamma prega per la tua vita,*" he continued, telling me that my mother had been praying to God for my life.

"*Sono vivo,*" I answered. I am alive, I will make it, I reassured him, realizing that it hurt to talk and even to breathe for that matter.

*My sister Brigida (left) and brother Pellegrino (right)
in Italy with Grandma Carolina Casoria.*

My chest felt heavy, as if a bag of rocks were set on it. Hearing my voice, my mother ran over to me in her hysterical way and knelt down, leaning over the cot. She stroked my hair back and looked into my eyes. I would have turned my head had I been physically able. Then came the yelling again, her voice filled with pity, "*Madonna mia! Grazie a Dio!*"

Across the room, a doctor stood next to my father. I overheard him say he had stitched up the back of my head, the left side of my rib cage, and my lower back.

"*Col tempo si guarisce,*" he told my father. I'd heal over time. Then he reminded him to keep my wounds clean to prevent infection and added that scarring was inevitable. "*Un giorno può mostrare le cicatrici ai figli,*" he muttered, shaking his head. I would have scars to show my children.

My body tensed when the doctor started walking in my direction. Looking down at my mangled body he asked, "*Come ti senti?*" He gave me no time to answer how I felt and began touching the dressing around my chest. "*Tutto andrà bene,*" he told me. Everything will be fine.

Again, my mother's disturbing screams started up. "*Figlio mio, figlio mio!*" The doctor walked toward my mother, and patting her on the shoulder to reassure her again, he repeated, "*Va bene, va bene. È fortunato, ma tutto andrà bene.*" I was lucky to be alive, but I would be fine.

CHAPTER THREE

The Departure

With the war and now my near-death experience of being thrown from the cart behind me, I was poised to gear up for yet another challenge. Although at the time I didn't comprehend what was happening, at the ripe age of ten, I was being prepared to leave this place I knew and loved, for another country—the United States of America.

My mother often told me how much better everything was in America. We could have so much more than we have here in Italy, she'd say. There were jobs for everyone, abundant food, and we could make money and live an easier life—not the backbreaking work we were accustomed to on our small bit of leased land.

She told us that in America, "*gli alberi d'oro*" lined the streets. Trees that bloomed with gold.

In Italy, I understood that our meals were simple: immense loaves of hard-crusted bread, boiled potatoes with olive oil, or rustic homemade *pasta fagiole*, pasta and beans. Our resources were utilized to the fullest. After the heavy rains, my brother and I were sent out to hunt snails, which my mother would boil, salt, pepper, and chop into small chunks. Then, like most everything, they would be pan-fried in hot oil and smothered in steaming tomato sauce.

While our crops were mostly sold for money, we sometimes had leftovers to add variety to our meals, and although we didn't starve, when it came to food, abundance was not something we knew. Still, harvesting the fresh vegetables and fruits from our land was gratifying, even though most of our stunning produce didn't make it onto our own table. The freedom of the hills and the feeling of dirt between my toes was truly a way of life that fit me well.

The tantalizing aroma that enveloped our piazza from the outdoor brick oven when my mother and aunts baked bread could lure me in from play, and when times were good, my mother would splurge, making a thick *focaccia* bread, sometimes with tomato sauce, anchovies, and mushrooms, or one of my favorites, topped with olive oil and onion.

Even with the simplicity of our everyday meals, I could always count on the holidays, Christmas and Easter, to come alive with my favorite foods. My parents and grandparents would go all out during the holidays, and my memories are vivid. Crunchy biscotti and fruit-filled panettone were my favorite baked sweets, and if my grandfather was able to raise a pig that year, we also enjoyed an array of salamis and sausages.

As fond as I was of eating chewy, peppered salamis, *soppressata* (my family's specialty), and fennel-spiced, fat-filled sausages, the ritual of the slaughter was gruesome. The family gathered in the piazza of Grandpa Giuseppe's home in Cicciano, a small neighboring town of Rocca, and my dad and uncles brought the farm-fattened pig to the middle of the square to meet its fate. As the rest of the family set the stage for the work that lay ahead, I averted my eyes, but I could hear the scuffle, the scrambling and squealing. I knew it was over when the bedlam came to an abrupt halt, and an eerie silence filled the air. I watched as the pig's lifeless body was carried to rest on a table in the basement of Grandpa Giuseppe's home.

Povero maiale morto. Poor dead pig. The thought ran through my head, and I couldn't help but feel sorry for the enormous animal. Then, as if he could sense my anguish, Grandpa Giuseppe would shout out, *"Bella! Che bella salsiccia!"* Beautiful sausage! He couldn't wait to get started. The family gathered around, and like lightning, knives began flying, carving. All in attendance were assigned a task, and everyone was awarded a portion of the pig.

Cutting, scraping, and separating all sections of the animal was the first order of business—not one ounce was wasted. Even the blood was drained into canisters for later use. My job was to cut large chunks of meat and fat into smaller pieces for grinding, which we stuffed into their appropriately sized intestine casings after the mixture was seasoned with salt and whole black peppercorns for salami and fennel seeds for sausage. Large intestines held salami, and small intestines were for sausage. The giant slabs of meat from either side of the pig's tail were salted and then hung to air dry for prosciutto, and the skin was cleaned and cut into strips. With the skin, my mother made one of my favorite dishes, *braciole*.

"*Fai il braciole quest'anno?*" I begged my mother every year. She'd laugh and sing out "*Certo!*" She knew I loved her braciole, made with a thin strip of the pig's skin or a slivered steak topped with garlic, breadcrumbs, *Parmigiano* cheese, and sometimes sliced prosciutto, then rolled up and tied around the middle to hold it together. My mother would first sear it in spitting-hot olive oil, then simmer it for what seemed like all day in a pot of tomato sauce. At dinnertime, the meat fell apart moist and tender, the combination of flavors undeniably perfect.

Even though as a child I enjoyed our simple way of life, I knew my mother wanted more for us than being at the mercy of the rich, miserly landowners, and she wanted a better home than our ancient apartment building, falling apart at the seams and cramped with family. I tried to understand my mother's words; I knew there were wealthy Italians living in homes with hot running water where you could bathe inside and relieve yourself in private without the nuisance of flies buzzing around your head and landing on your face and in your ears.

"*In Italia, i ricchi sono sempre più ricchi e i poveri sono sempre più poveri.*" In Italy, the rich are always richer and the poor are always poorer. I heard it over and over, but even so, I was happy.

The alluring countryside beckoned me as I set off on foot toward school, and more often than not, I found a reason to escape my teachers for the day. Untamed and carefree, I couldn't get enough of playing hard with my cousins and friends, rocks and sticks our toys, the gravel roads our soccer fields, transforming to fit whatever game we conjured up that day. I also never tired of the thrill and mystery of the outings with my father and grandfather, whether we were delivering produce, hunting game, or collecting our favorite wild mushrooms. I would stop at nothing to tag along and be at my grandfather's heels exploring the countryside.

I guess I was the chosen one, being the eldest of my siblings— lucky, so to speak, having dual Italian and American citizenship. My citizenship had been passed on to me through my mother. My maternal grandparents had been migrant workers in America, traveling by ship from Naples, Italy, in the early 1900s for a stint of work in Scranton, Pennsylvania.

There, my mother was born and her name put on a U.S. birth certificate, making her a dual Italian and American citizen. My mother was a young child when work ran out and her family returned to Naples. Again, luck played a role: I was born just three months before U.S. citizenship laws drastically changed. Children born between May 24, 1934, and January 13, 1941, could acquire the citizenship of either parent who was an American citizen, provided that parent had resided in the United States for any period of time.

On January 14, 1941, the law was changed and required that the parent passing on citizenship had to have lived in the United States for ten years prior to their child's birth; this is why my siblings would be Italian citizens only. My mother had not lived the requisite number of years in America to pass on citizenship to them. At that time, a person born between 1934 and 1941 could lose their American citizenship if they did not reside in the United

States for five years prior to their eighteenth birthday or take an oath of allegiance to the country at least six months before their twenty-first birthday. The laws on this have since changed, but as far as my parents were concerned, to secure my U.S. citizenship, they knew that they had to get me to America soon.

The day we went to Naples, the first time I had ever been into the heart of the city, was a slap in my face. I knew something was brewing. My father led the way, and my mother jerked my arm through masses of people as we made our way to the American Consulate. The city was loud and fast-paced—erratic. We walked through the front door of a huge stone building, and I was measured from head to toe and then blinded by the large bulb of a camera as I posed in a chair for a picture.

"*Metti la firma,*" the man behind the counter snapped impatiently. As I scrawled my name in the best unschooled handwriting I could muster, I noticed there were many words that I could not read. I would not know until years later that my passport gave me a rather bare description:

Height: 4 feet, 3 inches

Hair: Light brown

Eyes: Hazel

Distinguishing marks: None

The consulate general reaffirmed to my parents that if I didn't claim my American citizenship five years prior to my eighteenth birthday, I would lose it. I didn't know I was an American citizen, and I had no idea what all of this meant, but that day I learned that for my family and our future, I needed to move to the United States before I turned thirteen. My being nearly eleven at the time must have caused my mother to feel a sense of urgency; I'm sure it played a role in her ability to convince my father that it would be okay to send me by myself to America. To this day, I will never fully understand why I was sent alone.

My father never spoke of it, but I could sense his reservations leading up to my journey. It hadn't become real for him until the day I left. Understanding this vague idea of a better life was beyond my ten-year-old comprehension, and I had no desire to leave my home and my family. The day before I was to leave, my parents took me to visit my grandparents to say goodbye— Grandma Carolina and Grandpa Giuseppe Casoria, my mother's parents in Cicciano, and Grandma Nappi-Russo, my father's mother in Rocca. Grandma Nappi kissed me repeatedly. "*Un bacione dal Nonno*," she told me—a kiss from your grandfather. Grandpa Russo, the man for whom I was named, had been killed a few years earlier, and memories of him flashed through my head. I forced the picture of the last time I saw him out of my brain, the memory too painful. *Ci pensero piu tardi*, I promised myself. I will remember him later.

Little did I know this would be the last time I would see any of my grandparents.

My mother had dressed me in a man's collared shirt, a suit jacket, and a pair of men's slacks that she had cut off and sewn up at the hem. The pants were so big they hung off of my bony frame. They would have fallen straight to the ground had my father not cut extra notches in one of his belts to hold them up.

It was important to my mother that I look presentable for this significant occasion, and shoes were crucial, as they seemed to present themselves only for monumental occasions in my life: my grandfather's funeral, my First Holy Communion, and now again for the journey that would change my fate forever.

I'm not sure how well I wore that jacket or how pungent I must have smelled, my pockets stuffed with salami and provolone cheese. My mother thought having some of my favorite foods with me might help to calm my nerves. She wanted me to have something special on my trip. She also filled my suitcase with the same foods and instructed me to give those items as a gift to the family members who would be taking care of me in America.

On August 7, 1951, the air was hot, and the sun shone on the hills so unrelentingly, it burned to take a deep breath. Feeling awkward and uncomfortable in my oversized clothes, I boarded a bus that would take my family and me to the Bay of Naples. Angelo, an older gentleman who was an acquaintance of my parents, would be making the journey also. My parents had asked him to keep an eye out for me on the ship, and he promised them he would.

The ship I would be taking was an American ship—the SS *Independence*. My parents told me I would arrive in the United States, and my family would be there to take care of me. My mom's brother Michele was now "Michael" in America, and he would be the one to greet me in New York. Besides my Uncle Mike, I had no idea who the other people might be; I took my mom's word that they were family.

When we arrived at the Bay of Naples, there was a breeze

in the air, albeit a warm one, which gave some reprieve to the heat. I could taste the moist, salty air. We walked hurriedly to the docks together, not talking about the imminent event about to unfold. The SS *Independence* towered over the bay. As we got closer, it grew even bigger, and I became smaller than my already meager height of four foot three. The enormity of the ship was breathtaking; I could barely see the top. The hull of the ship was black with little white squares—windows—lined in rows along the edge. A red stripe that bordered the black hull disappeared as the ocean waves lapped the sides.

Realizing it was time to board, my parents, tears streaming, grabbed my face and began kissing me on both cheeks. "*Arrivederci, figlio mio,*" they kept saying over and over again. Good-bye, my son. My mother added some comforting words about the rest of the family following soon, and my father, with stilted speech, spoke of being brave through a painstaking look of uncertainty. Watching the toughest man I knew, tall and handsome, get choked up was unbearable. I looked up at my father and soaked in his features—thick light-brown hair set high above his head as if he were wearing a hat, deep-set hazel eyes, and chiseled face. I could not comprehend the word *soon.*

When would I see them again, and what did that mean?

My brother and sister kissed me too; my sister, six years younger and unaware of the significance of the moment, grabbed my arm and hung from it, almost dislocating my shoulder. My father, prying her off me, picked her up, and she laid her head on his chest and stared through me with hollow eyes.

Angelo, my parents' "friend," motioned his head at me and yelled, "*Muoviti, vieni, vieni!*" They hurried me along and nudged me toward Angelo as we entered a never-ending stream of people. My brother yelled, *"Arrivederci, Tino,"* one last time, and then my mother's shrill voice called out, *"Figlio mio, figlio mio! Non aver paura!"* Don't be afraid, my son! She continued screaming as we walked up the long, steep ramp to the deck of the ship.

Once at the top, I saw Mount Vesuvius looming with its plumes of smoke in the background, and looking down at my doll-sized family below, white scarves waving, it hit me: I could not do this. Nothing my mother had said to me in the months prior had adequately prepared me to leave the only family and country I had ever known. I was heartsick and in a state of shock. This was not a good idea, and I was not going to go.

I cried and screamed as hard and loud as I could at them below, *"Mamma, no!"* I reached toward them with my arms, but it was too late. There was nowhere to run in the masses of people and no way to get back down. Angelo, knowing what I was thinking, held on to me so I could not move. I would never have made it back down anyway. I would see Angelo only one more time in my seven nights and eight days on the SS *Independence*. He was not a man of his word. He did nothing more than show me where my bunk was. That ended his commitment to my parents that he would keep an eye out for me.

If there was one thing I learned from my sporadic Catholic schooling and weekly Sunday Mass, it was the definition of Hell: a fiery pit in the realm of the Devil where the damned suffer everlasting misery. Alone at the age of ten aboard the SS *Independence*, three floors below deck, disoriented, dehydrated, and lying in a pool of my own vomit, I was there. My mind was reeling. *Che cosa ho fatto per meritarmi questo?* What had I done to deserve this? I had one goal only—to survive.

I mostly stayed face down on my bunk, my head turned to the side, nausea overtaking my body in waves with the movement of the ship. I drifted in and out of delirious sleep, and at some point, day and night no longer had definitive boundaries.

Occasionally, I tried to leave the room and make my way up on deck, but the washing motion of the ship was sickening, and dry heaves possessed my body every time the smell of American food wafted from the dining hall. At times I forced myself to drink small amounts of water from a metal water fountain in the hall, and I nibbled now and again on the salami and cheese stashed in my jacket, more for comfort than for sustenance. Each day felt like twenty, the loneliness and pain showing no mercy.

Then one day, I awoke in a start from a particularly vivid dream, beads of sweat covering my face and chest. I was a child of three holding Grandma Nappi's hand, running in the dark through the countryside around my home. We were headed toward the hills trying to escape the bombing that was hitting Naples and the surrounding areas. The sky was full of enormous steel birds, and I could see the horizon light up in the distance and hear explosions so loud my ears were ringing.

It took me a moment to shake it off and remember my new nautical surroundings.

Something felt different. There was an excitement and hurriedness in the air. The ship no longer swayed with the waves, and a man's voice boomed over a loudspeaker, although I couldn't understand a word. People were grabbing belongings and moving en masse upward toward the deck. Instinct told me to join them.

When I reached the deck, there was a beautiful, bright sky which stung my eyes after so many days below, and I had to squint to see at all. Then I saw it, a sight that would burn itself forever into my memory.

Grandpa Giuseppe had told me about Lady Liberty.

"Quando vedi la statua di La Donna, stai in America."

When you see The Statue of The Lady, you will be in America.

On August 15, 1951, at the age of ten, I had arrived.

My passport, 1951

CHAPTER FOUR

Brooklyn

In a sea of people, I spotted my Uncle Mike immediately; he looked exactly as I had remembered. His olive complexion and thin build set him apart from the rest of the Casorias. His black hair was slicked back, and his straight Roman nose, his most distinctive feature, was prominent on his face. I instantly flashed back to Italy, playing with my cousin Carolina, his daughter, during the holidays. He jolted me back to present day by grabbing my face and kissing me on each cheek. My uncle held my face for a moment and stared hard at me.

"*Antonio! Nipotino! Figlio di mia sorella! Il viaggio è stato difficile.*" Calling me his nephew, the son of his sister, he guessed correctly that my trip had been difficult. Then he squeezed my shoulders in reassurance and said, "*Tutto a posto.*" Everything's fine now.

Uncle Mike decided straightaway that I needed to see a doctor. I sat on a steel table covered in a white sheet as the doctor poked and prodded me and then spoke to my uncle in English. To my surprise, my uncle replied in this foreign language. I was shocked and confused during the conversation I was not privy to. On our way out, Uncle Mike assured me that the doctor had said I was physically strong but that I needed to eat and drink.

"Dice che sei forte ma devi mangiare, bere," he said.

My head spun as the day continued, and we headed to my mother's sister's place.

As I was greeted by Aunt Marie, whom I'd never met, I was struck and somewhat comforted by how much she looked like my own mother. She was short and round with dark eyes and the trademark Casoria hair. She was missing my mother's albino strip, but her familiarity was calming.

I was introduced to three new cousins: Connie, the eldest; Carmine, the middle boy; and baby Caroline. Connie looked to be about my age, and she and Carmine were excited to meet me. They were talking loud and fast.

"Possiamo mangiare i salumi e il formaggio?" Connie asked, wanting to know if they could eat the salami and cheese I had brought.

"Sì, sono per voi," I said, telling her I had brought the food for them.

As daylight faded, Uncle Mike decided it was time for us to leave. Driving to his apartment, he told me that I would meet his lady friend, Eleanor. I was confused by this. I knew Uncle Mike had a wife and daughter in Italy, but I figured it was better not to ask any questions.

Eleanor turned and looked straight over my head at Uncle Mike as we walked in the front door of his apartment. She was standing over the sink in tall, pointy shoes, with the water running, her eyes heavily lined in black and her lips a crimson red. She smiled at my uncle as she walked toward us, tall and shapely, her wavy dark-brown hair pinned up in back. Completely exhausted, I didn't move as Eleanor kissed Uncle Mike.

"How are you?" she asked, taking my suitcase, which had been emptied of the salami and cheese, and placing it on the floor at the bottom of a hallway closet. I looked to my uncle for translation. "*Come stai?*" he explained.

"*Bene.*" Good, I lied, looking away from her face.

Uncle Mike with Eleanor (right) and his daughter Carolina (left).

My uncle lit a cigarette and then pointed to an old upholstered sofa in the living area, which is where he said I'd be sleeping. I took off my jacket and shoes but left my pants and shirt on when I lay down. The only clothes I had were the clothes on my back, and they connected me to home. I wasn't ready to let go of them just yet. Shaking his head, my uncle threw a blanket over the top of me, sending a waft of stale cigarette smoke up from the cushions. It turned my stomach, and I wondered how I was going to sleep at all that night, but being exhausted and on solid ground masked the smell, and it ended up being one of the best nights of sleep I'd ever had.

In the morning, I woke up to my uncle and Eleanor throwing words back and forth at one another in English. I was used to yelling, as this was the instinctive speech cadence for most of the adults in my family, but what I was hearing now was unnatural. Even though I couldn't understand their language, I knew it was hateful. I was afraid to get up from the sofa, so I stayed still until Uncle Mike came flying into the room flustered and tucking in his shirt, a cigarette hanging out of his mouth.

"*Eleanor ti porterà al negozio per comprare i vestiti nuovi,*" he said, informing me that Eleanor would be taking me shopping for new clothes. He went into the kitchen and put on a pot of coffee. I followed and thought about Eleanor.

She seemed nice enough, but I knew she was not family, and I was heartsick for my mom, dad, brother, and sister. At this point, America was far from being all the wonders that my mother had promised, and I wanted nothing to do with shopping for new clothes with Eleanor.

She did take me shopping and bought me new trousers, shirts, and undergarments. They were hot and itchy, but I knew I should

— 34 —

be grateful. I mustered up the energy to thank her.

"*Grazie*," I forced out. Eleanor mumbled something back at me in English that I couldn't decipher. I was not used to getting new clothes, and I knew it was a big deal, but it meant nothing to me. If I no longer had a family, what was the point? Feeling the walls closing in on me like demons as I realized I no longer had the freedom to run or trees to climb, I zeroed in on just trying to make it through one minute at a time.

My Uncle Mike was a caring man, and he had every intention of fulfilling his promise to my parents, but my days with Uncle Mike and Eleanor were numbered. Volatile and unlike anything I had experienced with my family in Italy, my living situation frightened me, and I learned to stay out of the way and do as I was told.

I couldn't fully understand their arguments, but I knew Eleanor was angry. I'm sure she had an inkling that my uncle was already married, had a wife in Italy, and had no intention of marrying her. I was starting to think some of their arguments were about me and the stress I had brought into their lives. Feeling dejected yet relieved at the same time, I was soon taking my suitcase from Eleanor's hand, and Uncle Mike was leading me out to his car.

Within the hour, I was opening my suitcase again at Aunt Marie's apartment. This time, instead of salami and cheese, I was unpacking new clothes. Connie and Carmine were excited to have me back, and I was happy that at least there were children here. After unpacking, I went to find my aunt, who was washing dishes.

"*Quando vedrò la Mamma?*" I yelled toward her back over the running water. I wanted to know when I was going to see my mother.

"*Ancora no,*" she said without turning around. Not yet. "*Vai a giocare,*" she added, turning for a second and waving me away with her hand. Go play.

Homesick and unwilling to give up on memories and live in the present, I traded one volatile situation for another. My Aunt Marie's husband, Antonio, was out of work, and his main hobbies at the time were drinking, sitting around the table with a couple of his buddies playing Scopa (an Italian card game I knew from home), and sleeping with his mouth wide open in his easy chair. For as much wine that flowed through my family's veins in Italy, the abuse of alcohol was something I'd never seen. Aunt Marie, on the other hand, worked herself into the ground cooking, cleaning, and leaving every day to bring in an income, in addition to taking care of her three young children. Adding me to the mix was too much, and very shortly, I found myself with suitcase in hand again.

My third destination was living with my dad's cousin Pasquale Mozzariello and his family. Pasquale's father, Pellegrino, owned a restaurant and bar in Brooklyn, and the majority of my time was spent in Pellegrino's kitchen washing dishes.

The sink was on the back wall of a long, narrow kitchen, and there I stood in my white apron, on a step stool, scrubbing away at food-encrusted plates. Pasquale often warned me, "*Se viene qualcuno, nasconderti!*" I was instructed to hide if anyone came in, as he didn't want anyone of importance to see me doing dishes. He was probably worried that I was too young to be put to work.

We ate our meals at a table they had set up in a room off the kitchen. There I tasted my first beer, offered by the adults during a meal. At the first bitter taste, I sprayed it all over the table.

Sporting a bow tie and my new clothes from Eleanor, I'm in the kitchen of the Mozzariellos' restaurant.

Everyone laughed, except for Pellegrino's wife, Concetta.

"*Guarda cosa hai fatto*," she hissed, pointing to the beer-doused food on the table. Look what you've done. I glared at her angry face. *La prossima volta, ti la sputo in faccia—con piacere*, I thought. Next time, I'll spit the beer in your face—with pleasure. My mind could see it clearly as I stared into her beady dark eyes.

Pasquale's wife Maddalena was overwhelmed with caring for their two sons, Vincenzo and Michele. Michele was bound to a wheelchair, and it took enormous effort to care for him. Although they tried, with a handicapped child in a small, cramped apartment, it was nearly impossible for them to accommodate me. Pasquale was a hard worker and highly committed to his sons, but I was mostly invisible there. Although my extended family in America meant well, they were all struggling to keep their own heads above water. I was packing again.

At my fourth and final attempt for a home with my family in New York, I ended up with a woman named Lucia DeFrancisco.

When I arrived at her apartment, Lucia came toward me wearing the required attire for most of the Italian women in my family: a knee-length dress with knee-high stockings that always looked to be cutting off the circulation. She had rounded features but was not quite as rotund as my own mother; her black hair flew away from her head in curls on the sides, and the rest was pinned up into a bun. She wore thick glasses, and her friendly smile showed off a large gap between her two front teeth.

"*Benvenuto, Antonio!*" she said, welcoming me into her home.

My mother's sister Lucia was married to a man named Felice D'Avanzo. Lucia DeFrancisco was Felice's sister, which meant she was my relation by marriage. She had a daughter and two sons, all in their late teens or early twenties, and they were all still living at home. Her estranged husband would come around about once a week to visit his children, and I watched with my face pressed on the apartment window as Lucia's three children would run down to greet him at the bottom of the stairs. Lucia didn't even acknowledge the visits, continuing on with her dishes or cooking.

"*Che stronzo,*" she'd mutter to me while I watched through the window. What an asshole.

Lucia was another hard-working Italian woman, still caring for her three grown children and also walking across the street every day to sew clothes in a factory. I could tell she wanted me to stay, and she tried to make it work. She enrolled me in a local school and made me a fried egg sandwich every day to take for lunch.

The olive-oil-drenched eggs between two thick chunks of homemade bread were delicious at first, but as they continued daily for what felt like weeks, the smell of fried eggs began to turn my stomach.

My school days in New York were a disconcerting mess. I still had not learned English, and I sat in a classroom packed with kids, confused and possessing a full-fledged disdain for my teachers and classmates. Lucia was struggling, too, with the demands of her family and her job; I knew she couldn't do it. During conversations with my Aunt Marie on the phone, I overheard sporadic phrases like "*istituto per l'infanzia*" (children's home) and "*è meglio così*" (it's better this way).

One day, a car showed up at Lucia's apartment. I knew it was coming. Behind the wheel was Aunt Marie's sister-in-law, one of the few women drivers I had ever seen. Lucia opened the door for me to get in the back seat and then sat in the front next to Aunt Marie. I stared at the back of the heads of the three frizzy-haired Italian women sitting in front of me as we drove, their conversation guarded.

Without turning around, Aunt Marie directed a comment to me. "*Andiamo a visitare un instituto per l'infanzia. Forse ti trasferisci lì. Ci saranno dei ragazzi della tua età.*" She explained that we were on our way to a children's home, that I might live there, and that there would be boys my own age there.

"*Sì,*" I answered, not knowing how else to respond.

Four different living arrangements in the nearly eight months since I'd waved goodbye to my family from the confines of that ship—it felt like years. I closed my eyes in the back seat of the car and envisioned myself at home in Italy on our farm, climbing to the top of a tree just to prove to myself that I could. I recalled a time when my foot snapped a dead branch, and I hit the ground with a thud, knocking my wind out and tearing open my side on a jagged branch on the way down.

My brother, anxious and green about the gills from the sight of blood, yelled at me, "*Lo dico alla Mamma!*" He was going to go tell our mother, but I knew she would whip me up one side and down the other for climbing trees. As I lay on the ground in agony, I threatened him within an inch of his life, but fortunately for me, he told her anyway. Undoubtedly, the gash in my abdomen needed attending.

I still carried my family in the forefront of my mind as I was trying to decipher the mess that my parents had gotten me into. Although I was sad and lonely, waking up every morning meant that I had survived one more day of being tossed from place to place. Life had been thrown at me from so many different angles, and this was just the next bend in the road. Since arriving in New York, I had a roof over my head and was being fed, but mostly I was detached and just trying to stay out of the way. Entering a children's home would not be much different.

We were greeted at the front door by a friendly woman in a gray skirt and jacket, her thick black leather shoes and laces matching the bun on the back of her head. Disconnected and numb, I toured the home with my aunts. We walked through a gym full of older boys playing ball, and it surprised me to see nuns wearing whistles and directing the game. My aunts seemed pleased with what they saw.

We then walked down a narrow hallway to tour the sleeping quarters. The rooms seemed to be separated by age, and the one we observed had bunks stacked three high. The smell of cleaning chemicals mixed with urine burned my nostrils, and when we walked back into the hallway, my aunts asked some

Each of these Italian ladies played a role in my upbringing. Left to right: Marie Casoria DiBernardo, Lucia D'Avanzo DeFrancisco, Teresa Casoria Russo, and Lucia Casoria D'Avanzo.

questions of our tour director. I tuned them out and thought about my brother and sister and all of my cousins and friends kicking the ball to one another in the courtyard of our piazza. Then I thought of Grandma Nappi and wondered if she had been roasting chestnuts as the evenings cooled. We piled back into the car, and Aunt Marie looked back, asking, "*Ti piace quel posto?*" She wanted to know if I liked the place.

"*Sì,*" I lied, staring out the window.

Back at Aunt Marie's apartment, it was dinnertime. Aunt Marie pulled out two loaves of homemade bread from under yellowed kitchen towels and tore it off in hunks. Heaping the steaming spaghetti into bowls, my aunt ladled bubbling-hot tomato sauce, rich from simmering on the stove all day, over the top. I hunched over my food, focusing intently on soaking my bread in the sweet sauce and trying to chase away thoughts about where I'd end up next. The phone rang loudly, startling me, and my cousin Connie flew from the table to answer it. Holding the phone away from her ear and speaking in English, she yelled to her mother, "Ma, it's Uncle Tony from Portland!"

My aunt stopped chewing for a moment and became still in her seat. Then she set her bread on the table and pushed her chair away, getting up to answer the phone.

"*Sì, sì, va bene.*" Then, "*Sì lo porterò all'aeroporto.*" Yes, I'll take him to the airport. I was trying so hard to overhear my aunt, but my cousins continued to eat noisily, clanking their forks on their plates and talking loudly.

When my aunt hung up the phone, she came back, pulled out her chair slowly, and sat down. Staring at me across the table, a tunnel seemed to form between her face and mine, shutting out the chaos of my cousins. She said in full Italian, "Uncle Tony is asking for you; he wants us to put you on an airplane to Portland, Oregon." Then, with eyebrows raised to emphasize the importance of her next statement, she said, "Portland is all the way across America. Cowboys and Indians live there!"

My curiosity spiked regarding the cowboys and Indians I was about to encounter, but somehow I had a feeling my circumstances were about to change for the better. That night I went back to Lucia's apartment; she didn't speak much, her lips were tight, and her face was splotched with red. Again, I found myself packing my suitcase.

Lucia sent her middle son, Bobby DeFrancisco, to drive me to the airport. While we were waiting for my boarding call, Bobby told me that he had heard that the land in Oregon was green as far as you could see and was covered with trees, mountains, and rivers.

"*Mi hanno detto che l'Oregon è bello come l'Italia,*" he said. He'd heard that Oregon is beautiful, as beautiful as Italy. Then he continued on, "*Un giorno ci incontriamo lì.*" Someday we will meet up there.

I didn't know quite what to make of his last statement, but as soon as he said it, a pretty young woman with white-blond hair curling upward on the ends and wearing a blue hat with a matching skirt and jacket came up to us and began asking Bobby some questions. I couldn't look her in the face, so Bobby, in his stilted English, told her that my name was Tony and that I would be traveling by myself.

She knelt down in front of me and looked at me. Avoiding eye contact, I noticed golden eagle wings pinned to her jacket. Then, touching my arm, she spoke, in the sweetest voice, words that I could not fully understand, but her tone told me I would be taken care of. She made me feel safe, and this was the happiest I had been since leaving Italy.

What was in store for me, I didn't know, but maybe this place called Portland, Oregon, would be the true beginning of my new life in America. And maybe there, the demons that seemed to follow me no matter where I went would be quieted.

CHAPTER FIVE

Portland

I wish I could say the plane ride from New York to Portland was uneventful, but nothing could be further from the truth. As airsick as I was seasick on the SS *Independence*, I was distraught and frightened again—the one difference being the entourage of kind ladies looking out for me. They kept attending to me even when we were grounded for the night somewhere in the Midwest because of a snowstorm. When the plane finally touched down in Portland, my energy level picked up, and although I was trudging into the unknown, I was excited to meet the man who had sent for me from all the way across the country. My new lady friends escorted me off the plane, and I began to look around for my uncle.

Standing still amidst the hubbub of the terminal, I saw a familiar-faced Italian man next to a lovely, light-haired American woman. He was stout, stood about five foot five, and had a round face and black hair styled in a way I'd become accustomed to seeing, slicked straight back. My uncle knew right away who I was. He threw his arms out toward me and sang out a long "*Ayeeeeeeeee*" as I approached with my escorts. When I was within reach, he grabbed my shoulders, and in a loud booming voice with a thick Italian accent he said, "*Ayee-a Tony Roos!*" From that day on, he often addressed me by my first and last name, dropping the o from Russo.

I then received the most hugs of my entire life. I was used to kisses on the cheek, but hugs were something new. My uncle hugged me first and then turned and introduced me to his wife, Gladys.

Although she was a bit larger than my uncle both in height and girth, she had a shapely form and a soft, kind face with light-brown hair touching her shoulders. My new aunt and uncle each took one of my hands, and we walked out of the airport together. Aunt Gladys spoke to my uncle in English.

I believe she said something like, "He seems small for his age, but he's very cute and sweet." I was pretty sure she liked me.

When we got outside, it felt as if we were walking right into a misty gray cloud. A cold, wet wind nipped my cheeks and rushed through my hair. My entire body woke up, but even through the mist I could see the green: pine trees, shrubs, and grassy fields. We loaded my suitcase into the trunk of my uncle's car and headed toward his home.

On our drive, Uncle Tony spoke to me in Italian, telling me they had purchased a bed and set up a room for me in their attic. I stretched my neck to watch out the window from the back seat of the car as we sped past farms, orchards, and berry fields— Bobby DeFrancisco may have been right, I thought, regarding his declaration of Portland's beauty. The terrain reminded me of my Italian countryside in many ways. Soon, we turned off a busy street onto a narrow road lined with small houses on each side.

The car slowed, and my uncle turned onto the gravel driveway of my new home on SE 115th Street, Portland, Oregon.

The house was small and painted green like the landscape of my new surroundings. It was encircled by dirt, and the yard had no trees, grass, or shrubs. As we entered the house, a medium-sized black and white terrier jumped up and put her front paws on my stomach, panting and begging me to pet her. My uncle shouted, *"No! Trixie, a-down!"* Then he turned to me, and shaking one hand in the air, he yelled, *"Trixie is-a da best-a dog! She got-a lost in-a da flood, and-a two-a months-a lade-a, we find. Good as-a new!"* He shook his head in disbelief.

My new home with Aunt Gladys and Uncle Tony on SE 115th Street, Portland, Oregon.

My uncle mostly spoke to me in full Italian, but he occasionally threw out a singsong English-Italian verbiage that was hard to follow. I was able to make out that their dog Trixie had been lost in a flood and somehow they had found her months later. I would learn down the road that my aunt and uncle had lost everything they owned in the Vanport flood and only months prior to my arrival were they finally able to purchase another home.

Aunt Gladys's parents, my new adoptive grandparents, stood in the middle of the room. Grandma and Grandpa Beard were both robust, and with the smiles they were wearing, I could tell they were happy to meet me. They smothered me between the two of them, and Grandpa Beard gave me my first ever toy: a cowboy holster with a shiny silver cap gun.

Grandma and Grandpa Beard, my new adoptive grandparents.
They gave me a toy gun immediately upon my arrival in Portland.

"*Grazie,*" I said in quiet admiration, turning the gun over in my hands. Then Grandpa Beard motioned for me to come closer. I moved toward him slowly, and he proceeded to help me cinch up the holster. Then he placed a cowboy hat on top of my head.

"You're a real cowboy now," he said, and they all let out huge belly laughs. I wore my hat, holster, and gun with pride for the rest of the day.

With Aunt Gladys and Uncle Tony on my first day in Portland.
I am wearing the holster and toy gun given to me by Grandpa Beard.

Uncle Tony took me up the narrow staircase that led to the attic, my new bedroom. We unpacked my suitcase into a small chest of drawers, and my uncle spoke again in his self-composed language, "*You sleep-a here. You keep-a dis room-a clean.*"

"*Sì,*" I promised, but my mind was reeling at the idea of having my own bed and my own space, and it was starting to hit me—

this would now be my home. Grandma Beard had cooked a meal of pasta with red sauce and meat, "To make you feel at home," she told me. We all sat around the dining room table, and Uncle Tony poured everyone a glass of red wine. We ate and drank heartily.

"A toast to celebrate your arrival!" my new aunt announced, raising her wine glass.

"*Salute!*" Uncle Tony shouted.

"*Salute!*" everyone called back to him. They took long drinks from their glasses, and it made me smile. I had never felt so welcome in my life. I slept well that night, and the next day my uncle didn't waste any time in showing me how I'd earn my keep. He taught me how to line the garbage can in the kitchen with newspaper and how to take it outside to dump into the large metal can. He also showed me how to clean up after Trixie and told me I'd be helping my aunt with the dishes.

After a few days of exploring my new surroundings, playing with Trixie, and getting to know my new aunt and uncle, I woke up one morning and could sense that things were going to be different.

"You are going to start school today," Aunt Gladys announced as she directed me to the car. I understood the word "school," so close to the Italian "*scuola*," and immediately my stomach tied itself into knots. We started down the road and ended up in the parking lot of Powellhurst School. Aunt Gladys walked me up the stairs of the giant concrete building and then into the main office, where she enrolled me in fifth grade with a teacher named Mr. Wunderlich.

My school attendance in Italy had been sporadic, and school was a less-than-successful venture for me in New York. I was not one bit happy about it, but in April of 1952, I started school in Portland, Oregon. I had come a long way since leaving my family in Italy nearly a year before, and now, living with my aunt and uncle, I was starting to see a glimmer of hope in this place called America. I thought about my family, and although I had not yet seen any trees blossoming with gold, I knew this must be what my mother was talking about. This must be the better way of life my mother wanted for her family.

My first class in Portland at Powellhurst School. I'm in the front row to the left of the boy holding the sign.

School kept my daily life in Portland going with a sense of stability and regular routine, but I missed my family so terribly, it physically hurt to breathe when they flooded my thoughts. At night, before falling asleep, I thought about my mom and dad, envisioning them sitting around our table eating, drinking wine, and laughing with my aunts and uncles. I always wondered what they might be doing and wrestled with conflicting thoughts:

Why am I here living this new life, and you are not? I'm beginning to love my new family and life in Portland, but I still love and miss you all. What will happen to me when you get here? Will we ever be together again?

It was comforting for me to play out different versions of what it would be like when we reunited: The smell of red wine and garlic would hit me as my entire family, parents and grandparents alike, would walk in the front door of my new Portland home. They would take turns embracing me and gush over me, telling me how much they had missed me.

This scene replayed itself on a loop in my brain even though I knew the vision of my grandparents together as one was not based in reality. I felt chills every time I pictured my grandfather lying so still in his casket. Thoughts of the man for whom I was named, Antonio Russo, the patriarch of the family, the man who cared for me like a father, invaded my mind often, but he was gone, and losing him left a void in me impossible to fill. As his firstborn grandchild, we had always shared a special bond; we had also shared a home, with my grandparents living on the bottom floor of our brick and mortar apartment home outside of Naples.

My grandfather had a charismatic personality and a following of loyal friends, many of whom looked to him for advice or help when they were in need. He was greatly respected in our small town and was known as an honest man with a tough-guy edge, protective of his family and those close to him. His personality, coupled with his tall, lean stature, thick dark hair, and piercing green eyes, contributed to his popularity. The resemblance between him and my own father was uncanny.

My grandfather loved to play rough with me, wrestling around in the small living space of our home. It was exhilarating, and I used to grab his legs one at a time and with all my might try to take him down. He had such a competitive edge, though, that he'd never let me win. Whenever he would get too rough, my grandmother would raise her voice in protest. "*È troppo piccolo! Stai attento!*" Be careful, she warned, I was too small to play with like that. But I loved every minute of it. We always ended up huffing and puffing and laughing, with my grandmother shaking her head at the two of us.

"*È un bravo ragazzo,*" my grandfather would announce to my grandmother. I was a good boy.

"*Sì, sì,*" my grandmother would answer, finally breaking down and laughing in agreement.

One summer, when I was about four years old and playing around outside, I noticed my cousins and the neighborhood children playing a game of hide and seek. I wanted so badly to be included, but as the youngest of the group, I was mostly invisible to the older children. It happened so fast; the whole lot of them scattered behind our homes and up into the hills that bordered our small piazza. I followed them in my quest to be part of the group and soon found myself alone amidst the rocks and olive trees that covered the rugged hillside, not a child in sight.

Continuing to play in an attempt to convince myself I was not lost, I realized not only was I alone, but I had also gone too far and was disoriented. Not knowing in which direction to go,

I hid under an olive tree, crouched down with my back pressed against the trunk. My heart raced and my body was frozen still; I stayed in that position for what felt like hours.

When dusk settled in and darkness surrounded me, panic coursed through my veins, every thought turning to stories of wild animals living in the hills around our village. In my mind, every sound I heard was either a mountain lion or a large venomous snake. My ears perked up when I heard the earth rustling softly and swiftly nearby; I buried my face in my hands as the sound got louder. It was closing in on me. I was convinced I would soon become the supper of a hungry oversized cat.

I closed my eyes tightly as the sound escalated, and then I heard it, my grandfather's strong comforting voice. "Tino!" he hollered, short for Antonio. I looked out from under my hands and tried to respond but found myself still frozen. Then, through the blackness I saw the dim glow of his small lantern.

"*Nonno!*" I yelled. "*Sono qui!*" Grandpa, I'm here! I sprang to my feet and ran into his arms. I had never held on so tight. All *Nonno* said was, "*Mi hai spaventato.*" I had scared him. He never once scolded me; instead, he lifted me above his head, put me on his shoulders, and carried me home down the hill. He swore my tiny bare footprints in the glow of his lantern had led him to me. As I fell asleep that night, I heard Grandma Nappi ranting to my grandfather about how my mother needed to keep a better eye out for me, but in my mother's defense, running off by myself and doing my own thing seemed to be an inherent trait of mine.

Returning in my mind to experiences with my grandfather was a comfort to me in my new Portland surroundings, but the final story of his life, as hard as I tried not to let it in, would haunt me forever.

As I've been told by my father and uncles more times than I can count, the night my grandfather was killed was no different than many others.

He had finished his deliveries of wheat and fresh produce to the silos, convents, and markets in and around Naples and then stopped off at the local bar for a drink of his favorite red wine. Like many times before, a game of cards ensued. In attendance that evening was a local man by the name of Salvatore Biancomano, known about town as a loudmouth and a cheat. He even had the look of a large rat with his thin, wiry mustache, nervous voice, and twitchy body.

My grandfather had won a sizable amount of money and had collected from all except Biancomano. Fed up with this man's games and knowing he wasn't going to pay up, my grandfather reached across the table and grabbed Biancomano by the throat. With a trembling hand squeezing tight under his jaw so as to terminate the man's breath, my grandfather lifted him off the ground and held him up with one arm. The men in attendance watched in awed silence.

Holding Biancomano up and looking into his eyes with a deep-seated contempt, my grandfather shouted, "*Tu rubi dalla famiglia e dagli amici. Vattene e non tornare più!*" You steal from your family and friends. Run away and do not return!

Upon releasing him, Biancomano dropped to the ground, humiliated. He grabbed his throat and fled the scene, wheezing and sucking in air as he stumbled out the front door of the bar. My grandfather, so focused in the moment during this altercation, didn't even hear the boisterous cheers that rose up from the group as this despicable man vanished from the building.

"*È un imbroglione!*" my grandfather sang out as the men settled back into their card game. He's a cheat! The game continued quietly for about an hour until Biancomano returned. He nervously walked in the front door with a crazed look in his eyes and beads of sweat dripping off his forehead. Everyone froze, and all eyes watched as he walked with an unsteady gait across the room and approached the table. He positioned himself right next to my grandfather.

As my grandfather pushed his chair from the table and stood up to face him—he towered over the rat-like waif of a man— Biancomano pulled out a large butcher knife in a mad flurry and stabbed my grandfather square in the gut while muttering, "*Tu paghi per l'infamità contro Salvatore Biancomano!*" You will pay for humiliating Salvatore Biancomano!

Leaving the knife buried deep, Biancomano ran, and everyone scattered except my father and uncles as my grandfather collapsed to the ground. They helped him up, removed the knife, and used their own shirts to cover his wound. My grandfather stumbled outside, hunched over, holding tight to his stomach. He made his way to the wagon, and my father and uncles lifted him into the back and laid him down.

"*Quell'uomo non scappa vivo!*" That man does not escape with his life! My father shouted these instructions—chase Biancomano down!

I had been asleep and awoke to screams and chaos when

they arrived home. The scene was terrifying. The sight of my grandfather being covered in sheets as he lay in the middle of our table was more than I could bear.

"*Che cosa successo al Nonno?*" I yelled out to my aunts and uncles who ran past me as if I did not exist. What happened to my grandpa? No answer. They were trying to stop the bleeding, but he had already lost too much. I stood there alone and helpless amidst the bedlam and watched in horror, listening to the cries from the women and wails from my grandmother as my grandfather bled to death.

The entire town mourned the loss of my grandfather Antonio Russo, and all were in attendance at his funeral. This would be the first time I can remember wearing a pair of shoes, and I hated those shoes because of the meaning they held. For years to come, I knew that my father, uncles, and their loyal friends were on the lookout for Biancomano. I knew without a doubt any one of them would have killed him if given the chance. But from that fateful day on, nobody in town ever saw or heard from him again.

Several different stories circulated about him. One such story was that he had been jailed for another crime in a neighboring town and, when up for parole, begged to stay locked up, knowing he was a marked man. But according to other stories, he may have fled the country or possibly been killed for pulling the same scheming antics somewhere else.

My father would never speak of it. And in all honesty, I don't know whether or not he was ever able to hunt down Biancomano. Some think he did, but it will forever remain a mystery, and I'll always wonder if my father avenged my grandfather's death.

Thinking about my grandfather brought back memories of my life in Italy with a vengeance, and even though I tried not to, I occasionally asked Uncle Tony about my family. He had gotten a few sporadic letters and phone calls regarding their status and whereabouts. My mother could not read or write, so I knew the letters had been written by my father.

I thought of the family I left behind all the time, and then one day, while I was in the backyard throwing a stick for Trixie, my Uncle Tony had been on the phone for some time. I sensed a heightened tension but didn't know why.

He called me in from outside and spoke in full Italian this time. *"La Mamma è arrivata in America."* My mom had arrived. Chills shot up my spine.

"Quando la posso vedere?" When can I see her? I wanted to know. This question seemed to anger my uncle, and he threw his arms in the air and yelled, *"Nooooo, non la vedrai ancora. Lei va a lavorare al ristorante dello Zio Mike in Arizona."* She was going to go to work in Uncle Mike's restaurant in Arizona, and I would not be seeing her.

He explained that shortly after I had arrived in Portland, my Uncle Mike had moved from New York to Arizona and opened an Italian restaurant in Tucson. My dad, brother, and sister were still in Italy, and my mom, knowing she could earn more money in the States, was trying to stockpile enough so that when the rest of the family arrived, they would have an easier time of it. Knowing my mother was so close yet so far away and that I still could not see her didn't make sense to me. It was heartbreaking.

In the end, she didn't make any money working with Uncle Mike. His restaurant closed, and he ended up paying her way back to New York; she was penniless.

Meanwhile, school was becoming increasingly difficult for me. Although I could sham my way through many lessons, the language gap was a hindrance that made for misunderstandings with the other children. I developed a defensive edge and an attitude and was finding myself in physical altercations. Physicality was natural for me. Having learned to wrestle and fight from my grandfather at a young age, I knew I could handle myself against anyone, and that was how I began to define myself at school. It is also what helped me shake off some of the demons, the stresses I was dealing with, such as being separated from my family and struggling with English—but my behavior only brought more problems.

One evening, I heard a knock at the door and was shocked to see a man from my school, dressed in a suit and tie, standing there in our doorway. I had seen this man on occasion in the school office and sometimes in the halls; he scared me. We made eye contact, and I froze. What was he doing here? I didn't think teachers were supposed to leave their school buildings. My aunt and uncle welcomed him in while I bolted up the stairs to my bedroom. I wanted so badly to hear what was being said that I lay on my stomach with my ear pressed hard against the floor. I heard murmurs but couldn't make out a single word.

I finally heard the door shut, and Aunt Gladys called me downstairs into the living room. Uncle Tony stood off to the side as if unsure what to think, while my aunt did the talking.

"Your principal says you've been fighting at school," Aunt Gladys said. I nodded. "He says you're not learning English well enough to complete your school work properly." I nodded again. "You're not learning to read, he says, and your spelling is bad," she continued, looking at me sternly. I just nodded again.

I already knew my aunt didn't like it when my uncle and I had full conversations in Italian without including her. She hated it so much she was picking up Italian quickly so she wouldn't be left out. Then she said something completely shocking.

Pointing her finger and staring me hard in the face, she said, "That's it! From now on, at home you will speak only English."

I looked over at my uncle. He shrugged his shoulders and nodded his head yes. I couldn't believe it, but I agreed to try to behave better at school. I promised to try harder to sound out the English words. I felt angry and confused that this was happening, but mostly I was surprised that this man had ventured outside of the school walls and showed up at my house.

Uncle Tony was always full of big ideas, and he had huge plans for me and my future. He often talked about my career as a doctor.

"*Dottori make-a so much-a money,*" he'd say to me. Then, switching gears down the road, he decided I needed accordion lessons because I might just be an up-and-coming Dick Contino.

Money was extremely important to my uncle, and he often had more than one job. At one point he worked as a short-order cook for fishermen, which took him to Alaska for months at a time.

"You-a help-a your aunt while I'm-a gone," he'd spit out while holding me by both shoulders and nodding his head hard. I knew his absence was difficult for my aunt, and I did try to help her out around the house, but we still managed to have fun while he was off working, creating our own daily rituals.

While he was gone, Aunt Gladys would make popcorn, set up board games, and then send me to the gas station on the corner of 115th and Powell to buy ten-cent Cokes. Each time I put in a dime and pulled an ice-cold Coke out of the machine, it was like winning a prize, and I usually had enough money to do it four times over. I'd wrap my arms around the glass bottles and run as fast as I could the couple of blocks back home to play games, eat popcorn, and drink Coke with my aunt.

Other days, we would walk to a market called Holgate Farms, halfway between our house and Grandma Beard's. We'd meet Grandma Beard at the market, buy food for dinner, and then walk to Grandma's, where we'd sit down and eat together. One time, I was given the privilege of carrying the watermelon home from the market; I had made it nearly the whole mile, all the way to the sidewalk in front of Grandma Beard's house before dropping it. It hit the ground and splattered into pieces.

"What in the world!" Aunt Gladys shouted. "You are ten feet from the front door!" I stared at the carnage on the sidewalk in front of me, and as much as I loved that fruit, this would be the second time in my life I would incur punishment by watermelon.

After one of my uncle's stints in Alaska, he had money and went right out and bought me a brand-new red Schwinn bicycle with thick whitewall tires. I was crazy about my new bike, and I rode it up and down our street and all over the neighborhood. After a week of breaking it in, I was riding around on the street and started to get an itch to go fast, so I decided to see just how fast I could make my new bike go.

I rode down to the end of our street, stopped at the corner, and then turned the bike around, facing the direction of our house. I grabbed the handlebars, leaned forward, and started pedaling madly. I kept pushing faster and faster until the pedals were spinning my legs instead of my legs spinning the pedals. As I got closer to our house, I realized I was completely out of control and wasn't sure what to do. If I continued straight ahead, I'd end up riding right out onto Powell Boulevard—not a wise decision. I was also afraid to hit the brakes hard because I didn't want to fly over the top of the handlebars, so as I approached our driveway, I made a split decision to turn the handlebars sharply to the right. I miscalculated and turned just before the driveway; the tires slipped, the bike flew out from under me, and with no way to stop myself, I was catapulted through the air.

I hit the ground with a thud and dug a trench with my face right down the middle of my uncle's freshly planted lawn. With new trees and shrubs, my uncle's yard had become his sanctuary, and I knew this would be considered a major offense. I lay there, afraid to move, until I heard my aunt come running out the front door. I stood up slowly, my face caked in dirt, to see Uncle Tony so furious he couldn't speak. He was holding a shovel in one hand, and he had the other hand on his head as if trying to figure me out. His lips were pursed so tight and his face was escalating to such deep shades of red, I wasn't sure if he was breathing.

My aunt had seen everything through the front window and again, Uncle Tony let her do the talking. Her voice was fading in and out, and I was trying hard to listen and made out phrases like "be more careful" and "think before you act" and "pay attention," but I was holding back an uncontrollable urge to spit, and all I could think about was getting the grit out of my teeth. Needless to say, I wasn't sure if I'd ever see my bike again.

"You won't see the likes of that bike for one full week!" my aunt yelled, and Uncle Tony concurred, solving that mystery. I was so happy to only lose my bike for a week that I nearly smiled—but thought better of it.

CHAPTER SIX

Finding My Way

In spite of the stability that came with my aunt and uncle taking care of me, a home to live in, and regular schooling, the demons in my head kept my life in Portland continuing in a roller-coaster fashion. With the birth of my aunt and uncle's first child, Joey, and going on three years of separation from my family, my life in Italy was becoming a more and more distant memory. I still missed my family terribly, but I seriously questioned if we would ever be reunited. I knew on a deeper level that Aunt Gladys and Uncle Tony loved me, but I had been thrown away by my own family. How could anyone truly love me? This had to be the biggest demon haunting me.

I continued at Powellhurst School, and Mr. Wunderlich's initial efforts had paid off a little, but I was still having trouble. As difficult as school was for me, I did look forward to the social aspect as well as the games and sports I was learning during recess and physical education class. Being at school meant I wasn't at home doing chores, although, to me, sitting at a desk was painful. Reading was confusing. I could sound out words but didn't understand a thing I had read, and spelling was near impossible. The language was still a barrier for me, admittedly somewhat by choice. To say I was struggling academically would be an understatement.

My internal conflicts created a chip on my shoulder large enough to weigh me down and get anyone's attention. I was continuously at a hot simmer with the potential to boil over at any given moment. When teased by the other kids for how I talked or dressed, throwing punches seemed to be the most effective way for me to settle any miscommunication.

During science class one day, my teacher, Mr. Foos, sent Johnny Demonte, a hotheaded boy regarded by most kids as a bully, to the back of the room to sit at my table. He looked like he could be of Italian descent with his dark features: thick, dark eyebrows and jet-black hair. He was stoutly built and about a head taller than I. As Johnny approached my table, I must have been looking at him the wrong way, because the next thing I knew his chest was blown up like a balloon, and he was in my face spouting off.

"You better wipe that look off your face," he said smugly.

"Shut up!" The only words that came to mind spat out of my mouth, and I lifted my chin to appear taller.

"You think you're some kind of tough guy, huh?" he said. Then he threw his hand down in disgust and murmured, "Ah, you're nothin' but a pansy."

He pulled out his chair to sit down at the table, but I was infuriated. I couldn't let it go. I pointed my finger in his face and said in the deepest, toughest voice I could muster, "You better watch it."

"Oh yeah?" he said, staring at me with a smug grin.

"Yeah," I said, standing up and still trying to sound tough. He stood up as fast as I did and out of nowhere, crack! I felt a blow so hard it shook me to the core. He had punched me in the side of my head, square in the temple.

Everything got blurry, and my knees buckled underneath me. I grabbed the edge of the table to keep from hitting the ground, and when I gained my focus and realized what had happened, his snide grin stared back at me like he was greatly impressed with his boxing skills. But it wasn't over. I clenched my fist hard and, with everything I could muster, clocked him across his left eye. My knuckle sliced his eyelid just below the brow, and blood spurted everywhere.

"Aaaahhhh," he screamed as he put his hand over his eye and barreled head first into my stomach, pinning me against the edge of the counter.

I was on fire. Instinctively, I hooked him under the right armpit, elevated him into the air, and threw him to the ground onto his back. His head slammed the tile floor, and the class erupted. I used all my strength to keep him pinned to the ground. I wasn't going to let him up for anything. The satisfaction that came with holding him to the ground was filling a need inside of me, chipping away at my demons.

The next thing I knew, I was being lifted off my enemy by the back of my shirt. Mr. Foos was a large Irishman with arms like an orangutan and biceps to spare. He picked us up, one in either hand, and dragged us like ragdolls to the principal's office. After Johnny's bloodied and beaten-up face had been butterflied, we were called in to tell the principal our side of the story—one at a time.

As I waited outside the principal's office, one of the secretaries came over and kindly offered me a bag of ice. I just glared at her and shook my head. *I don't need any ice*, I thought. We were both sentenced to one week of after-school detention. Staying at school got me out of my chores, but having to sit still in a desk, trying to focus on homework, was near torture.

Johnny and I didn't look at or speak to one another the entire week. Then, the last day, just after the detention monitor excused us, he came up to me and said, "Hey, you should come over to my house sometime. I just made a new bow and arrow, and I can show you how to shoot it."

I shrugged my shoulders and said, "Sure," wondering if he might be contemplating shooting it at me. I took off for home that afternoon hoping to keep myself out of the detention room for a while.

My middle years at
Powellhurst School.

I did end up going over to Johnny's house, and he showed me how to make a bow and some arrows. In his backyard he had a pear tree with long, skinny sprouts growing up around the trunk. He used his pocketknife to cut the sprouts off at the base and then showed me how to cut a notch in each end of the stick and tie string to it for the bow. For the arrows, he sharpened the end of the stick until it came to a fine point. We shot around playing "Cowboys and Indians" in an open field behind his house. From then on we were fine, never the best of friends but with a mutual respect for one another.

I tried to stay out of trouble at school, but for some reason it always had a way of seeking me out. During a recess break one morning, I was throwing rocks at a chain-link fence near the playground. I loved to throw things at a target, and I thought back to when I struck that blackbird dead with my friend Michele back in Italy. I was aiming at one fence post in particular, wondering what Michele was up to—if he was in school and if he still saw my family. The rocks began flying harder and faster. Many of them were going through the chain-link to the other side of the fence, but occasionally, one would hit the post dead on. The high-pitched clank of the rock connecting with the post completed something inside me. I didn't mean to cause any trouble, but one of the rocks hit the post at an odd angle and ricocheted off much farther than the others had—and hit a girl square in the forehead.

She grabbed her head, screaming and crying. My heart sank, and I ran up to her to apologize. There was none of the rush I had felt when I nailed the bird back in Italy. This was horrible.

"Are you okay?" I asked nervously as she continued to wail. The playground supervisor ran toward me. Looking at me disapprovingly and pointing at the building, she said, "Take yourself into the office. I'll be right in." I walked across the playground and into the school with my head down and my hands shoved deep in my pockets. I sat in a familiar chair and waited to give my account to the principal.

The teacher came in with her arm around my victim, red-faced and still sobbing. I felt lousy. All the women in the office scrambled to get her ice and then took her straight into the nurse's office. As I was sitting there, I saw the playground supervisor go in and talk to the principal. When he finally called me in, he had a look of anger I hadn't seen before. I sat in a chair across from his desk; he asked me if I had been throwing rocks at the other kids. I tried to explain that I had just been throwing them at the fence and that I hadn't meant to hit the girl. I knew he didn't believe me.

"You could've caused more harm," he yelled, shaking his head in disgust. "And it doesn't matter who or what you were throwing them at. You never throw rocks!"

I sat and stared at him as he fumed; his head looked as if it might actually burst into flames. His eyes darted over to the side of his desk where a large paddle hung by a leather strap from a nail sticking out about a half inch. I had heard about the paddle, and I knew what he was thinking.

My insides were burning. I wanted to lash out. *Pazzo bastardo!* I thought. Crazy bastard! *Stupido!* But my time had come, and I didn't say a word. This was a combination sentencing, the paddle along with another week's detention. My reputation continued to build in the wrong direction.

Although I was proving a complete failure in school academically and behaviorally, I did find one place where I could actually shine: in physical education. I had made a connection and had a way of hyper-focusing during any kind of physical game or activity. I would go all out every time. My energy levels always seemed to be too high for the kids playing with me, though. The only sport we played back in my hometown in Italy was soccer, but by now I'd learned baseball, basketball, and American football, which we had our own recess version of that entailed chasing, then tackling anyone with the ball. Above all, though, I had been introduced to the sport of wrestling.

The combative nature of wrestling fit me like a glove; I couldn't get enough. It was the first time my intensity had been met head-on. I could pour out my aggressions on the mat, pushing away all thoughts of missing my family, struggling with the language, and getting along in school. My first introduction to wrestling was during a unit in PE in which my teacher, Mr. Elliott, threw down a bunch of thick gray mats in the gym and, with little instruction, blew his whistle and sent us out to battle. I thought I was pretty good, scrambling and flailing mostly, but somehow keeping my opponents in a defensive mode. I knew one thing for sure: I couldn't get enough.

When I found out I could stay after school to be involved in these different sports, I begged my aunt and uncle to allow me to join, but they wouldn't hear of it.

"Your responsibilities come first," my aunt responded, and my uncle nodded in agreement. My responsibilities at that point, along with my chores at home, included mowing lawns, doing yard work, and performing other odd jobs around our neighborhood. What little money I earned went directly to my Aunt Gladys, and she would put it away. I know it helped out when I needed new clothes or school supplies, and it may have even bought groceries at times. I never focused on the money, though. I knew it was necessary in order for me to have the things I needed, but it was never a driving force. I worked my neighborhood jobs more out of loyalty than anything else. I wanted to do a good job to please these neighbors who were becoming a part of my extended family.

The Azlins and the Skibblys were the two main families I worked for. I spread sawdust under trees, trimmed lawns with a push mower, cleaned, did the edging by hand, and pulled every last weed. At the Azlin home, my job had an added benefit, as I got to take care of Mr. Azlin's hunting dogs, his beloved German shorthaired pointers.

Flo and Leonard Azlin owned a restaurant called the F & L Cafe in the South Park Blocks of Portland. Leonard looked just like Santa Claus minus the white beard, and he had a quirky personality. He had a newly acquired electric razor he was quite impressed with, and he'd sit in his easy chair wearing nothing but his long johns, his rotund stomach resting on his lap and his razor touching up his round face, all the while instructing me on my list of chores for the day.

He didn't always get along with the other neighbors, and before he got to the end of my list he would spout off, "Mr. So-and-So this and Mr. So-and-So that!" I just nodded my head and waited for him to finish, and then I'd go out and get started. Flo was as thin as her husband was round, and she was remarkably kind. She would invite me to the F & L Cafe for tomato and rice soup with bread. It reminded me of the food I used to eat in Italy, and I savored every spoonful.

Leonard's hunting dogs were his pride and joy. He had a large male that he'd named Sandy after the Sandy River, and a small female named Linda. I'm not sure who Linda was named after, but she was the prettiest little dog I'd ever seen. It was my responsibility to clean out their kennels and to exercise them. Running the dogs was the one thing I couldn't wait to do—they loved it, and it served a purpose for me also, out in the open fields, the fresh air, no one around but the dogs, my mind free to try and make sense of things I didn't know if I ever would. It took me back to roaming free in the Italian countryside, but the dogs always brought me back to the present, pointing at birds and even large bugs along the way.

One day, Uncle Tony was hanging around shooting the breeze with Leonard while I was hosing out the kennels, and Leonard decided he wanted us to take the dogs out for a run. He yelled over to me, "Junior, let's go. I'll show you a great place to run the dogs." He and all the neighbors had taken to calling me "Junior" as my uncle and I shared the same name.

Leonard opened the trunk of his shiny black 1952 Buick, and he called the dogs over. They came running and jumped right into the empty space in the trunk. His method for transporting the dogs shocked me, which Leonard could tell by the look on my face. He motioned for me to come closer and showed me the breathing holes he had custom cut into the door of the trunk so that the dogs could get fresh air. I have to admit I wasn't sure how much "fresh" air those dogs were actually getting.

Leonard told me to hop in the front, and I slid across the leather bench seat as he got behind the wheel. My uncle opened the passenger side door and squeezed in next to me from the other direction. There was no room in the back seat as it held all of Leonard's hunting and fishing gear. My uncle and Leonard were of a similar build, which meant the space between them was nonexistent.

I managed to fit somehow, although so tightly that my arms were glued to my sides. Just after we pulled out of the driveway, Leonard removed a big brown stogie from his pocket and offered it to my uncle. I had seen my uncle smoke cigars on occasion, but it was usually in the backyard where the smoke would dissipate and float off into the sky.

Leonard and my uncle both lit up, and the next thing I knew, my head was enveloped in the most rancid cloud of smoke I'd ever encountered. To make matters worse, the windows were rolled up tight, and I was too shy and too scared of both of these men to say anything.

I tried to hold my breath and just take in little bits of air as needed, but it didn't help. My lungs were about to burst, and I could feel myself turning green. When the Buick pulled off the road and came to a stop, Uncle Tony opened his door and got out of the car.

As soon as I saw an opening, I bolted out into the middle of the field, stopping only for my guts to spew out of me. I couldn't hold back. I heard them both laughing, although my uncle stopped just long enough to shout, *"Tony Roos! What's-a matt-a you?"* He and Leonard found hilarity in my misery, and they stood back leaning on the car, smoking cigars, their giant bellies shaking with laughter.

As time went on, my uncle and I began to accompany Leonard regularly on his hunting and fishing trips. My favorite times with Leonard were fishing on the banks of the Sandy River and hooking large rainbow trout or steelhead. Being outside in nature always took me back to Italy and my excursions with my father and grandfather. I thought about how much my father would have loved these outings and the terrain.

With Leonard, the dogs were always in tow, and on one particular excursion to eastern Oregon, we somehow lost track of Linda. I was horrified at having to return home without her. To our surprise, about a week later, Leonard received a phone call—someone had found her! I was thrilled to make the trip back with Leonard to retrieve her. Later that year, Linda had a litter of puppies. But no matter how much I pleaded, my aunt and uncle would not hear of letting me have one. Aunt Gladys had taken Leonard's lead and was now raising dogs of her own. She was more interested in blue merle border collies, and we now had two blue merle pups sharing space with Trixie. It didn't matter to me; I still wanted one of those pointers.

CHAPTER SEVEN

Dr. Hare

My internal bodily systems had been out of whack much of the time since arriving in Portland. I got sick often and had an altogether impossible time calibrating my stomach to certain American foods. My aunt liked to make me bologna sandwiches with a half inch of mayonnaise spread on the bread—far from the plain, rustic food I was used to in Italy. The first time I ate mayonnaise, my stomach lurched, and I was nauseated for the rest of the day, but Aunt Gladys didn't care whether I liked it or not. That wasn't the point as far as she was concerned, and she was a stickler when it came to eating. I sat at the table until I had finished my entire meal.

Before long, I realized Trixie trolled the floor during meal times, so I seized the opportunity. I became savvy at pretending to eat, all the while waiting for the precise moment Aunt Gladys would look away or get up from the table. With baby Joey around, the distractions were plenty, and at the exact second of any commotion, Trixie would go into stealth mode, inhaling the food I dropped under the table and then sitting back and looking wide-eyed and innocent. Uncle Tony was too focused on his own meal to notice anything except what was right in front of him, and Aunt Gladys would sit back down to finish her meal none the wiser. This method worked, and unbelievably, I never got caught.

I had also been riddled with chronic sore throats and ear infections. They were painful for me and stressful for my aunt and uncle. Extra medical costs were not in their budget. Although I never missed school, constant ear pain and pressure did not help with my contrary attitude.

One morning before school, Uncle Tony informed me he had talked to Leonard Azlin the previous day about my ear and throat troubles. Leonard told him that one of his hunting and fishing buddies was a doctor. He told my uncle that he would ask Dr. Hare if he could do him a favor and have a look at me.

"I don't need a doctor," I protested.

Uncle Tony grunted with a look of disgust and yelled, "*You-a need a dottore!*"

I wasn't thrilled in the least to hear Dr. Hare had agreed to see me. Regrettably, he decided the best course of action would be a tonsillectomy. Leonard must have put in a good word because Dr. Hare said that he would do the job himself and keep the fees way down for my aunt and uncle.

I was admitted to the hospital, which was unlike any environment I'd been in. Never before had I seen any place so clean or so white. I was wheeled away on a stretcher with an ether mask over my nose and mouth, getting drowsy and scared to death about what was happening to me. As I drifted off, Aunt Gladys's face faded in and out as she peered over the top of me.

"Everything will be okay," she said. "When you wake up you can eat all the ice cream you want." Ice cream was the last thing on my mind. I was seeing myself at home in our piazza in Rocca, the grown-ups intoxicated and holding hands with the children, dancing and singing in a furious mob.

My tonsillectomy was routine until I was on my way out to the car. Aunt Gladys was hooked on my one arm and Uncle Tony on the other. As we walked slowly toward the car in the middle of the parking lot, I felt a tickle in my throat and an overwhelming urge to cough. I tried not to unleash, but it happened despite my efforts. I felt a tearing pain on one side of my throat as I spit out a small amount of blood. Almost instantly my mouth was flooded, and I couldn't breathe. Blood spewed out all over the asphalt, and Uncle Tony panicked.

"*Oh my-a God! Oh bull-a shit-a!*" he yelled loudly, throwing his hands in the air. I started crying. The blood scared me. They turned me around and rushed me back inside. Nurses grabbed my arms and strapped me to a gurney. I was wheeled off again, and then, with nurses holding my mouth open, my throat was singed by a hot steel rod, cauterizing the tear and earning me one more night's stay in the hospital. Unfortunately, my tonsillectomy was not the last time Dr. Hare would perform his handiwork on me.

During the previous year, the television had made its debut in Portland, and I had taken a liking to two radically different shows. Every Friday night we went over to Grandma and Grandpa Beard's house to watch live professional wrestling. Grandpa Beard and Uncle Tony loved watching "Gorgeous" George Wagner. Into a microphone, he announced that not only was he the greatest wrestler that ever lived, but "I'm also the most beautiful!" Then he professed he could beat his opponent without displacing a single hair on his head. His actions were over the top, and we were all enthralled with his villainous performances. His ring valet used to spray the entire wrestling ring with a giant perfume bottle before it was fit for "Gorgeous George" to step foot on the mat. Truly ostentatious.

We got caught up in the matches as if they were real fights. Grandpa Beard would adopt Uncle Tony's flailing arm movements and butchered English, both yelling at the television, "*Kill 'em-a, kill 'em-a!*" with their fists pumping in the air. The whole room came alive. I later learned that George Wagner was actually a skilled freestyle wrestler and also the inspiration for the persona of boxing legend Muhammad Ali. Little did I know at this point what my future would hold in the sport of wrestling. Although the style of wrestling I would compete in was drastically different from what we were watching, Uncle Tony would nevertheless cheer me on in this same fashion.

The other show I had become engrossed in was about as far as one could get from professional wrestling: *Lassie.* I had made a connection with the dogs in my life, Sandy and Linda, Leonard's beloved pointers, and Trixie at home, so I could relate to Lassie, the collie. I could also relate to her owner, Jeff. He was a boy about my age who had lost his father in the war and struggled in school. In every episode, he encountered a problem and had a choice to make. Jeff always overcame the obstacles in his life and made the right decisions with the help of his beautiful dog, Lassie. When I heard on the news that Lassie had a new litter of puppies and the Campbell's Soup Co., sponsor of the show, was holding a contest to give them away, I became fixated on winning one of Lassie's puppies.

The contest rules stated that you were to send a letter to the company with suggestions for naming one of the pups. If your name was picked, you would receive $2,000 and a bona fide Lassie pup. I finished my letter, and my aunt helped me find a three-cent stamp and address it to the Campbell's Soup Co. She and my uncle had promised me that, even with Trixie and the blue merles they had taken up breeding, I could keep the puppy if I won the contest. I went to bed that night just knowing I was going to win.

With beads of sweat dripping down my face the next morning, I opened my eyes and could feel I was lying in a puddle of sweat. Sitting up slowly, I felt a stabbing pain shoot through my lower right side, and I leaned over the edge of my bed with my arms wrapped around my stomach. Dry heaves started in. I tried to stand upright between heaves but couldn't.

I moaned down to my aunt, "Aunt Gladys ... I don't feel good!" My aunt did not like climbing the stairs to the attic, so she yelled up, "What's wrong? Come on down." I grabbed the blanket off my bed, wrapped it around my shoulders, and somehow made my way down the stairs.

Aunt Gladys couldn't figure out what was wrong with me.

She thought I had the flu and had me lie down on the couch. I spent the day in misery with fever and chills, hugging my pillow tightly, trying to ease the pain in my stomach. When Uncle Tony got home and spotted me on the couch, he walked toward me and asked, *"Whats-a matt-a you?"*

"I'm hot," was all I could muster. He looked concerned and told my aunt to call Dr. Hare. I could hear her dialing the phone.

"Noooo," I moaned. "No doctor!"

As Aunt Gladys hung up she said, "Dr. Hare wants you to meet him at the hospital." My uncle didn't waste any time; he put me in the car and drove me to Good Samaritan Hospital. Dr. Hare was in the emergency room waiting for us. I sat down in a chair, hunched over and shivering, and pulled the blanket tight around me. Dr. Hare approached, knelt down, and, staring over the top of his glasses, took his huge hands and felt my face, then started probing my stomach.

He got to the lower right side, and when he released his hand, a stabbing pain shot through me. I winced, and he looked at my uncle.

"It's his appendix, and with his fever this high, we need to take it out now."

The next thing I knew I was waking up in a hospital bed again, and Dr. Hare was standing next to Aunt Gladys and Uncle Tony. After looking at his clipboard, he turned toward them and said in a lowered voice, "We got it just in time. His appendix was hot and bulging—any longer and it would have ruptured."

My aunt let out a deep sigh. "Thank you very much," she said in a breathy tone.

Uncle Tony grabbed Dr. Hare's hand and shook it hard, and

then, hitting him on the side of the arm, said, "*Thank-a you! You take-a good-a care of-a my neph-a-yew.*"

As much as I appreciated Dr. Hare taking good care of me, I could have done without my time at Good Samaritan Hospital. Lying in my hospital bed, I remembered the *Lassie* contest, and I asked Aunt Gladys if she had sent out my letter. She said yes, and I hoped and prayed I'd win. Weeks later, I got a consolation letter in the mail with an autographed picture of Lassie.

After all that I'd been through, with my nearly burst appendix and losing the *Lassie* pup-naming contest, I finally got some kind of reward that summer. Jeff and Lassie made a guest appearance at the Molalla Buckaroo Rodeo in Oregon on the Fourth of July. Uncle Tony took me, and I couldn't believe I got to watch the real Lassie and Jeff ride around the arena in a shiny red convertible.

I still would have preferred the puppy, though.

CHAPTER EIGHT

The Reunion

In June of 1955, I would be graduating from the eighth grade at Powellhurst School. For the previous month there had been a buzz in the air, and I remember Aunt Marie calling from New York and putting my mom on the phone to talk to Uncle Tony. I never spoke to my mother on the phone while she was in New York. Long-distance calls were expensive, and I don't think Aunt Gladys and Uncle Tony saw any purpose in my speaking to her. Thoughts of my family still went through my head daily, but time and distance had pushed the dream of reuniting with them into the far reaches of my mind.

My mom, after her failed attempt at working in Uncle Mike's restaurant, had been plugging away at a sewing factory in New York. I wondered who had been taking care of my brother and sister back in Italy. I worried about my father and how he was getting along, alone with the two of them. I especially worried about my little sister, Brigida, being so young and without a mother. Shortly before I left Italy, my family had moved from

Rocca to the neighboring small town of Cicciano, within walking distance of my mother's parents. I wondered if Grandma Carolina and Grandpa Giuseppe were helping take care of my brother and sister.

I still had an incredible desire to be reunited with my family, but after four years in Oregon, I had become part of a new family—a family I loved. My aunt, uncle, and baby cousin Joey all gave me a level of comfort and stability. I struggled with these conflicting thoughts daily, and at times they kept me awake at night.

My graduation in early June came on a beautiful Oregon day. It was cool and refreshing with sparse clouds, the previous day's rain compelling the sun to glisten off the newly budding foliage. So much had changed since I had arrived in America. I had grown more than a foot since signing my passport in Naples, but I wasn't as bony—I was sinewy. Living with Uncle Tony and Aunt Gladys, I had eaten and drunk just as the doctor in New York had recommended.

Still, my uncle would say, "*You-a shkinny! No meat on-a da bones.*"

Also, my hair had darkened over the years, and I now had it cut in the typical 1950s American fashion, tight on the sides with a short wave of bangs across my forehead. For graduation I wore dark-gray slacks with a red button-down collared shirt. It pinched at the neck and wrists, but I knew my aunt was pleased that I was adorned in proper attire.

"Antonio Russo," voiced the microphone as I sat in alphabetical order among my classmates. I stood and crossed the stage, shook hands with my principal, and received my diploma. Aunt Gladys was clapping and snapping pictures wildly, so proud I had made it to this point; Uncle Tony was at work, and Joey was home with Grandma and Grandpa Beard. Aunt Gladys was my only family there, and I waved to her as I stepped down from the stage.

Walking the loop to sit back down with my classmates, I had thoughts running wildly through my brain. By the middle of my eighth grade year I had convinced Uncle Tony that after-school activities would be good for me. Luckily, he somehow convinced Aunt Gladys, and I'd made some friends through those activities. After the last name for diplomas was called, we stood around in groups in the gymnasium, mingling and talking about what we'd be doing that summer. Susie McKee, a girl from down the street, came up to me, giggling.

"Hi, Tony," she said, continuing to laugh.

"Hi," I answered, shoving my hands deep into my pockets.

"Look at this!" She pulled her arm out of her sweater and posed, resting her chin on her shoulder. Spelled out across her upper arm was the name "Tony."

"Nice," I said.

"I sunbathed with your name in stencil letters on my arm," she explained.

I had no idea how to respond to this. "Wow, I like it," was the best comeback I had. Luckily, she ran off to find her parents—I had no skills in dealing with girls.

Next year, I'd be joining Susie as part of the second class to attend a brand-new high school built in Southeast Portland called David Douglas. The school was named after the Scottish botanical explorer for which Oregon's Douglas fir trees are named.

On our way home, Aunt Gladys looked over at me. "I need to tell you something," she forced out. I knew what was coming. I could feel it in the pit of my stomach.

"Your father and your brother and sister have arrived in New

York. They've moved into an apartment with your mom in Brooklyn."

I didn't respond. We pulled into the driveway of our home; several familiar cars were parked near the house. I got out of the car quickly and ran through the front door before Aunt Gladys could say any more.

Uncle Tony stood in the living room with Grandma and Grandpa Beard. Baby Joey, a typical toddler, had taken to running everywhere. His head had been topped off with a small hat, which made him look like a miniature Italian man, and as I entered, he was cutting circles around his dad's legs. Uncle Tony reached out, scooped him up on the fly, and, swinging him through the air, landed him on his hip.

Cousin Joey as a baby.

Mr. and Mrs. Azlin and Mr. and Mrs. Skibbly were mingling with some familiar faces from my aunt's side of the family. Aunt Gladys walked me over to the table to show me my graduation cake, but I knew exactly what this was really about. The cake was cut and served, but I could barely choke down a piece.

As the evening wore on and guests started leaving, my agitation level rose. I knew this would be the last time I'd see these people. I had done this once before, waving goodbye to my family from that ship, and I did not want to do it again. I fought back tears as I shook hands and hugged everyone. Grandpa Beard would not look me in the face; Grandma Beard was visibly shaking when she came over to hug me.

"Take care of yourself," she sobbed.

I couldn't believe this was happening all over again. Grandpa Beard suffocated me with his barrel chest. I remembered the day I met him and how much I loved that toy gun he had given me.

"Be good," was all he said, and they were gone. The house was still.

"*You-a sleep!*" Uncle Tony yelled, pursing his lips and throwing his chin in the air toward my bedroom. Aunt Gladys walked over to me and put her hands on my shoulders. She was calm.

"Why don't you get some sleep? You can pack in the morning," she said, and I turned away and walked toward my room.

"I will be back," I told her as I was walking up the stairs, trying to sound convincing. There was no reply. I didn't change my clothes; I just lay down and cried myself to sleep.

I woke up on Saturday morning, and Aunt Gladys had a suitcase opened up on the sofa in the living room. She had already begun putting my things in it, although there wasn't much, mostly clothes. I thought about my bike, the boxing gloves my uncle had surprised me with for one of my birthdays, and also the picture of Lassie taped up on my wall. *I don't need to bring it all with me,* I thought. *It'll be here when I get back.*

Except for Joey's babbling, the drive to the airport was silent. As we pulled into the parking lot, I flashed back to the day they picked me up and how happy I felt walking hand-in-hand with the people who cared enough to send for me from all the way across the country and take me in. We arrived at the gate and waited. Joey's wide eyes watched the planes land and take off. He kept the atmosphere light.

When we heard my boarding call, Aunt Gladys started sobbing out loud, and I couldn't help it; I did too. My uncle had wet eyes but maintained his composure. They both hugged me tightly, and I told them again, "I'll be back." I knew they didn't believe me.

"Love you, Tony," Aunt Gladys choked out as I started walking away, and I noticed Joey waving goodbye as I made my way up the staircase to the plane.

The flight attendant took me to my seat near the center of the aircraft. As I looked through the tiny window, the broad silver wing of the aircraft with its lightly moving propellers obstructed my view; I could barely see my Oregon family standing and waving. As the airplane began to turn, I got a closer look at them. My aunt wiped tears from her face with a handkerchief my uncle had handed her. I began to sob loudly. I now had the hiccups, but I didn't care, although I was trying hard to catch my breath and get my emotions in check. The flight attendant who had helped me to my seat came by and placed her hand on my shoulder.

"Are you alright?" she asked in a soft voice. Without speaking or looking at her I lied by nodding my head.

The reality that I was leaving another family behind suddenly struck me hard. I felt heavy in my seat. These were people that I loved; this was a step in the wrong direction for sure. My fear of flying and motion sickness entered my mind but only for a second. The demons swept back into my brain, and questions blinked like neon signs. Nothing else mattered. Would I be back? Would I ever see Uncle Tony, Aunt Gladys, Joey, and Grandma and Grandpa Beard again? What would reunited life with my family be like? Would New York treat me better this time around?

As the giant bird began to taxi toward the runway, the roaring engines got even louder. The props were spinning so fast, all I could see out the tiny window was a blur.

Within seconds the airplane was suspended in midair, and although I could no longer see my Oregon family, what I did see was beautiful: clear, majestic, green. Mount Hood and the Columbia River, places I had grown to love through my fishing and hunting excursions, had become part of me, and I was now viewing them from a new perspective.

As I soaked in the stunning picture below, I told myself that somehow, some way, I was going to find my way back.

How my biological family was going to receive me, I didn't know. It was now June of 1955. I had waved goodbye to them from that ship in Naples as a ten-year-old boy four years ago. My brother and sister were so young when I left. The picture that flashed in my mind continuously was of the four of them standing below me, white handkerchiefs waving and tears streaming as I peered down from the huge ship.

I wondered what they would look like now and if they would recognize me. I wondered about my mother and father and how they would react toward me now that I was becoming a young man. I did know one thing for sure: I loved them all, and regaining our family was something I still desired. There was never a day or night that went by without thoughts of them. As I reflected on my first sight of the enormous buildings and the giant lady holding the torch, my tumultuous experiences in New York came rushing back to me in a flood.

Those memories were dark and lonely. Nobody had wanted me, and I did not want to return there. Still, I was thankful that during that time I had a roof over my head and was grateful to the people who took me in. They did their best to take care of me during those months, even though they were struggling with burdens and hardships of their own. And even though this time in New York I would be with my own family, the unknown was frightening, and all I could do was sit and wait.

I leaned back into my seat with my eyes closed. Once again, the wheels of my mind began to spin. I had made up my mind that no matter what, no matter how hard it might be, I was going to convince my mother and father to move to Oregon. I had to formulate a plan that would get them to listen. I knew it was a near impossible task, as they'd have no reason to leave New York and start over again in Oregon. I just had to convince them otherwise—and I would.

The airplane's jerking motions startled me. My stomach lurched as the plane descended. Looking out the window, I saw it all again—the lady, the buildings, the water. Beads of sweat gathered on my forehead, and my anxiety increased as we approached the ground. We touched down on New York soil, and I entered the flow of people, making my way down the narrow aisle. When I got to the doorway and stood at the top of the stairs, I looked down and immediately saw them—my family, Aniello, Teresa, Pellegrino, and Brigida, standing in a row waving hello just as they had waved goodbye from the Bay of Naples four long years ago.

The crew that greeted me upon my return to New York. My mom and dad are to the far left of the back row, and my sister is to the far left of the front row. I'm not sure why my brother didn't make the photo.

CHAPTER NINE

The Power Of Persuasion

Choked with emotion, I ran down the steps of the plane toward my family. I fell into my mother's arms, and she embraced me tightly. My brother and sister grabbed me around the waist, and my father patted me on the shoulders. Tears of joy sprang from our eyes, and smiles spread across all our faces. My mother placed her hands on each side of my ears, pulling me down to her level, and kissed my cheeks over and over.

"*Mio figlio Antonio! Come sei cresciuto!*" she shouted at the top of her lungs. "*Sembra cent'anni da quando ci siamo visti!*" It had been a long time since I'd been fully immersed in my native language, yet I understood every word. She said, "My son, look how you've grown! It seems like a hundred years since I've seen you!"

This brought more tears, and my brother and sister kept repeating my name, "Antonio, Antonio," and holding onto my hands. My father grabbed my face, kissed me on both cheeks, and said, "*Come stai? Ti trovi bene in America!*" He asked how I was and noted that America had been good to me.

All I could think of in response was, "*Sì, sto benissimo e vi voglio bene!*" I told them I was doing well and that I loved them all.

My parents looked much the same as I had remembered, with my dad towering over my mother in height, although the difference between his lean six-foot stature and my mother's round four-foot-nine build seemed even more pronounced. My brother and sister were growing up. Pellegrino was taller but small and compact. He reminded me of myself when I left Italy and was the exact same age: ten years old. His hair was cut very short so that none of his curls showed, and I noticed his right ear was swollen and purplish-green in color. I wondered what had happened but didn't ask, figuring I'd find a better time later. I remembered Brigida as a porcelain doll when I left her in Italy. Now a girl of nine, she was beautiful but had an air of sadness and anger about her. She reminded me of Grandma Nappi, petite yet sturdy, with the same striking dark features.

After our kisses and hugs, the rest of the family, Aunt Marie, her sister-in-law, and all of their children, joined in. I had not seen Aunt Marie since she had taken me to visit the children's home in 1952 just before Uncle Tony brought me to Portland. I shuddered, and my thoughts turned to the promise I had made to Aunt Gladys and Uncle Tony before they put me on the plane. I knew I had to somehow keep it.

I clenched the handle of the small case I had brought with me from Portland as we walked through the parking lot. We all piled into one vehicle. Aunt Marie's sister-in-law drove us to 148 Withers Street, Brooklyn, New York.

It was a tight one-way street with cars lining both sides, and I could feel the concrete closing in on me.

I already missed the freedom of Portland's expansive green landscape. Vivid memories were hitting me as I got out of the car with my family and looked at the face of our apartment building. As I climbed the few steps to enter the front door, I gripped my suitcase in one hand and squeezed the railing tightly with the other. My father told me that this was the third place they had lived.

"*A noi piace questo posto,*" he said. They liked it there. Then he continued in Italian, "Your mother and I can walk to work, and everything we need is here." I nodded in agreement, knowing he was looking for my approval. Just before entering the front door of the building, my father turned and motioned with his head toward all the buildings around us. Proudly, he stated, "*In questa zona tutti parlano italiano.*" He motioned up and down the street with his hand. Everyone around here speaks Italian.

We walked down a hallway to the front door of our apartment, a narrow, rectangular one-bedroom flat. My brother and sister showed me where I'd be sleeping. Along with my parents, they spoke in full Italian, and I realized that it didn't take much for me to be drawn right back in.

"*Il divano è anche un letto; noi dormiamo qui,*" my brother said, explaining that the sofa was also a bed, and that's where we'd sleep. Then he continued, still speaking in full Italian, "Brigida gets a bed to herself," and he pointed to a small cot next to the sofa.

"*Va bene,*" I said. Okay.

As I began to unpack, I realized I truly had thought this day would never come. I couldn't believe my family was together again. Portland, Uncle Tony, Aunt Gladys, and Joey were still in the forefront of my mind, but I now felt I had another family to reunite with. I had to somehow combine both families, and that was my plan.

The huge impact of our family reunion was short-lived, and no time was wasted in getting everyone to work. My mother worked sewing clothes in a neighborhood factory. She had been a hard worker all of her life; she started working as a young girl, and bringing money home was her number one priority.

"If you work hard, good things will happen," she would repeatedly preach, although school wasn't necessarily a priority for any of us. Most young women in our area of Italy, including my mother, didn't go to school, so she never learned to read or write. My father, on the other hand, who had attended school until he was about eleven, could read and write quite well. In fact, when my mother went to apply for her passport to come to America, my father had to help her sign her name. Hand over hand, he guided her to spell out "Teresa Russo."

The man behind the counter assisting my parents with my mother's passport was watching this closely. "Why are you going to America? You can't even write your own name!" he mocked pretentiously.

Holding up both of her hands, my mother replied, "Do you see these hands? These hands work hard! These hands can do anything!"

Before I knew it, I found myself working with my father at a construction company, a job his cousin Luigi Mozzariello had secured for him. Luigi was the brother of Pasquale—I had lived with him and washed dishes at his restaurant during my first stint in New York. My father and I were on the same construction crew. Our family's daily routine was that my mother, father, and I would leave for work every morning while my brother and sister, still too young to work, stayed at the apartment together. Brigida loved when the milkman left glass bottles of milk in the hallway outside our door, and especially when my mother would have Orange Crush soda delivered. Pellegrino brought it in and put it in the small refrigerator. Brigida was not required to do much that resembled work; she was in many ways still considered a baby. We all protected her, and she was very private and quiet. She stayed mostly in the background.

I came home from work one day and decided it was time to ask my brother the reason for his damaged ear.

"*La Mamma mi fa pagare le bollette,*" he said. I could see where this was going when he told me our mother made him pay the bills. He had gone to pay the electric bill with the twenty dollars cash our mother had given him to take care of it. He had put the money securely in his pocket, or so he thought, but when he got to the billing office, it was gone.

"On my way home, I was scared to death," he continued, still speaking our native tongue. "Mom grabbed my ear so hard she almost ripped it off the side of my head."

"*È pazza!*" I said. She's crazy. Luckily, she had left his ear intact, but there was definite damage that would take a while to heal.

My brother was also still healing from a dog bite. A German shepherd had attacked him while he was out playing, and he opened his shirt to show me where it had taken a chunk right out of his chest.

"*Guarda la cicatrice,*" he said, proudly jutting his chest out toward me to show me his scar. I winced. Then, looking at the ground, he murmured, "*Odio le punture.*" He had been receiving a series of rabies shots, and since he had always been queasy about any kind of physical trauma or medical treatment, I knew the shots must have been unbearable for him.

In my time away from New York, Lucia DeFrancisco's son Bobby, who had taken me to the airport four years prior, had become a taxi cab driver; he took my mom and dad wherever they needed to go in the city, and he also treated my brother to his first baseball game at Ebbets Field, about ten blocks from their second New York apartment on Ryerson Street.

Bobby was a diehard Brooklyn Dodgers fan, and this rubbed off on Pellegrino, who became obsessed with baseball and the Dodgers. He talked about Gil Hodges, Jackie Robinson, and Duke Snider nonstop. One of his favorite players became Carl "Reading Rifle" Furillo, the right fielder known for his strong, accurate arm. Bobby had taken Carl home in his cab several times, and he took my brother to see the high-rise where Carl lived.

Bobby loved baseball so much that many times he'd join the kids for a game of stickball, which Pellegrino and I played with neighborhood kids in a nearby empty lot every chance we got. He could connect with the ball like none other, even with his non-muscular build and Coke-bottle-sized eyeglasses.

My brother's passion ignited my interest in the game. We began watching baseball on television and studied the game to help fashion our stickball sessions. I picked my team, and because my brother had claimed the Dodgers, mine became none other than the Dodgers' archrivals, the New York Yankees. My players were Mickey Mantle, Yogi Berra, and Whitey Ford.

My mother somehow attached the name Mickey Mantle to baseball and then associated it with any baseball game. Even years later, whenever my brother and I were watching a game instead of helping out with chores, she'd yell "*Basta con Mickey Mantle. Aiutate vostro padre!*" Enough with Mickey Mantle, she said. Go help your dad!

My brother and sister also took a liking to all of the cowboy TV shows, and I introduced them to my favorite, *Lassie*. They were picking up English quickly, and I have to say I was enjoying my time in New York. We had a neighbor who liked to show us the local attractions, and he would take us to Coney Island, the Boardwalk, and even the beach. My mom's sister Aunt Marie occasionally walked with us and her three children to the movies. *Love Me or Leave Me* with Doris Day and James Cagney was playing one time; I identified with James Cagney's raspy voice and tough-guy demeanor.

Things were generally going well, but during the nights, tears streamed down my face over the loss of my Oregon family. I was still focused on my number one goal of returning to Portland and the family I had left behind. I began to have tunnel vision, obsessed with my mission, and after a few weeks in New York, I missed my Oregon family more than ever.

I needed to get my parents to understand what they were missing in Oregon: the green landscape, the open space, the rivers, and the mountains, much like what we had left behind in Italy. I knew the exact spot on Mt. Hood where I would take my dad and brother mushroom hunting, and I couldn't wait to show them my favorite fishing holes.

I had to convince them, but I was aware that it was going to take more than bountiful fishing and hunting. I knew my parents' first priority would be jobs, so I had been formulating a plan, and my ace in the hole was Uncle Tony. I had an idea that my uncle would be able to secure work for my father in Portland. I didn't know this for sure but thought if I could at least get my father to ask him, it might work.

After Uncle Tony gave up working as a short-order cook and making trips to Alaska, he secured a fantastic job building railroad cars at Gunderson Brothers Inc. in Portland through his friend Johnny Gibbons. Johnny was a crew chief at Mixermobile, a company in Portland that built tractors for mixing and pouring concrete, and was friends with the head boss at Gunderson, George Okeson. Johnny had convinced George to hire my uncle. Uncle Tony proved to be a hard worker and soon became a favorite of the head boss. The three of them, George, Johnny, and Uncle Tony, became good friends, socializing frequently on weekends; I figured between the two companies, Uncle Tony would have some leverage in getting my dad hired somewhere.

I practiced what I would say and finally worked up the courage to hit my parents with it. One evening as we were eating dinner, I burst out across the table, "*Ci dobbiamo trasferire a Portland con lo Zio.*" I told them we had to move to Portland with Uncle Tony. My parents were shocked. They both stopped eating, mouths half-open, full of food, and looked at me for a moment, saying nothing.

My mother ripped off a hunk of bread with her mouth and then broke the silence with bread crumbs flying: *"Noooo, abbiamo posti di lavoro, amici e famiglia qui. Non possiamo lasciare tutto!"* We have jobs, friends, and family here. We can't leave! She was adamant; I had been defeated in one swift blow. Although he said nothing, I thought I saw some receptiveness in my father's eyes as he continued to eat, and this gave me a glimmer of hope.

My father's job had gotten increasingly more physically demanding, and we had recently been separated onto different crews. I knew his excellent mechanical skills were not being utilized, and the work he was doing in New York was backbreaking, lugging buckets and wheelbarrows of cement back and forth at the different job sites. We had come to America for a better life, less burdensome, and I knew this wasn't it.

One morning, about a week after my mother's outburst at the dinner table, my father and I were headed to work, and I mustered up the courage to ask him about the suggestion I had made.

"Have you thought about moving to Oregon?" I asked in full Italian.

"Sì." His response caught me off guard. I smiled but kept my posture, hands in my pockets, looking down at my feet as we walked. I was elated but did not want to show too much excitement so as not to jinx it. My dad's consideration of my proposition motivated me to keep my plan in motion. The wheels in my head started working double-time; my plan had to work. Maybe my idea of joining both families could really happen.

Lying in bed one night, I was bursting inside when I overheard my parents discussing the possibility of Uncle Tony getting my dad a better job. My mom was concerned that my dad would come up short if he checked out job possibilities in Portland and lost his stable income here. She insisted my father first find out if he could have his job back if things went badly in Portland. I lay there in bed, pleased with my plan, as it seemed to be taking shape.

It was early July, and one hot Saturday evening, we were all getting dressed in our best attire to attend the wedding of one of Luigi Mozzariello's daughters. As we headed out the front door, I flashed back to when I was fresh off the ship from Naples, trying to carve out space in the apartment of Luigi's brother, Pasquale.

When we arrived at the wedding, hundreds of people were already crammed into the pews of the Catholic church. The kneeling, standing, and praying of the Mass dragged on, and the wedding programs became fans, my mother's flapping madly at about a hundred miles per hour. We were all sweating profusely by the time the bride and groom finally made their exit as husband and wife.

A reception followed, and the hordes of sweaty Italians were more than ready to cut loose. There were gallon jugs of red wine on each table and music blaring, and everyone was dancing, singing, and partying to the fullest. I sat at our table while my brother and sister ran around and played with the other children. I watched the madness while chewing on candy-coated almonds conveniently placed in a bowl within my reach.

A man approached our table with a pretty young lady by his side. He told me he was one of my father's friends from work and then introduced me to his daughter. She had curly, light-brown hair and looked to be about my height. She shook my hand and then shouted over the music, "Do you know how to dance?"

"No," I stated, not intending to budge from where I was positioned.

She would not take no for an answer and grabbed both of my hands, pulling me out of my seat. With an overstated smile plastered across her face, she yelled, "It's easy! The Tarantella!" while dragging me onto the dance floor.

The dance floor was brimming with people, and at this point everyone was holding hands in a circle surrounding the bride and groom. The music was rhythmic and upbeat; the circle moved to the right, then to the left, and then in toward the bride and groom and back. I tried to make sure I was going in the same direction as the group, and I had to admit to myself, I was having fun. I spotted my brother and sister peering over the top of a table snickering and pointing in my direction.

As the dancers began to disperse, my new friend ran off to her family, and I went back to our table. Steaming-hot plates of lasagna were being served, and everyone was eating and drinking, with forks, spoons, and glasses clanking loudly.

My dad had been drinking all night, and holding up his glass of wine, he began to tell everyone at the table in loud, slurred Italian, "Tomorrow I'm going to call Teresa's brother in Portland. To see if there are any jobs." Eyebrows seemed to raise as he explained that his job here in New York was fine but that he wanted to do something with his hands.

"*Io potevo fare tante cose!*" he said, now holding his fork in the air to accentuate his words. I have skills! He was touting their broad range and implying they weren't being utilized fully in New York. Hearing my dad talk like this gave me the feeling that my plan was real—and now in full swing.

Sunday following the wedding was long and boring after the craziness of Saturday night. That week everything seemed to go on as usual—we went to work in the mornings and came home to my brother and sister in the evenings. The subject of moving did not come up, and I was in a holding pattern, afraid to mention it. I sensed my parents had contacted my uncle during the week. We didn't have a phone in our apartment, so they must have used Aunt Marie's.

July came and went, and August arrived. I was getting nervous because I knew if we started school in New York in September, we'd never leave. Then one evening, as we were finishing dinner, Aunt Marie came over with the news that Uncle Tony had told her he thought he could get my dad a job in Portland.

I jumped up from my chair. *"Perfetto!"* I yelled. Everything was falling into place!

My parents called him back the next day and started piecing together how we would manage this expedition. They decided it would be best if my father and I went to Oregon together by train. My dad made sure with his foreman that if things didn't work out for him in Portland, he could have his construction job back, so that comforted my parents.

By now, speaking English came easily for me, and since my dad spoke primarily Italian, I would be able to navigate us across the country. My mom, brother, and sister would stay in New York so my mom could keep working while my dad figured out his job prospects. I was thrilled. All the pieces of my puzzle were fitting together. I could see Portland more clearly than ever in my mind, and the trip by train sounded like a wild adventure. We would work through the end of the week, pack on the weekend, and leave Monday morning.

As beautifully as my plan was coming together, that very next day the rug was nearly jerked out from under me. In mid-July, my mom's younger sister Lucia D'Avanzo (who had cared for me as an infant), along with her husband, Felice, and their two sons, Antonio and Aniello, had arrived from Italy.

They made their journey on an Italian ocean liner called the *Andrea Doria*. One year later, almost to the day, the *Andrea Doria* would sail her last voyage, sinking to the bottom of the ocean. My Aunt Lucia talked for years about how they had almost waited one more year to make their journey and thank God they hadn't.

"*Madonna mia!* We'd be swimming with the fishes!" she'd say, shaking her head.

Of all my mother's siblings, she and Lucia had the closest connection. My mother hadn't told her of the plan for my father to check out job prospects in Portland, because in my mother's mind, that's all we were doing, just checking it out. Aunt Lucia felt differently.

We were preparing to sit down for dinner when the front door of our apartment flew open. Aunt Lucia burst in on a rampage. She threw her hands in the air and started yelling at my mother in Italian so fast I could only make out about every other word. I got the point very quickly, though.

She had come all this way to be with her sister and our family. We were to start a new life together, and now the sister she was closest to was leaving—not just down the street but all the way across the country. Aunt Lucia was making herself very clear: "*Noi stiamo insieme! Una famiglia sta insieme, non separati!*" she shouted. Stay together as a family!

Aunt Lucia must have heard the news from Aunt Marie. My

mom kept trying to comfort her, saying, "*Calma, calma, calma.*" She tried to assure her sister they could work it out.

Aunt Lucia suddenly stopped and said to my mother matter-of-factly, "*Mio marito va con Aniello.*" She insisted her husband go with my father.

"*Va bene, va bene,*" my mom answered back. Okay. Grabbing her sister's hands, she told her they would call Uncle Tony tomorrow and ask about a job for Felice.

That was it, the new arrangement: the three of us traveling by train across the country from New York to Portland, hoping there might be work for my dad and uncle there. My plan had been altered, but it was playing out nonetheless, and I was ready to go.

CHAPTER TEN

The Train Ride

The day of our departure arrived. We headed off toward 42nd Street to board the train at Grand Central Terminal. Both families were in tow, and everyone was nervous about what was going to transpire. I was the only one of the three of us who spoke English, so it would be my sole responsibility to organize the trip. We were traveling lightly; knowing that the trip to Oregon was just a trial, each of us carried a single suitcase and one extra case for wine and food.

The week prior, I had worried that the trip would be long and that we would need food and extra money. Aunt Lucia and my mother got busy baking bread for our journey. They filled an old suitcase from Italy with their homemade bread, provolone cheese, salami, and of course, my father's treasured red wine.

I was nervous about how Uncle Tony felt about Uncle Felice coming with us. I knew my parents had talked to him about it, but they hadn't told me what he had said. I had an idea that

Uncle Tony wasn't completely open to it based on their facial expressions and murmured discussions.

The stationmaster prepared our tickets and booked us from New York to Portland with only one exchange in Chicago. After he explained all of the details to me, I translated to my dad and Uncle Felice.

It was time to board, and both families were troubled. Nobody knew what the outcome of our trip would be, and nerves were getting the best of everyone. After the conversations seemed to calm down, both my mother and Aunt Lucia began to give me instructions.

My mom told me to look out for my dad and uncle and to keep an eye on all our things, especially "*i soldi*," the money. I shook my head and told them not to worry.

"*Non ti preoccupare!*" I said, trying to sound convincing.

As we began to board, the tears came again. My brother and sister were holding on to my arms, and it sent goose bumps up my spine as I realized their anguish. I hadn't thought about it until now, and I knelt down to hug them both and said in Italian, "Don't worry, we will live together as a family again."

I stood to board the train, and my mother's voice rose into a scream in unison with my aunt, "*Arrivederci, state bene! Vi vogliamo bene!*" Goodbyes, good wishes, and love all around.

Their voices faded as we entered the passenger car, and I immediately heard the wheels start chugging along. My family again disappeared out of sight, and I hadn't realized until that moment the burden of responsibility bestowed upon me. I started to question what I had gotten my father into. I knew both families were frightened and had no idea what lay ahead for us.

From New York to Chicago, the journey went rather well. Our food case was accessible, and my dad's wine jug was placed within reach under his seat. We sat still and did not move around much. My father and uncle kept asking me questions: *Dove siamo? Quando arriviamo? Tutto bene?* They wanted to know where we were, when we were going to get there, and if everything was okay. All of these questions so early into the trip made me nervous. All I could think of saying was, "*Tutto bene.*" Everything's fine.

As we approached the train station in Chicago, I began to worry about our transfer. I knew I had to do some reading to find our way to the new boarding area. We exited the train with a crazed mob and followed the crowd toward the center of the station. Men wearing button-down jackets and round hats with shiny black bills worked behind a large counter enclosed with glass windows. We made our way up to one of the open windows. The stationmaster in New York had told me, "You are paid in full. Show your tickets in Chicago and then board the train from Chicago to Portland."

As we approached the window, the man behind the counter eyeballed the three of us up and down and immediately began looking around nervously as if to see if anyone was watching. He looked at my dad and uncle in a peculiar way and then asked me, "Where are you headed? Do you speak English?"

I handed him our tickets. "Yes, I do, but my dad and my uncle don't. We are headed to Portland," I added. Again, he started looking around nervously, and I knew I had just made a terrible mistake.

He looked at our tickets, leaned down on his elbows, and

looked me straight in the face. "You owe another forty dollars to get to Portland," he stated.

I took a deep breath. "The man in New York said we were paid in full," I stammered.

"Well, son, he made a mistake. You owe forty bucks to switch trains." I knew he was cheating us, and I felt my face flush and tears begin to sting my eyes.

My dad and uncle realized there was something wrong. "*Che è successo?*" My dad asked what the problem was. His face turned red and tightened with anger as I explained we needed to pay another forty dollars to switch trains. I was worried because I knew my father was capable of reaching through that window and squeezing the life out of that oily fraudster, and right now, that was the last thing we needed.

My father was a reserved man, but if there were a reason for him to be otherwise, as was the case now, anything could happen. If an altercation occurred here, we could end up in serious trouble. Trying to reason with my father, I told him to just pay the man so we could be on our way. We were trapped at this point, and all I knew was that we needed to get on that train to Portland. Reluctantly my dad asked my uncle about the money.

"*È un mariuolo,*" I heard him say to my uncle in disgust—this man is a thief. Then he asked him where the money was. "*Dove sono i soldi?*" My uncle handed him what was left of our extra cash. I felt sick knowing it was all we had.

My father held on to it for a minute and, sensing his hesitation, I pleaded with him, "*Papà, per favore, pagalo.*" Please, just pay the man.

He handed over the money, and the man placed a stamp on each of our tickets, then pointed in the direction we should go. Not wasting any time, we grabbed our belongings and headed toward the turnstiles. I showed one of the stationmasters our tickets, and he escorted us to the train we would be getting on. Union Pacific Railroad line to Portland, Oregon. Direct. No more exchanges. I was relieved.

After we found our seats this time, I knew we were here for the duration. We placed the food case under the seat, and once again the wheels started rolling forward. Finally, we were off. We did get up to use the bathroom, but that was the farthest any of us would stray from our seats. I quickly realized this was going to make it a long and tedious trip. Standing up to stretch our legs and my father and uncle partaking in their wine helped a bit, but mostly we were grumpy and deliriously tired. Every time we got out the salami and provolone or the bread, my dad and uncle took long, hard swigs on their wine jugs.

After a couple of days of being glued to the same seats as we moved along the tracks, their restlessness increased. Pointing out the window, I told them to enjoy the beautiful scenery. "*Mamma mia, quanto grano!*" I said, urging them to look at all the corn.

"Hrrrmph," they'd growl back at me, and I realized I was a complete failure at my attempt to impress them. I knew we were somewhere in the Midwest because corn and wheat fields stretched as far as the eye could see. Miles and miles of flat land.

During a particularly long stretch of boring terrain, one of the porters making his rounds spotted my dad drinking from his wine jug. His eyes got big as he pointed at it and then pointed under the seat to let my father know he should put it away. My dad made a motion to the porter offering him a drink, and he vehemently shook his head in refusal. He walked in our direction, and I was worried that we were going to be thrown off the train. When he reached our seats, he leaned down and whispered in my ear that the wine needed to be kept out of sight. I told my dad in as stern a voice as I dared use toward my own father, "*Nascondi il vino!*" Hide the wine!

As the days wore on, my dad and uncle started to wonder whether we would ever get to Portland. The questions came on full force: Where is this Portland? When will we arrive in Oregon? I assured them it had already been four days on the train, so we had to be there soon. They were agitated and annoyed because they'd had no idea how long the trip really was. As the porter walked by from time to time, he informed us of stops and states we were approaching. Finally, when word came that we were coming into Oregon, my dad and uncle lit up and got excited—and so did I. I started scanning the view for familiar scenery: trees, rivers, mountains, Mt. Hood in particular.

My dad and uncle looked out with me, and I kept saying, "*Tutto e' bello,*" assuring them that everything was beautiful. They looked at me questioningly, and then my father yelled, "*Niente case, niente persone, non c'è niente qua!*" No houses, no people, nobody lives here! They were worried, but I kept reinforcing the point that Oregon is a beautiful place to live and soon we would see many homes, many buildings, and a lot of people.

The scenery started to look familiar—the Columbia River Gorge, the high cliffs and mountains, and Multnomah Falls. My excitement was building as we edged closer to Portland. At times, the train was so close to the river I felt like I could reach out and touch it.

I knew we would soon be in a more populated area. My father and uncle were regaining their strength, realizing we were approaching our final destination. Then, there it was: the Willamette River, the Portland skyline, and the Union Station Clock Tower staring right at me.

Excitedly, without even thinking, I lunged out of my seat toward the window and yelled, "*Siamo arrivati! Questa è Portland!*" Both my dad and uncle flashed big smiles and huge looks of relief that our journey by train was finally over.

CHAPTER ELEVEN

Day-Old Donuts

As we exited the train, a huge burden was lifted from my shoulders. My feet were once again on Oregon soil, and a rush of energy shot through me. I instantly spotted Aunt Gladys and Uncle Tony. My aunt was jumping up and down and waving at us, her beautiful smile spread across her face. It felt like years since I'd seen her. She pulled me close to hug me, and I held on tightly. My uncle was happy to see us too; he had not seen my dad since he was a young man in Italy. Kisses on both cheeks were mandatory. Even though Uncle Tony had open arms, I could swear he shot Uncle Felice a side-eye glance. I was pretty sure something had gone down years ago in Italy, and though I had no idea what it was, it was apparent there was no love lost between the two.

We piled into Uncle Tony's Chevy and headed east on Powell to SE 115th Street, to the home I'd lived in for the past four years. I couldn't wait to see Joey. I was coming home! Waiting at the house were Grandma and Grandpa Beard with my young cousin; he looked older even though it had only been a few months since I'd seen him, and my dad bonded with him instantly.

"*Che bel ragazzino!*" my dad yelled out, touching his face, calling him a beautiful little boy. I remembered back to my first meeting with Grandma and Grandpa Beard and could still feel the thrill over that toy gun Grandpa Beard had given me.

As Uncle Tony was introducing everyone, Grandpa Beard seemed to get nervous and quickly explained, "No kisses are necessary. In America we shake hands." Uncle Tony translated to my dad and Uncle Felice, "*Niente baci, qui in America ci stringiamo le mani.*" Handshakes followed all around.

Uncle Tony worked quickly to make final plans for my father's job. As the three of us unpacked in what used to be my attic bedroom, I heard Uncle Tony on the phone with his friend Johnny Gibbons.

"*You come-a here for dinner on-a Sunday,*" he told Johnny over the phone.

That Sunday afternoon, Mr. Gibbons was impressed upon meeting my dad. He saw a big man with huge hands who was friendly and ready to work hard. Uncle Tony told my dad, "*Lavori con strumenti,*" you will work with tools, which my dad was excited about.

They hit it off right away, and Mr. Gibbons hired my father on the spot and asked him to show up for work the following day. I couldn't believe it had all happened so quickly.

Uncle Felice also needed employment, but at the time, Mr. Gibbons had only one position available at Mixermobile. However, he told us that Hyster Co., which specialized in building forklifts, was also hiring, and he encouraged Uncle Felice to check into it. Uncle Felice was hired at Hyster but only ended up working there for one week; heavy machinery did not suit him. In Italy he was a talented baker, and that's what he wanted to do. One day, when he was downtown buying bread at Pierre's Bakery, he found out they were hiring—and Uncle Felice was the man for the job.

Both my dad and uncle loved their work and decided they would not be going back to New York. They sent word back to my mother and Aunt Lucia and were in a hurry to get the rest of the family out to Oregon. As much as I liked it, I knew we couldn't stay with Uncle Tony for much longer, partly because the tension between him and Felice was escalating. In the evenings, when the nightly wine-drinking ritual set in, Uncle Felice took his glass and slunk away into the other room; he and Uncle Tony pretended the other didn't exist.

We immediately made plans to get the family moved out to Oregon; they would travel by bus to save money, and we would move out of Uncle Tony's house by the end of the week when everyone was scheduled to arrive. My dad and I secured an apartment at the end of Uncle Tony's street, on the corner of 115th and Division, and Uncle Felice found a rental home in the nearby Parkrose area.

In the meantime, I picked up right where I had left off with the Azlins and the Skibblys, mowing lawns, pulling weeds, and taking care of the dogs. I welcomed the familiarity of working for these families again, and I especially loved being back with the dogs; Sandy and Linda slobbered me up one side and down the other the day I showed up to clean their kennels.

When my mother's bus was due to arrive in Portland, Uncle Tony drove us to the Greyhound station. As we walked into the station, they were already standing in a group waiting for us: my mom, brother, sister, Aunt Lucia, and her two sons. They all looked haggard and worn out. We greeted each other with kisses, and although we were happy to be together, their smiles were forced, and the look in my mother's eyes told me she was not thrilled to be here.

"*Mi fa male la spina,*" my mother spat into my father's ear with a frown as they said hello. Her back hurt. This made me nervous, and I had a strange feeling that I would be hearing more about this bus ride they had just endured. I hoped my mother's sour attitude and aching back weren't an indication of what her overall opinion of Portland would be.

At Uncle Tony's house, after pouring wine all around and then introducing the families, Uncle Tony raised his glass, toasting, "*Grazie a Dio! Thank-a God,*" he continued in English. "*You all-a here in-a Port-a-land! Salute!*"

All glasses were raised, tensions were eased, and I started to see some smiles. I had done it, really done it. My two families were together in the place that had become my home. Uncle Tony then directed the D'Avanzo family into his car and drove them to their rental home in Parkrose. Even though we had found an apartment, my family remained at Uncle Tony's. It was crowded, but it was easier to stay there for now, and Uncle Tony and Aunt Gladys didn't seem to mind. Although my aunt and uncle were gracious in sharing their home, Aunt Gladys was now expecting her second child; adding the five of us made for cramped living space. It was far from an ideal situation.

Money was tight. I added to the family income with my yard work, and my brother went out and got a paper route to do his share. My mother didn't have a job yet but was inquiring about some possibilities. A few weeks later we decided it was time to move out of Uncle Tony's and began transporting some of our things to the new apartment.

During that week, my brother burst into Uncle Tony's house after his paper route one day and shouted in Italian to anyone who would listen, "There's a house for sale on 118th Street!" We all walked down Powell to 118th to take a look.

"*È perfetta!*" my father said before we had even toured the inside. The asking price of $7,100 was out of our league, but the owners were willing to sell it to us on a contract.

My parents got out of the apartment lease, and that was it. It was unbelievable, and I was overwhelmed over the purchase of our new home, only three streets down from Aunt Gladys and Uncle Tony. I had accomplished my goal. I would have the best of both worlds—my two families together in Portland, Oregon.

The transition happened quickly; the sellers wanted out, and we wanted in. Our new home was quite small actually. Inside the front door, the kitchen was on the left, the dining room was on the right, and straight ahead was a bathroom. To each side of the bathroom were identical bedrooms; my sister claimed hers, and my parents took the other one.

The attic, which had a long flight of narrow stairs leading up to it, became a shared bedroom for my brother and me. The house had a detached garage and a large lot, which gave my father a place for two of his favorite things: a spot to make his red wine and enough property to have a large garden.

My father Aniello Russo in the front yard of our new home in SE Portland.

My mom was still on her quest to find work. We'd had a phone installed right away, and she and my Aunt Lucia talked every day about her need for employment. Aunt Lucia had already found a job at Scarpelli Macaroni Co., but my mom was still out of luck.

The D'Avanzos had met some Italian people in the Parkrose neighborhood where they were now living, and one of their friends, Pasqualina Vitiritti, had told my Aunt Lucia that her company, ShedRain Umbrella, was hiring. They needed workers to sew umbrellas, and it was no secret that my mother knew her way around a sewing machine.

Aunt Lucia called my mother and told her what Pasqualina had said: "If you can get yourself there, ShedRain will hire you." And they did.

My mother, Teresa Russo (right), with a coworker at ShedRain Umbrella Co.

My mother didn't drive but she was determined, and Aunt Gladys showed her how to navigate the Portland bus system. She found the bus route that would get her to ShedRain, and it conveniently dropped her off right in front of the building.

She had to walk a couple of blocks down the street from our house to catch the bus, though. The stop was on the corner of 118th and Division, which happened to be the parking lot of Marshall's Donut Shop. She quickly realized the donut shop sold their day-old donuts for twenty-five cents a dozen, so she began leaving early to buy them for us kids to eat for breakfast. She'd walk them home and then head back to catch the bus. When my brother, sister, and I got up for the day, we'd have an array of "choice" day-old donuts awaiting us every morning.

Surrounded by both of my families, though, I didn't care how old the donuts were. It was great to be home.

CHAPTER TWELVE

Breaking Ground

The hallways at David Douglas High School were frenzied, with kids bumping into me right and left as I tried to get from one class to another. September 1955, the beginning of my freshman year, was rough; kids hung out in groups, and somehow they all seemed to already know one another. There were only a couple recognizable faces from my days at Powellhurst School. My summer in New York had created a divide I was not prepared for.

To make matters worse, my mother had bought me a black leather jacket in New York that made the journey with her to Oregon by bus. It had a large collar and big silver zippers, one up the middle and one on each side pocket. She had seen these jackets on kids in Brooklyn and was proud to give it to me so I could wear it to school. I was thrilled to have it. The jacket was impressive; it matched my black leather boots and reminded me of Marlon Brando in two movies he had been in recently that I related to: *On the Waterfront* and *The Wild One*.

My jacket made a statement at school to say the least—and unfortunately not a good one. By the looks I was getting, I understood black leather jackets with large zippers were not popular in Portland, Oregon, yet. Sadly, I started leaving my jacket at home, though I felt bad since my mom had worked so hard to provide it.

Lunchtime in the cafeteria turned out to be even worse than trying to navigate the halls. It was buzzing with kids and earsplittingly loud. I would try to find the least crowded table and sit at the very end, usually the best place to avoid interacting with anyone, but also the best place to eat my lunch in private. My mother would take a large hunk of her homemade bread, hollow it out, and stuff it with salami and cheese or whatever had been left from dinner the night before: peppers and onions fried in olive oil, tomatoes, or meatballs in red sauce. These were my favorite foods, but I could feel the spotlight on me when I'd pull out my daily offerings and try to eat with any dignity.

I would look around to make sure no one was watching and then hunch over and quickly take a bite. The crust on my mother's bread was thick and crunchy, making it impossible to take in small chunks, and my mouth would be stuffed full. It was difficult to keep the contents from spilling out onto the table. I tried to use my hands to keep everything where it was supposed to be, but it was no use. Enduring this humiliation for a couple of weeks was as much as I could take. I begged my mother to buy sliced white "American" bread like Aunt Gladys, and to my surprise, she did. She began making my sandwiches on this deflated, insipid bread, and I just knew it was going to be the answer to all of my troubles. I was wrong.

At home I was beginning to feel like a big shot. I had been

responsible for uniting my two families, and now that I was living with my biological family, I seemed to be considered more of an adult. I didn't have the same discipline enforced on me that I'd had while living with Uncle Tony and Aunt Gladys. I enjoyed my new freedom, and it did seem I was living the best of both worlds. My aunt had recently given birth to her second child, a girl they named Susan, and I was honored when my aunt and uncle asked me to be her godfather.

The church, glowing from the dim lighting and bit of sun diffused by the stained glass windows, set the mood, and the ceremonial event was humbling. The baby's scream as the priest doused her head in holy water made me cringe. I was nervous and not feeling quite worthy of this new position in my life.

"You will always be a part of this family," Aunt Gladys told me as she hugged me after the ceremony.

Holding my goddaughter Susan on the day of her baptism.

Uncle Tony was at our house daily, as he drove my father to and from work. When he brought my father home at the end of the day, he'd come in for a few glasses of red wine.

"*Porta il vino!*" Bring out the wine, he'd shout, throwing his hands in the air. He always spoke in full Italian to my father.

"*Che cosa c'è da mangiare?*" Uncle Tony would ask. What's to eat? Many times it was one of my mom's specialties like *pasta e fagioli*, pasta and beans.

"Teresa," my dad would shout, "*porta la pasta e fagiul!*" My mother would serve the men their food; they'd eat, drink, and shout to one another across the table. Shouting was the norm in our house, the decibel level directly proportional to the amount of wine that had been consumed.

School continued on for me in the same manner. I was trying to fit in but having trouble, so I picked up where I had left off at Powellhurst—by emitting as much attitude as I could. My first fight, in the boys' locker room, was inevitable. After a PE class, a senior started giving me some lip.

"You're an Italian idiot, you know that?" he said, trying to get a rise out of me. I didn't reply. "You heard me, you pansy ass. Walking around like you're some kind of tough guy." He started to mock the way I walked.

I put my foot up on the PE bench and pretended to tie up my boot. Looking directly at my foot, I drew in a deep breath to try to contain myself, but this guy would not let up.

He walked over to me and bumped his shoulder into mine

and, putting his mouth right up to my ear, whispered, "I could kick your ass any day of the week."

That was it. I turned in a fury with both my hands on his chest and drove him back into the lockers. His head slammed against the doors, and the crashing sound brought a mass of onlookers. He flailed around, trying to punch at me. I drove my left forearm across his throat, digging my elbow in as hard as I could below his collarbone. His eyes were wild with a look of fear and surprise, and my intensity rose as I increased the pressure across his throat.

Mr. Miller, our PE teacher, must have heard the commotion from his office and came running out to find my adversary blue in the face. He pulled us apart, pushing away my enemy, and then, grabbing me by the back of the arm and squeezing, forced me into his office, pushed me down into a chair, and sat behind his desk. He stared at me for a moment with his elbows on his desk and his fingers interlocked. Then he got up and knocked on the window.

"Get out of here!" he shouted, pointing to the door at some students who were lingering. "Get to class, there's nothing more to see." He sat back down behind his desk. "You like to fight, do ya?"

I shrugged my shoulders, not looking him in the eye. *This guy doesn't know me*, I thought. And I had no intention of talking.

"There is a place where you can fight if that's what you like to do."

I shrugged my shoulders again.

"Have you ever played football?"

I shook my head. I was finding it hard to keep my legs still in that chair. I was still fired up inside, though I could tell he was trying to calm me down.

"You know, I'm the head football coach here, and we have a great freshman program. Why don't you think about joining the team?"

I still didn't say anything even though I wanted to respond. I had seen the guys out on the field, and I was envious.

"Don't worry, I'm not going to turn you in this time," he continued. "Go ahead and get to your next class, but try to control yourself, and give football a thought."

I got up out of the chair to leave, and on my way out the door, I turned back to face Mr. Miller. "I will," I said. "I think I would like to play football."

He gave me a half-smile and nodded his head in approval.

When I mentioned to my mother that evening that I wanted to play football, she began to scream in Italian, "*Noooo, no play this-a game!* After school you start the sauce and put coal in the furnace."

She would not hear of it. She had no idea about organized sports and didn't care one way or the other about the game of American football. She was mostly concerned that I come home after school and get the house ready for the evening.

"*Quando arrivo a casa sto morendo di fame!*" She pointed out that she was always starving when she got home from work.

I pleaded with my mom and dad. "I will still finish my work. Pete and Patty can start the chores, and I will finish when I get home."

Pete and Patty were, of course, my brother and sister. Since starting school in Portland, they had both come home with new American names. My brother came home one day and simply announced, "*Da oggi mi chiamo Pete!*" He explained that there was a tall blond boy at school named Pete, and that was to be his new name. I'm not sure how my sister went from Brigida to Patty.

I continued to plead my case for football with my mother, and she finally reluctantly agreed, but not without a threat. If I missed any chores, there would be no more football.

"We are not here to play games," she added. "We are here to work hard!" She was not happy.

That next day I checked in with Mr. Daggett, the freshman football coach, in the locker room after school. He gave me a bunch of gear, and I watched the other guys suit up so I knew how it worked. The only thing I didn't have were the right shoes; all I had were my boots, which was embarrassing, but I had no other choice. We ran out onto the field and did a warm-up and then split into groups. My group was at the blocking sled, and when it was my turn to drive the sled forward, my boots were slipping out from under me. I saw Coach Daggett zero in on my feet, and he motioned for me to come over.

"Take this kid to the locker room and get him a pair of shoes," he said to the manager. I followed the manager to the locker room, and he gave me an old pair of cleats. They smelled like leather combined with sweat, and the scent struck a nerve, reminding me of the few times I had worn shoes as a child in Italy. I put them on and was ready to go.

Mr. Miller, my PE teacher, had been right. I loved being out there hitting and running. It was difficult to keep up with my chores at home, but there was no way I was going to give up football. Somehow I managed.

My academics were a different story altogether. I was struggling, and even though I could speak English fluently at this point, language was still a hindrance, especially in terms of reading and writing. My spelling was particularly dreadful. The classes were brimming with bodies, and I was lost in the shuffle. Most of my teachers were empathetic toward me and tried to help, but it was football that kept me going back every day. Even though I was only playing sparingly on defense, I appeared in every single game. I had the skills down, tackling being my favorite, but I still really didn't know much about the game. I only weighed about 125 pounds, but I loved to hit and I didn't care about getting hit. Going hard during practice satisfied my aggression needs.

During one practice about halfway through the season, just as everything with home and football seemed to be meshing, I jumped into the air to receive a pass, and the defensive back put his shoulder pad into the left side of my rib cage and laid me out flat. I heard something crack and hit the ground hard. As I lay there, I tried to tell myself I wasn't really hurt, but when I tried getting up, I only made it to my knees and couldn't straighten out my torso. The trainer came running over and helped me stand.

"You might have a couple of broken ribs," he said as he was helping me off the field.

Tears flooded my eyes, not from the pain but because I feared my mother. I knew exactly how she would react if I got injured, so when I got home I pretended to be okay, trying to go about my chores in a normal manner. But I was favoring my left side and moving more slowly than usual, and of course my mother noticed immediately that something was wrong.

"*Che cosa è successo?*" she yelled. "*Ti sei fatto male?*"

I downplayed it and told her I was just a little hurt.

She started screaming again, "You quit this ball! You come home after school!"

I started crying, not from the pain as my mother thought but because I did not want to give up football.

She came over and put her arm around me. "*Domani andiamo al dottore.*" Tomorrow we're going to the doctor.

"We have a doctor for the team," I explained to her. "I will see the team doctor, and you don't have to pay."

"*Bene,*" she said, nodding.

The next day, instead of going to practice after school, the trainer drove me to 148th and Division to see Dr. Dale R. Browning. Doc Browning was the team doctor for most of the sports teams at David Douglas High School. He was a broad-shouldered man, about five foot ten with a muscular build. He had medium brown hair and wore squared-off glasses. I sat on the exam table. He crossed his arms and looked me in the face as he asked me what happened.

I gave him the scoop as he lifted my left arm and started pressing on my rib cage.

"Yep, we'll X-ray it. But a couple of broken ribs for sure," he said. "And you've probably torn all the muscles across the left side. At least you'll be healed up in time for wrestling season," he added, chuckling to himself at this last statement.

"I don't know," I sputtered, trying to process what he meant by that comment. "When can I play football again?"

He looked at me over the top of his glasses and replied, "I'm sorry, but you're out for the season, son."

Disappointed, I nodded, knowing full well that once I was healed up, I was going to have to re-convince my mom to let me play anyway.

I was still thinking about his wrestling comment. "I have wrestled in PE," I told Dr. Browning, "but I don't know about the team."

"Give it some thought," he said. "You look like a wrestler."

Then he shook my hand firmly and said, "Nice to meet you, Tony Russo. Take care of yourself."

I took an immediate liking to Doc Browning, a far cry from my experiences with Dr. Hare.

All hell broke loose at home after I explained my injury to my mother.

"*Basta con questo gioco!*" she yelled. Stop with this game! She insisted I was finished with football.

That next week after school I came straight home instead of checking in with my coaches at practice. I couldn't play anyway, and I tried to convince myself that this was somehow different than quitting. My decision appeased my mother, but the looks and grumbles from the other players told me I was wrong; I knew exactly what they were thinking. I had to change my mom's mind.

I decided to talk to my dad, telling him that the boys at school were calling me a quitter. I pounded my chest with both fists for emphasis.

"*Oh, bull-a shit-a!*" he yelled. My parents had quickly picked up the word bullshit from Uncle Tony and, of course, added an Italian flair. "*Mio figlio non si arrende,*" he added, pointing his finger in my face. My son is not a quitter. "*Non preoccuparti della Mamma.*" He assured me I shouldn't worry about my mother.

He did convince her, and I played in the final game of the season, but she was adamant: "When it's over, you are done with this game!" That was her final word.

When football season ended, my mother was happy I was coming home after school again to do my chores. I hated it, and I missed staying after school for practice. In PE we had started a unit on wrestling with Mr. Hiebert, one of several PE teachers.

He was also the junior varsity football coach as well as the head wrestling coach. He was young and handsome and stood nearly six feet tall. He had a lean, athletic build and his straight, dark hair was cut short on the sides in a classic men's fashion.

Mr. Hiebert sat the whole group of us boys down at the beginning of the wrestling unit and gave a speech about how David Douglas was a new school and that he was trying to build a program. He was animated and passionate about wrestling, and as he got fired up, his face went beet red. He said we had the kind of athletes at David Douglas that it takes to build an outstanding wrestling program, and he was encouraging all of us to come out for the team.

As he was talking, I thought back to my days at Powellhurst School; wrestling had provided a means to work out some of my frustrations and was an activity that for the first time in my life had met my level of intensity. I recalled the sheer raw power and intense focus it took to control my opponent, and even though my ribs were still sore from my football injury, I was champing at the bit to get started and show Mr. Hiebert I had some skills.

The unit started with the fundamentals: the stance, the take-down, escapes, reversals, and pinning combinations. We worked on these every day. Mr. Hiebert had a systematic way of breaking down each skill, and I picked them up quickly. After drilling and going over the basics, we ended each class with an aggressive mat game. Then, about a week into the unit, he started to pair us up against one another. Some boys in the class had substantial wrestling experience and were already signed up for the team. I was determined to show Mr. Hiebert I could hold my own against those boys.

One of them was John Loomis. John was a tough, skilled wrestler. I knew if I could stay with him in a match, Mr. Hiebert would notice me. He had been taking some of the guys off to the side and talking to them about joining the team, and I really wanted him to come to me. One day, during a match with John, I noticed Coach Hiebert watching and decided to go all out. I shot in for a takedown, lifted John off the mat, and threw him straight to his back. I was working as hard as I could for the pin, and Coach Hiebert walked over to get a better look. John ended up fighting his way off his back, and the rest of the match was a head-to-head brawl. After class, Coach Hiebert called me into his office.

"You've got some talent," he said. "I'd like to see you come out for the team."

I wanted to join the team so badly I could taste it, but I was still conflicted about what was going on at home. My parents were working hard to make a new life for us, and I felt it was my responsibility to help with chores and continue working to bring in money.

"I'd like to, but my mom didn't like me playing football, and I know she won't want me to wrestle," I admitted to Hiebert.

"I'd be happy to come over and meet your parents," Hiebert told me. "I can explain the sport to your mom."

My stomach knotted up; the last thing I wanted was this man showing up at our house and finding out that my parents didn't even speak English. "No, that's okay," I said quickly. "I'll talk to them tonight."

That evening in the kitchen, after my dad had started in on his wine, I started in on him about wrestling.

"I can wrestle at David Douglas. It's like fighting," I told him. "The coach says I'm good."

"*Sì?*" My father raised his eyebrows and smiled.

I could tell he was receptive to the idea. My dad was a tough guy, and I had heard stories of fights in his younger days. He had an impressive ten-inch razor blade scar down the middle of his back from a brawl that had happened before I was born. Now he was more reserved and had mellowed over the years, but if someone truly angered him, he'd just as soon take them out. Remembering the night my grandfather was stabbed to death, I knew my father would have killed that man had he found him.

"Teresa!" he shouted from the kitchen. "*Antonio farà la lotta a scuola.*" Tony will wrestle at school.

"*Noooo, non va bene!*" she screamed back at him. No way!

"*Sì, va bene!*" my dad yelled back with finality.

My mother, the only person I knew not afraid of my father, walked toward us from the other room. Pointing a finger in our faces, hissed at the both of us. "*Sei non lavori, tu fai solo la lotta con il diavolo!*" You are wrestling with the devil if you don't work hard! Then she continued on sharply in Italian, "We need to work hard to make it in this country!"

My dad looked over at me and nodded his head. "*Tu puoi fai a lottare.*" He assured me I would wrestle. I decided this was a yes even though I was nowhere close to having the blessing of my mother.

I did go out for the team, but without my mother's approval I felt like somewhat of a sneak, and I found it hard to commit. I left practice early every day to appease her and start my chores, and I never went to any of the away matches. Coach Hiebert wrestled me in a few home exhibition matches, though, and I won them all. When the season ended, Coach Hiebert asked me into his office.

"You know, Tony, you've got talent in this sport," he said. "Wrestling might just be your thing, but nothing's going to come of it if you don't commit yourself."

I knew exactly what he was saying. This was my sport, and I knew it. All season I had been idolizing a senior wrestler by the name of Hershell Green. He was a Black Adonis, godlike with his 190-pound build and perfectly etched physique. He was David Douglas High School's first-ever individual state wrestling champion. I knew when I saw him with that gold medal, a champion, that I wanted to be there. I needed to make a commitment to myself that I would step it up next season regardless of the reticence from my mother. I had my dad on board, and that was all I needed.

When summer started, so did our jobs. My brother, Pete, had his paper route and had come up with an ingenious plan to add to his earnings. My father had built a fence along the border of our back yard, and he'd deliberately put in a gate so that we could go out that way and kids from the other side could come through our yard to play in the fields across our street. My brother set up shop at the gate each afternoon and charged each traveler a dime to pass through the gate. I'm not sure how many friends he made that summer, but it definitely added to his pocket change. I was still doing yard work and odd jobs for the same families.

My sister, Patty, didn't work, but she helped around the house and played in the nearby open fields and farms with the other kids her age. Behind us was a dahlia farm owned by Mr. Benedict, who lived on our street. Occasionally he would pick up my brother and me on the way to his farm; we'd work all day for nearly nothing.

One afternoon my sister came home from her escapades outside with a dog in tow. A neighbor had given him to her, and she really wanted to keep him. He was cute and looked like he might be a beagle/terrier mix.

"Please, can I keep the dog?" she begged my parents. My mother groaned, but my dad had a soft spot for my sister and did not tell her no very often.

"*Sì, lo puoi tenere,*" he told her. You can keep him. My sister started jumping up and down.

"*Grazie, grazie! Si chiama Lucky!*" She wanted to name him Lucky, and both my parents liked the dog's name and could pronounce it easily. He would become the first of numerous "Lucky" dogs to join our family.

ShedRain Umbrella Co. kept my mother busy. She was paid by the piece, so we would help her get her needles threaded and ready the night before to give her a head start on the next day. She was competitive, and not only did she want to make the most money she possibly could, she also wanted to out-produce her coworkers.

Even with her job at ShedRain, my mother decided that on the weekends during the summer she would pick berries, or anything for that matter, to make extra cash. The three of us would go with her to one of the many local farms or berry fields and pick all day. My mother would holler at my brother and sister to work hard if she caught them playing. "*Lavoro, lavoro, niente gioco!*" No playing allowed! They didn't especially enjoy being out in the fields all day picking berries; neither did I. One Saturday morning my mother told us she couldn't go out and pick that day.

She laid out the plan for us. "*Voi raccogliete le fravole e poi portatemi i soldi,*" she instructed. We were to pick the berries, then come home and deliver the money to her. We stared at her in shock. That meant we had to get on the bus and find the fields by ourselves.

"We don't want to go without you." I spoke for the three of us. She stood her ground and handed us the lunches she had already packed.

"*Andate, andate,*" she said, shooing us out the door.

When we started to see berry fields out the window of the bus, we got off at the next stop. The three of us stood there watching the workers entrenched in their rows, picking furiously. Nobody seemed to notice us standing there, and none of us were confident talking to people in general, let alone strangers. We ended up sitting on the bench where the bus had dropped us off and talking about how angry our mother was going to be if we didn't bring home any money. Time passed, and we were bored and getting hungry, so I suggested we go ahead and eat our lunches and then wait a bit more.

"When we get home, we'll tell her there was no work today," I suggested. My brother and sister agreed, but we all knew what the outcome would be. She would be spitting mad.

We boarded the next bus that came by, and when we walked in the door, the first thing my mother said, rubbing her fingers together in my face, was, "*Dove sono i soldi?*" She wanted the money.

"*Non c'era lavoro oggi.*" I lied, telling her there had been no work, and she knew it. The rage in her eyes was frightening.

"*Sei pazzo!*" she yelled. You're crazy! She popped me on the head with her open hand. By now I had grown much taller than my mother, and she had to reach up to get to my head.

"*Figli disgraziati!*" she screamed at us. We were disgraceful. She had asked us to do one thing, and we hadn't delivered. She was fuming and kept rambling on about how lazy and ungrateful we were. The three of us scattered to avoid our mother for the rest of that day.

CHAPTER THIRTEEN

Rebel In A Blackboard Jungle

Summer ended, and school was upon us again. My brother and sister were growing up. Pete was entering seventh grade at Powellhurst School, and Patty would be in fifth grade. Pete was doing well, and he looked like a miniature version of myself. If it weren't for our size difference, we could pass for twins with the same haircut and similar facial features. Our mannerisms, gestures, and voices were alike, too, and we had an identical gait in our stride.

Patty, on the other hand, did not like school. She was becoming even more beautiful but was struggling with her academics and having trouble adjusting. Earlier that year we had started watching a new television show called *The Mickey Mouse Club*. My sister, with her wavy dark hair, dark eyes, and petite build, was the spitting image of Annette Funicello, one of the Mouseketeers.

Missing school was becoming a trend for my sister, and my parents, coming from a place where most girls didn't attend school anyway, did not see the danger in it. I was worried about Patty, but I tried to stay focused on football and my goals for the upcoming wrestling season.

By this time, I had made some friends and could now walk down the halls of my school with confidence. My two best pals were my wrestling teammates, Louie Day and Mike Elia. Louie thought he was the toughest guy at David Douglas High School; he could have been a member of my own family with his jet-black hair, thick eyebrows, and angry, deep-set eyes. He stood only about five foot two, but he was muscularly ripped and had outstanding athletic ability. He was also the only boy I knew who could sport a full beard whenever he wanted. Louie was always one step away from crossing the line in any given situation. His favorite thing to do was to see how many fights he could get into during a day.

Mike, taller, thinner, and as far as I could tell, smarter, followed Louie's tough-guy lead. The three of us were always getting into trouble, and our behavior had been greatly influenced by the release of two movies in 1955—*Blackboard Jungle* and *Rebel Without a Cause*. We were impressed by the rebellious acts of the kids in those movies, and we tried to emulate them. In fact, we pretty much thought we were those kids. Nobody was going to tell us differently, nobody was going to mess with us, and as a result, trouble met us head-on around every corner.

As mid-wrestling season rolled around, I was living up to the promise I had made to myself to be committed to my sport, working out hard in the practice room and going all out in every match. I was undefeated in the league, and my goal this season was to make it to the state tournament. My "Blackboard Jungle" attitude was helping me out on the mat, and Coach Hiebert was happy with my work ethic. As hard as I was working in the wrestling room, Louie, Mike, and I were matching that with our level of mischief on the weekends.

School had let out for winter break, and this would be the first time my family would enjoy Christmas in the full American fashion, although I couldn't help remembering our Christmas celebrations in Italy. Christmas had been drastically different there. On Christmas Eve we always had a quiet meal at home with the family, consisting of *baccalà*, salted cod. We would then attend midnight mass at Sant'Agnello, a church near our home. My brother, sister, and I would get excited on Christmas Day to help my mother fill baskets with the special breads and cakes she had baked. We would deliver them to friends and family, and in return they would present us with baskets filled with different types of breads, and sometimes there would be salamis, meats, and cheeses, too. Christmas in Italy focused on family and delicious food, not gifts. Our entire extended family celebrated together, talking, eating, and drinking around a giant table.

My parents had learned the American tradition of a Christmas tree and gifts on Christmas morning from Aunt Gladys. On the morning of December 25, 1956, we were all excited. My brother, sister, and I had opened some gifts of clothing and items that we needed, and then my dad handed me a long, heavy box.

"*Buon Natale!*" he sang out, wishing me Merry Christmas.

I thought I knew what the box contained right away, but a voice in my head said, *No, it can't be.* I opened it up, and sure enough: my very own Sears & Roebuck J.C. Higgins shotgun.

"Wow, *grazie!*" I turned the gun over in my hands. *It's the real thing this time*, I thought.

"*Sei bravo!*" my dad said, nodding in my direction. You're a good boy, you have worked hard and you deserve this. My mom chimed in and told me to have fun with my new shotgun. She was laughing; they were both happy to give it to me. I wasn't sure I deserved it, but I was more than ready to get out there and give it a try.

All of my hunting trips to date had been either with relatives or friends of relatives. I always had to use someone else's gun, and I was usually the fetch-it guy for the adults. Now, I would finally get to go hunting on my own. It was perfect timing because school was out for Christmas break, and all I had going on was wrestling practice.

That next day at practice, I told Louie and Mike about my gun and that I knew the perfect spot to go duck hunting on Sauvie Island.

Louie was game. "I'll borrow my stepdad's car and pick you guys up in the morning," he said.

We were all pumped up about our plans. I told my mom before I went to bed that night that I needed to be up at four in the morning because I was going hunting with Louie and Mike. My mom always got me up; she never set an alarm clock since she was always up at the crack of dawn no matter what.

Louie and Mike pulled into my driveway at four thirty. They were laughing and hell-bent for trouble.

"What's going on?" I asked as I threw my gun into the back seat and then squeezed in next to Mike in the front.

"I just stole the old man's car," Louie said, slapping the steering wheel and laughing. "He left the keys out. It's his own damn fault."

"You kiddin' me?" I asked. "I thought you said he'd let you borrow it."

"The old man's a jerk. He said I couldn't use it, but I don't give a shit. He's not my dad. I can kick the crap out of him anytime I want, and I have."

I shook my head. "Let's go."

Louie backed out of the driveway, and I directed him to Sauvie Island. It was dark and foggy, and the closer we got to our destination, the thicker the fog seemed to get.

"Man, you could cut this fog with a knife!" Louie said, and I could tell he couldn't see three feet in front of him, but he didn't care. He drove out of control as I shouted directions to the farm where I'd been duck hunting with Aunt Gladys's cousin Kenny Brooks. I was Kenny's bird dog; he used to make me run and bag up the birds after he'd shot them down. He knew the property owners, and as long as I told them I'd been here before with Kenny, we'd be fine.

We arrived at the property and turned down a long dirt road until we reached a clearing, and Louie parked the car. The three of us got out quickly and grabbed our stuff out of the back seat. Louie and Mike had their own guns, and I was raring to break in my new J.C. Higgins. It was still dark and foggy, but we were able to make out a brushy area where we could take cover. There was no way we could see anything in this fog.

"How are we gonna get any ducks if we can't see 'em?" Mike whispered.

"Hell," Louie said. "They're flocking right toward us! When you hear 'em, just aim and shoot."

That's exactly what we did. Ducks were dropping from the sky like rain. In about an hour, the trunk of Louie's car was packed full. I was nervous about it, to say the least.

"We better go," I told them. "I don't know what the limits are. Let's get out of here."

The three of us were still in a crazed state of mind, especially Louie. It was now about six in the morning. The sun had not yet risen, and the fog was still blanketing the ground. Louie was driving even more recklessly than he had on our way in. I was holding on to the dashboard with both hands as Louie's foot pressed the gas pedal closer and closer to the floor. We were flying. All three of us were thrown to the side around every corner, and I kept getting pinned up against the passenger side door. Before I knew it, we were going head-on for a telephone pole. Louie had no time to react. He veered to the left, and I heard a deafening blow as my door slammed into the pole.

I came to with a police officer staring me in the face. He sat me up, and I put my hand over my forehead and felt a divot where a piece of my scalp had been. My eyes blurred as blood started streaming into them, and I started to panic about what my parents were going to say. I was scared to death and sick to my stomach.

"Can you stand up?" the cop asked me.

"Yeah," I said, getting out of the car.

"What are you boys doing out so early?"

Louie was standing there with both hands clasped behind the back of his head looking at his stepdad's car.

"Shit," he kept saying over and over, kicking the dirt.

The cop looked ticked off. "I asked what you boys are up to," he said with irritation in his voice.

"We were duck hunting," Mike told him.

"Do you have a license for that?"

"Not with us," Mike replied nervously.

I was pretty sure I didn't have a license at all. I just kept standing there with my hand over my head trying to keep the blood from running into my eyes.

"Open the trunk." The cop motioned to Louie.

When he saw the ducks, he shook his head and slammed the trunk. "I'm going to need to see your license and registration."

Louie didn't have his wallet on him, and he had no idea where the registration was.

The police officer was pissed. "What the hell were you thinking?" he said, looking down at Louie. "Get in the car!" He motioned his head toward his squad car, and then, grabbing me by the shoulder, he added, "We need to get you to the hospital."

We sat in the back seat of his squad car, not making a sound all the way to the hospital. After being checked in at the emergency room, we were separated; I was taken to another room and had nineteen stitches put into my scalp. The injury was so jagged that the doctor had to cut it to straighten it out before stitching it up.

I later found out that Louie and Mike were released right away, but I spent the day in the hospital. When my parents arrived, they were more grateful that I was alive than angry.

"*I fucile dov'*è?" I asked my dad. I wanted to know where my shotgun was, but he shut that door fast.

"*Scordatelo!*" he answered. Forget it! I didn't bring it up again.

I was shaken up from the accident and knew I could have been killed, and I felt guilty that my parents had no idea Louie was driving recklessly. At practice, we told Coach Hiebert about the accident, and he was understanding. Nobody knew the extent of it, which added to my guilt.

"We don't have any matches until after the break," Hiebert said. "You should have your stitches out by then. For now you just need to focus on running and conditioning."

I did run, and I conditioned myself into oblivion. I ran the stairs and jumped rope, anything to sweat out the demons until I could get back on the mat. When the stitches came out, I was more than ready to start wrestling again.

By the time school was back in session for the new year and we had wrestled our next dual, my anxiety over the accident had begun to wear off. Louie, Mike, and I were right back in the saddle of waywardness. I was having a highly successful season and winning most of my matches by pins. I was loving it, and it fueled my attitude of rebellion.

We were now in the middle of January with one dual meet left before the state qualifier. Coach Hiebert was trying to elicit support for the wrestling team by having us wrestle in front of the student body. He scheduled our meet against Sandy High School during an assembly period at the end of the day. The gym was packed with students, and the tension and energy levels were through the roof. Because parents had also shown up to watch the match, the gym was overflowing—and to add to everything else, the fire marshal was visiting.

Our principal, Mr. Horner, was a nervous wreck and beside himself with worry. He was pacing all over the gym and kept distracting Coach Hiebert before the match with minor issues. Coach was trying to warm us up and motivate us for the competition.

"There are too many people in this gym," Mr. Horner chirped nervously into Coach Hiebert's ear. "The kids are out of control."

Putting a hand on Mr. Horner's shoulder, Hiebert kept a calm, steady voice and said, "Don't worry about it, Howard. I've got a handle on it. Just go back to your office and be a principal."

Luckily, Mr. Horner listened to Coach Hiebert and left the gym.

Coach told the fire marshal, "If you see a man wearing a suit and tie trying to get in that door, turn him away. The gym is already filled to capacity." He laughed out loud, and the fire marshal shook his head and grinned.

Both teams lined up across the mat, each wrestler facing his opponent. As our names were announced, the crowd erupting with each one, we ran to the center of the mat to shake hands. We all knew Sandy didn't have much of a lineup except at the 125-pound weight class, which was Louie Day's spot. The match began, and our 98-pounder started it off with a bang. He pinned his kid, as did our 105-pounder, and at 115 it was another blowout for David Douglas. We were now up to the 125-pound weight class, and Louie was ready to kill, but the Sandy kid was tough.

Louie was handling him well, ahead by two points going into the third round. The third round started with Louie in the up position, which means his opponent was on all fours (down position) and Louie gripped him from the top. As the whistle blew to start the round, for some reason, Louie let his opponent go, and the crowd went wild. The Sandy wrestler was awarded an escape, which meant he got free, and both wrestlers were now in a neutral position. This gave the Sandy wrestler a point, and now Louie was only up by one.

Hiebert stood up from his chair yelling, "Get your two! Take him down!" With one slip, the Sandy wrestler could take Louie down, and he'd lose the match by one point.

Time was ticking down as both wrestlers danced around the mat, and with three seconds left, we thought Louie had it won. The ref raised a clenched fist and warned Louie for stalling, and the next thing we knew, the Sandy wrestler shot in for a single leg takedown. Louie lost his balance and dropped to the mat.

"Two, takedown!" the ref yelled. He awarded two points to the Sandy kid, and the match was over. Louie was out of his mind. They raised his opponent's hand as the victor. Louie threw his gear and cursed in a rage. He went off into a corner and started kicking the wall.

The dual meet continued, and the rest of us won our matches. I pinned my kid at the 136-pound weight class, and when it was over, I saw Louie bouncing on his toes, saying something to his opponent with his finger in the guy's face. The humiliation was more than he could take. He found me when the match ended as we started rolling up the mats to clean up the gym.

"Hey," he said as he jumped in next to me to help with the mats.

"Yeah?" I answered.

"We're gonna kick the shit out of these guys before they get on the bus."

"What?"

"Yeah, we're gonna show them that they should've never shown up here!"

"Okay," I said. It seemed as if I often said yes to Louie when I should have said no.

He ran off into the hallway, and I grabbed Mike and told him what Louie had said.

Mike was excited. "Let's check it out," he said, and we both ran into the halls where Louie had disappeared.

We heard something going on in the boys' bathroom, so we ran in. Louie was going at it with his opponent. Several wrestlers from Sandy were watching, and Mike and I were like gasoline on a flame—we jumped into the action with no hesitation. The room exploded with bloody lips, and body parts were flailing all over. A rush of teachers came in and pulled us apart to break the whole thing up. They told us to calm ourselves down and go our separate ways.

We huffed our way out of the bathroom and went straight down into what we called the dungeon, a basement area under the school that housed the locker room.

"I'll be damned if this is over," Louie snarled as we sped down the stairs.

The visiting team's buses usually parked behind the school, and there was a door that led straight out from the dungeon. We picked up our speed and ran through the door to the back of the school. A huge group of people, wrestlers and parents, had gathered in front of the buses, and some of them were already boarding.

Louie spotted his rival, made a beeline for him, and popped him across the face with his fist. The whole place blew up and turned into a flat-out brawl. I didn't know who I was hitting or who was hitting me. I heard a whistle, and the Sandy coach was in the mix throwing kids off to the side.

"Break it up!" he was yelling. Parents were also trying to intervene. I escaped the action and ran over to the side of the building. Coach Hiebert grabbed Louie by the collar of his T-shirt and twisted it tightly around his throat as he pushed him toward the door.

"That's uncalled for—and unsportsmanlike!" he yelled as he pushed Louie forward. "You're goddamned lucky there are no administrators here. You'd all be expelled!"

My decisions up to that point in my life had not been upstanding ones, and I didn't feel good about them. If I were expelled from school I'd be devastated; I didn't know what I would do if I couldn't wrestle.

As my mind replayed some of the more recent events, I tried to get all of that out of my head and concentrate on the upcoming district tournament. Sweating hard helped bring things back into focus, and I trained insanely with one goal in mind: to make it to the state tournament. I wanted it badly, and I had a mental image of Hershell Green from the previous season on top of the podium.

Coach Hiebert gathered us in the wrestling room before the tournament. We sat on the mat in a group facing him.

An early team photo of the DDHS squad. Coach Marv Hiebert is to the far right of the second row with Louie Day and myself to his left. My buddy Mike Elia is fourth from the left in the second row, and Hershell Green, the first state champion at DDHS, is directly in the middle of the top row.

"It's been a great season, and some of you have done more than I could ask with the skills you came in here with," he said. "Go out there and contribute in any way possible. If that means you don't get pinned by the toughest guy out there, that's a contribution. If that means you pin your opponent instead of winning by points, that's a contribution!" His voice escalated as he went on.

The team score in wrestling is kept by how a match is won or lost. During these years, the point breakdown was as such: three team points for a decision (a win by points), five team points for winning by pin, and two points for each team in a draw. I knew exactly what Hiebert was talking about, and I closed my eyes to whisper a prayer: "Lord, let me win all of my matches and make it to the state tournament. Amen." I quickly made the sign of the cross, and Hiebert called us into a huddle and shouted, "Champs on three."

"One, two, three—champs!" we shouted in unison. I was ready to go.

I won my first match in a flurry with a fast pin. Nerves were beginning to hit me, so I ran to sweat it out, making sure to be fully warmed up and covered in a light sweat before every match. As I won my way through the 136-pound weight bracket, I wasn't taking anything for granted. In the semifinals, I would meet a tough kid who had gone undefeated this season and had been to the state tournament before.

All I need to do is win this one and I'll make it to state, I told myself. My semifinal match. Jumping rope off to the side of the mat, I had the perfect light sweat going. I was fully prepared.

I ran to the center of the mat to meet my opponent, and we shook hands. The whistle blew, and I went in lightning-fast for a double leg takedown.

"Two, takedown!" the ref called out. My opponent was flustered. That wasn't supposed to happen. He scrambled to his feet. "One point, escape!" the referee yelled. We danced around, both with a sense of caution. I tried for an inside trip, but he held his stance. The round ended with the score in my favor 2–1.

I was in the down position to start the second round. If I reversed him, it would put me up by three, but as hard as I tried, I could not reverse the guy—that is, to go from the down position to a position of control over my opponent. The next thing I knew, he had an arm bar on me and began to turn me onto my back. I rolled through, but the ref awarded a two-point near fall anyway.

Hiebert was going crazy. "That was no near fall! He rolled through! What the hell?" he screamed at the ref.

I scrambled to my feet to get a one-point escape, and the score was now tied 3–3.

It was my opponent's turn for the down position to start the third round, and at the whistle, he started working for his one-point escape. I was trying to hold him as the clock was ticking down. Then Hiebert yelled, "Let him go and take him down!" I knew what I had to do; I pushed my opponent out from under me and let him stand up.

"One point, escape!" the ref yelled. The score was now 4–3 in favor of my opponent. I needed a takedown to win the match. I was looking for my opportunity as Hiebert yelled, "What are you waiting for?" I went in for the takedown, and my opponent fell to the mat.

As he was falling, his upper body crossed the out-of-bounds line, but both his knees hit the mat in bounds. The ref blew the whistle calling out of bounds and threw both his hands to the side. "No points!" he yelled.

Hiebert came unglued. He paced back and forth yelling, "Time out! Time out!"

The ref went over to Hiebert's corner and stood with his hands on his hips. Coach's hands flailed with his explanation, but the ref kept shaking his head.

He called us back to the center of the mat with seconds left, and we were both in the up position. I scrambled as hard as I could to get another takedown, but the whistle blew. Time was out—and so were my dreams of going to the state tournament.

I had lost by one point. I couldn't believe it. Devastated, I hung my head. My dad and brother were across the gym, but there was no way I was going over there. I grabbed my gear, ignoring the quips around me from my teammates—"Nice try Tony!" "You had that won," and "You've had a great season." Everyone meant well, but I couldn't hear that right now. In my mind, I had failed. I found my way to a dark, secluded area behind the upper-level bleachers. I sat against the wall with a towel covering my head and face. I didn't want to see or hear from anyone. At least a half hour passed, and then Hiebert's voice cut through the dull roar of the crowd.

"Tony!"

I looked out from under my towel.

Coach Hiebert was crouched down to my level. "I'm proud of you," he said, smiling. "You came out of nowhere."

I couldn't believe he was still proud of me.

"You've had an outstanding season," he continued, "and you've got some kind of instinct for this sport. Your accomplishments this year are unheard of."

"Thank you," I said under my breath. "I wanted to go to the state tournament, Coach."

"I know," Hiebert replied. "And believe it or not, damn it, you should be going. But you still need to get yourself out there! You need to contribute to your team!" He kept going, raising his voice and using his hands as he spoke. I listened to every single word.

"I need you to get out there and win as many matches as you can. You need to place as high as you can for your team!"

I was inspired and ready to shake it off and face the world. As I stood up, he put his arm around me, squeezed my shoulder, and said, "You're only a sophomore. There's plenty of time for the state tournament."

CHAPTER FOURTEEN

The Defining Moment

The remainder of the school year flew by, and throughout the summer, Louie, Mike, and I lived on the edge the entire time. We were out late most nights cruising 82nd Avenue or Broadway downtown, hitting the burger joints and looking for fights. My mom always knew when I got home regardless of the time. Sometimes I'd come in at one or two in the morning, and she'd always tell me the next day what time it had been. *"Tu venuti troppo tardi!"* You came in too late!

"Naaaah," I'd reply, drawing it out nonchalantly, trying to keep her calm to no avail.

"Tu sei pazzi!" You're crazy! She threw her arms in the air. *"Non va bene!"* This is no good!

Usually, after our nightly escapades, Louie would go home, but Mike would come in, and we'd finish off cold pasta in the kitchen. Mike loved my mom's cooking. He'd eat whatever she had made, and he didn't care that it was cold.

The work cycle for my parents carried on as it had when we first arrived in Portland; they both still worked for the same companies. There were times I knew my parents would have been much happier if I'd quit school to go to work so I could contribute more to the prosperity of the family. Work was their priority, and they left early for their jobs every day.

My dad now knew how to drive a car and owned a 1953 Pontiac. Uncle Tony had driven him to and from work for a year or so, and then my dad decided he needed to get a license. He hadn't driven anything in Italy except a horse and cart, so this was a Herculean step for him.

Uncle Tony took him out to buy a car, but they made the colossal mistake of buying a manual transmission. That car never left the driveway. For the life of him, my dad could not get the hang of the clutch. Uncle Tony took him to trade it in for an automatic, and that did it; he had no desire to learn how to drive a stick shift and from that point on would only own cars or trucks with automatic transmissions.

Driving a car was not even a consideration for my mom. Most of the Italian women I knew didn't drive, and she was no exception. She had the bus routes memorized for anywhere she needed to go and could now walk to buy groceries. A new store called Fred Meyer had been built off of Division Street behind our home on the property where Mr. Benedict's dahlia farm had been.

The first time in the store, my mother somehow convinced the employees to loan her a cart to take home. They agreed, and it stayed parked on our patio. When we needed groceries, my mom, barely able to see over the top of the cart, pushed it down the street and around the corner, did her shopping, and then wheeled the full cart all the way home.

Pete continued to excel in school. I talked to him about wrestling, but he wasn't interested. Baseball was his favorite sport and had been since he'd fallen in love with the Dodgers back in New York.

"You need to wrestle," I'd tell him.

"Nah, I'm a baseball player," he'd retort. I was disappointed that he didn't even want to try it. He only weighed about eighty pounds in eighth grade, and I knew that as a freshman he could really dominate as a 98-pounder. Coach Hiebert wanted me to get him out for wrestling; I had about a year to work on him.

Patty's academic issues continued to snowball. Now she rarely smiled, and many days my parents didn't know whether or not she had attended school. Coming to this country so far behind because of her lack of schooling in Italy was a hurdle that my sister couldn't seem to clear. She needed one-on-one attention to catch up, and because her attendance was so poor, she wasn't getting it. She was also becoming more and more introverted and beginning to take a liking to my dad's wine. My parents were starting to worry.

In the fall of 1957, my junior year was underway, and football season was going strong. I was hustling during practice and playing on the swing team as a defensive linebacker. I played both JV and varsity. Coach Hiebert was the JV football coach, and I loved playing JV because I was on the field for a full three quarters. We were also on a winning streak. I'd have to sit out the fourth quarter because they had me dressing for varsity on Friday nights, and the five-quarter rule applied. No one could play more than five quarters in a week. Hiebert would play me three, and that would leave my playing time open for two quarters during the varsity game. I much preferred my JV playing time, as the varsity squad was taking some serious blows this season.

Plugging away at football was my way of ensuring I'd be in the best possible shape for wrestling season. I was obsessed with making it to the state tournament after coming so close the year before. I knew this was my year—not only could I make it to state, but I had a good feeling that I could also place once I was there. Hershell Green was still the only individual state champion from David Douglas. I was burning inside to accomplish that for myself, and I would do whatever it took to get there.

Academics were still not my strong suit, although somehow I was holding on to a 2.7 grade point average. Many of my teachers liked me and always offered up extra help. I embraced this as much as I could, and it got me through some difficult classes. I did well in assignments that required creativity, but spelling and reading were still foreign, and I wasn't sure if those subjects would ever come naturally. I have to admit—I was also good at soliciting help from some of my smarter friends.

One class I didn't have trouble with was metal shop. I started in metals as a freshman and had been working my way up the ladder of classes, pulling A's the whole time. My teacher, Mr. Crisp, put full trust in me, as I was one of his best students.

"Nice work, Russo," he said as he approached my station. I was building an iron flowerpot shelf for my mother; Mr. Crisp encouraged my progress. I thought it would sit perfectly on our patio, and I couldn't wait to finish it and get started on welding something new.

As football season ended and wrestling season began, I was in my element. Sweating profusely during practice and winning matches every week, I couldn't get enough. Our team was tough to beat; we were in line for the league title, and this added to my fervor. My vision was an individual title along with a team title at the end of the season. I pictured it day in and day out and knew exactly what I needed to do to attain it. Although I had an intense focus on my wrestling goals, my actions and behavior off the mat were still not in alignment.

One Friday after practice, Louie, Mike, and I were finishing up in the locker room, and Louie asked what we wanted to do that night.

"I'm not getting very far on my tank of gas," Mike replied. "And I'm flat broke. I'm not going anywhere."

"What do you mean?" Louie said, "It's Friday night! Hell, we'll get you some gas. All we gotta do is siphon some. The clubs will be packed tonight. No one'll see us."

I knew it wasn't a good idea, and I knew it was wrong, but the word that came out of my mouth, as if on autopilot, was, "Okay."

"I'll borrow the old man's car and pick you guys up. We'll get the gas and then fill your tank," Louie told Mike. He had it all figured out.

Mike gave me a ride home, and I tried to eat with the family, but I was jumpy, and my nerves were getting the best of my stomach. I was watching my weight anyway. I liked to hover right around 140 pounds. Hiebert moved me anywhere from the 135-pound weight class all the way up to 157, depending on who we were wrestling and where he needed me in the lineup.

Louie pulled into the driveway with Mike and honked the horn. It was eight o'clock. My brother and sister were watching television, and my parents were getting ready for bed.

"See you later," I said to anyone who would listen.

"*Non fai tardi,*" my mother yelled from the bathroom, warning me not to stay out too late.

I ran out the door and jumped into the car.

"Hey, we need an empty gas can," Louie announced the minute I shut the door.

I ran back into our garage and grabbed a tall rectangular gas can.

"Got it," I said, jumping back in.

We took off down Powell Boulevard and headed toward the city. There was a nightclub called The Grove on the left not far from my street, somewhere around 112th and Powell. Right behind it was a drive-in movie theater.

"This place is perfect," Louie said. "It's jam-packed. I'll keep a lookout, and you guys go get the gas."

"Stay close by so we can get back in the car quickly," I told Louie.

"Yeah, yeah, I will. Just go." Louie rushed us out of the car.

Mike grabbed the hose, and I had the gas can. There were hundreds of cars parked in rows, and it was dark except for the light from the huge screen of the drive-in.

It illuminated our crime scene, fading in and out as the movie played. Crouching down and overwhelmed with the number of cars, I spotted a fairly new Oldsmobile and figured it looked nice enough to be filled with gas.

"How 'bout that one?" I asked Mike, pointing at the Olds.

"Sure, looks good. Let's go," he said. We stayed low and made our way to the car. My heart was pounding out of my chest, but I stayed focused on the task at hand.

When we got to the car, still crouching, Mike opened the gas tank and stuck the hose in.

"Hurry up," I whispered.

Mike put the end of the hose in his mouth, took a long draw, and the gas started flowing. We quickly got the hose in the can and let it go. I glared at Louie waiting for us in the car on the far side of the parking lot. The gas stopped, but Mike got it flowing again, and then I felt it—a presence behind me.

Mike looked up from the can and froze. I knew something was wrong, and fear pushed the air out of my lungs.

Then, I felt my collar cinch up, and the next thing I knew, I was being pulled to my feet.

"Stand up, you little bastards." The voice was cold and erratic. Mike dropped the hose and stood up slowly. A Paul Bunyan of a man wearing a security guard uniform was staring down at us, gun cocked. Mike and I were now side-by-side, our arms in the air like statues.

"Of all the cars in this lot, you two bastards pick mine?" he said with a crazed look. My mind was reeling. *Should I run?* I thought. Mike stayed motionless, and I decided to do the same.

"If I don't kill you tonight, the least you hoodlums are gonna get is thrown in jail." He motioned his gun toward the building and said, "Let's go."

We walked toward the back of the nightclub, and he followed with his gun directing us to the back door. He kept the gun steady in one hand and reached around us, opening the door with the other.

"Get in there and sit down," he said, pointing across the kitchen.

There were no chairs, so we sat on the floor with our backs against the wall.

"Hands behind your heads," he barked.

We followed his instructions. I couldn't believe it had come to this. I felt weak. What was I doing? The question echoed inside my head. Floods of memories engulfed me. My journey from Italy, having been to hell and back on that ship, coming within a shred of moving into a children's home, my Uncle Tony who sent for me all the way across the country and took me in, and my Aunt Gladys who loved me like her own child and made me the godfather of her daughter … I thought about my parents, how I'd waited for them for four long years, and how hard they'd worked to make a good life for us in this country. And now it had come to this. I was going to jail.

I closed my eyes tight and prayed, *Please God, help me!* I wanted to make the sign of the cross, but I didn't dare move. I knew I needed divine intervention now more than ever, and it was nobody's fault but my own.

The security guard who had been staring down his gun at us sent one of the kitchen workers to get the manager of the club.

"Whoa, hold on," the manager said as he walked in, motioning with his hands toward the crazed security guard. "Put down the gun. Let's get to the bottom of this." The security guard put his gun inside the breast pocket of his jacket.

"These two shit-for-brains were siphoning gas out of my car. They're going to jail."

The manager looked at us. "Is that true?" he asked.

We nodded.

"You look like good kids. Have you boys ever been in trouble before?"

"No," we lied.

"Put your arms down," he said and then asked us where we lived and went to school.

My voice was shaking, and my mouth felt full of cotton; it was hard to speak, but we answered as best we could.

I had a sense the manager felt sorry for us and didn't want to send us to jail. *Maybe he cares*, I thought. It didn't matter. My heart sank when the security guard piped up, "Hey, we need to call the paddy wagon. They're goin' in."

"Give 'em a call," the manager replied, seeming to forget that he might feel sorry for us, and then he turned away and walked back into the nightclub. I couldn't believe that after all the adversity I had overcome, it was going to end like this. I knew this was not the way I was meant to live my life.

The security guard answered a knock on the back door, and standing there were two police officers. He told them everything, then emphasized that we were little punks who needed to be taught a lesson. "Some jail time would do them good," he added.

The cops walked over and grabbed each of us by the arm. They stood us up and cuffed our wrists, sealing our fate, and escorted us back outside to the car.

I was humiliated and felt tears starting to sting my eyes as they opened the car door and threw us into the back seat. The door slammed, and the car pulled away. I knew I had messed things up beyond repair this time. What would Coach Hiebert think of me now? When we got to the exit of the parking lot, the car stopped, waiting to pull out into the street. My mind focused on the turn signal blinking rhythmically. A knock on the driver's side window snapped me out of it. The cop rolled down the window to reveal the malevolent security guard. We didn't know what to think.

"Let 'em go," he said.

"What?" the cop answered. "Are you sure? We're ready to take these guys in."

"I changed my mind. I'm not gonna press charges," he said.

I couldn't believe what I was hearing. I made a promise to myself at that moment that if I got out of this one, things were going to be different.

The cop behind the wheel stepped out of the car and opened our door, shaking his head. After letting us out, he unlocked the cuffs and said, "I guess it's your lucky day, boys." He got back in the car and drove away, but the security guard wasn't done with us.

"I know where you live," he said, staring us down with his crazy eyes. "And I still have half a mind to send you to jail." Mike and I didn't move. The man went on, "Get the hell out of here, and if I ever see the likes of you two again, I'll make sure you do time. Do you understand me?" He spoke in staccato, emphasizing every syllable in each word.

"Yes," we answered. We knew he wasn't lying, and taking that as our cue, we turned and started running down Powell Boulevard in the direction of my house. We didn't have far to go. As we were running, we realized a car was following close behind us. Mike looked back. "It's Louie," he shouted. We stopped running, Louie pulled over, and we jumped in.

"That was crazy!" Louie shrieked.

"Take me home," was all I could say. When Louie got to my driveway, I sensed Mike was thinking about coming in for cold pasta.

"I'll see you later," I said, slamming the car door and running straight into the house and up to my room. Lying there awake all night, I saw my life flash before me: my grandfather for whom I was named, my childhood in Italy, my journey, the people I loved, and my struggle to unite my family in Portland. It was all I could think about. *This isn't the way I want to live my life. I'm not a criminal.* I kept repeating it in my brain.

From now on, things were going to be different. I would make sure of it.

That next day, as happy as I was that things turned out the way they did, I couldn't shake the pit that was grinding away at the bottom of my stomach. I stuck to my dad like glue, following him around, trying to help out with anything he needed. He went into the garage, so I followed, and we began to change the oil in his car. It felt good to be working with my hands.

"*Quando fai la lotta ancora?*" my dad asked me. He wanted to know when I'd wrestle again.

"This coming week," I told him, and then added, "*È un torneo importante.*" The David Douglas Invitational was indeed a big tournament.

"*Voglio vincere*," I said. I want to win.

He stopped what he was doing, looked over at me, and said, "*Tu vincere*," You will win.

Winning a match for the DDHS Scots my junior year.

CHAPTER FIFTEEN

A New Agreement

The entire family came to watch me wrestle in the David Douglas Invitational Tournament—the first time my mother would see me wrestle in a match. Unfortunately, the drama was too much even for my mother, so this match would also be her last. When I got to the center of the mat and shook hands with my opponent, I heard my mother screaming from the bleachers, "*Madonna mia! Dio mio! Dio mio!*"

She was basically on a loop yelling, "Mother of God, my God! My God!"

Oh man, I thought, *I'd better get this over with quickly*. I wrestled my opponent to a quick pin, and when they raised my hand to the crowd, I looked to my family standing in front of the bottom row of bleachers.

My dad was red-faced, smiling and clapping wildly, and my mom had both her hands reaching out toward me yelling, "*Figlio mio! È troppo violente questo sport!*" She thought wrestling was too violent, too rough, and she wasn't happy at all.

I ran back to my team and across the gym as my dad escorted my mother out. She never came to another match, but she always asked how I did when I got home. Although she couldn't watch, she liked to hear about it. And she liked it best when I won.

I felt invincible through the rest of the David Douglas Invitational. Everything was clicking, and I beat all of my opponents soundly, winning my bracket.

We also prevailed as a team, edging out the opposing schools for the first-place trophy. Coming out on top and standing on the podium holding a large blue ribbon whetted my appetite for victory. I was pumped up and more than ready to finish my season strong at the district tournament.

I had made an agreement with myself back on the night that crazed security guard nearly sent me to jail, that I would redirect my life and focus all of my energy on three things: wrestling, school, and work. I knew the moral standards of my family, and I was determined from now on to live up to them.

About this time at school, Mike had been talking to me about his parents having trouble at home.

"I think they might be getting divorced," he told me one day during lunch. "I don't want to have to move."

He was down about it because he wanted to finish out his wrestling season and graduate with his class from David Douglas. Mike was a year ahead of me and was set to graduate that spring of 1958.

"I'll ask my parents if you can stay with us until you graduate," I told him. "They probably won't mind. My mom likes you because you always rave about her cooking."

"Yeah, I love her meatballs," Mike agreed, patting his stomach.

I ran it by my mom and dad one evening, and they didn't think twice about it; my parents were always willing to help those in need. It seemed like the next day Mike moved in. He had brought a mattress from home, and we put a makeshift bed together for him up in the room where my brother and I slept. It was a great situation for both of us because Mike had a car and took me to and from school, and he was grateful to have a place to stay and be able to finish out his school year. As an added bonus for me, he was also willing to help me with my homework.

The season was winding down, and the week before the district tournament, we were training hard in the wrestling room. Things were still clicking for me. I had an untarnished record, and my body felt strong and technically prepared. I could visualize myself winning district and, who knows, maybe even winning state. I had defeated at least two wrestlers that season who had placed at the state level in previous years.

Toward the end of practice one day, we were grouped by weight class, and Hiebert was wrestling us at full speed. The room was packed with fifty to sixty guys in there like sardines; we were supposed to be focusing on stand-ups from the bottom position. My drilling partner was John Loomis, the same boy I had wrestled as a freshman in PE class when I was trying to prove to Coach Hiebert that I was worthy of a spot on the team. John and I had remained around the same weight class over the past three years.

I got my stand-up quickly and was on my feet trying to break free from Loomis's grip so I could escape and turn to face him. Before I knew what hit me, Loomis tripped me from behind and, attempting a throw, he lifted me off the mat. As I began my descent to the mat, everything started moving in slow motion, and the mat was rising up to accost my face.

Loomis had my arm trapped, so I knew there'd be nothing to break my fall. I tried futilely to free my arm before impact. With the combination of our weight, everything exploded right through the tip of my left shoulder. I heard a loud pop and felt a balloon burst inside my shoulder, then found myself being crushed beneath a mob of wrestlers; not only had my own wrestling partner landed on me, but simultaneously, the adjacent group had lost their balance and landed on me also.

It was a freak occurrence.

Everyone disassembled slowly, and I lay there flat on my back.

"Aaaaah," I moaned.

Hiebert's whistle echoed through the wrestling room as he ran toward me.

"What the hell is going on over here?" He sat me up. "Can you stand?"

"I think so," I said. There was a burning pain in my shoulder, and I could feel it starting to swell. I knew it was bad, and reality was beginning to set in. The trainer made his way over to me.

"Check him out, get some ice on it," Hiebert spat out.

The trainer began walking me toward the locker room, but then Hiebert must have decided not to waste any time.

"Hey!" he yelled in our direction. "Get him over to Doc Browning. He needs an X-ray, damn it! This doesn't happen in my room. Line up for down and backs," he yelled at the group. "We're gonna run!"

In the locker room, the trainer called Doc Browning, and he

was able to get me in right away. I don't remember how—the trainer might've driven me—but somehow I made my way to Doc Browning's office.

"Separated shoulder, Tony," Doc said when he walked back in the exam room with my X-ray.

My face was red from holding back tears. "Can I wrestle this weekend?" I asked, not willing to accept his diagnosis.

"Well, I can shoot your shoulder up with some cortisone. See how it goes."

I nodded. "Yeah, let's do it."

"You need to know," he said, looking at me through his large rectangular glasses, "it'll kill some of the pain, but you're not going to be a hundred percent."

"Okay," I said. "But the district tournament is this weekend. I have to wrestle."

I called my dad to pick me up at Doc Browning's office. As he pulled up in the parking lot, a look of concern came across his face when he noticed my arm in a sling. By this point, my dad had developed a love for the sport of wrestling, and he had become engrossed in my success. Although quiet, he was highly competitive in his own right, and if I ever lost a match, when I got home he'd yell at me in Italian, "You be stronger! That's all!" He could never see any reason for me to lose.

I got into the car, and the first words out of his mouth were, "*Che cosa successo?*" He wanted to know what happened.

"I hurt my shoulder." Sensing his anxiety, I added quickly, "Doc Browning will fix it so I can wrestle."

"*Va bene,*" he said and nodded.

At home I couldn't eat; I was in pain, and my mind was numb.

I kept praying my shoulder would heal up in two days and that I'd be fine to wrestle. I wondered if this was a punishment from God for some of my prior delinquent choices, but I shook off the thought. As much as I prayed and willed it to be, I knew my injury was not going to heal quickly.

I got in to see Doc Browning the day of the district tournament, and he shot me up with cortisone. It did kill much of the pain, so I was ready to give it a go. My first match was rough; I won it by a small point margin, but my shoulder did not hold up well. It was weak, fatigued, and intensely painful. I knew it was too soon for another cortisone shot, so I kept telling myself to suck it up and get tough.

Preparing for my second match, I couldn't jump rope to warm up, so I was trying to shake out the nerves as best I could. Hiebert came over and rubbed my shoulders, warning, "If it gets bad out there Tony, I'm gonna call it."

I couldn't believe what I'd just heard him say. "No, don't," I said curtly, looking him straight in the face.

I ran out on the mat and shook my opponent's hand. Word of my damaged shoulder had gotten out, so I knew he'd be gunning for it. I tried to protect my injury while looking for an opportunity to score, but the first chance he got, my opponent reached for my left arm and, with a sweeping motion, dragged it hard across my body. I felt my shoulder come apart as I fell to the mat.

"Two, takedown!" the referee yelled out.

That was it. Hiebert stood up, motioning for time-out. "It's over," he said.

I was crushed. The whistle blew, and my opponent jumped up and raised both arms in victory. I sat up on the mat and put my hands over my face, trying to keep from sobbing, but I couldn't hold back.

The ref leaned toward me. "Let's go, son. It's over."

I stood up, and my opponent's hand was raised to the crowd.

It was only the second match of the district tournament, but it had just become my final match of the season.

CHAPTER SIXTEEN

Figs And Famiglia

Since we'd arrived in Portland, my parents had gotten involved with an Italian club in the area called Club Paesano, through which they had made many new friends. These new Italian friends helped my mother decide that it was okay for her to call Portland her new permanent home. When she got off the bus after her cross-country trip from New York back in 1955, she was spitting mad and had an aching back. She did not take to Portland right away, and it was these Italian friends who became extended family members that changed her mind.

Carl Trentadui was one of my father's new friends. He lived three houses down from Uncle Tony on 115th Street and shared my dad's hearty passion for drinking red wine, an activity they often enjoyed together. Even so, work always came before wine.

"*Prima il dovere, e poi il piacere,*" my father would tell me. Duty first, then pleasure, or in other words—work, then wine.

On weekends my dad always had ongoing projects of some

sort. One task was digging out underneath our house to put in a basement. My parents wanted to equip the basement with a full kitchen and bathroom, and Carl, a fix-it man, was helping them accomplish it. He often came over to help my dad with whatever he was in the midst of. When they would finish, Carl's wife, Marguerite, would walk over, and they'd stay for dinner.

Our house filled up with family and friends around noon on most weekends, especially Sundays. My parents were determined to return kindness to anyone who had done something nice or neighborly for them. No matter how small the favor, my mom wanted to cook for them, and my dad would offer up wine or produce from his garden. Our kitchen and dining room became a path of destruction around one o'clock, as Uncle Tony, Aunt Gladys, Uncle Felice, Aunt Lucia, and all of their children also joined us for our midday meal. At times the bedlam was unimaginable.

"*Fuori! Andate a giocare nella strada!*" my mom yelled to the kids from the kitchen as she slaved over the steaming pots and pans on the stove. Go play in the street! She just wanted us out of her way.

We always had ample pasta and bread thanks to Aunt Lucia's position at Scarpelli Macaroni Co. and Uncle Felice's work as a baker at Pierre's; they brought bags of pasta and bread home that were for whatever reason not fit to sell. This worked out well for us, and my mom always cooked some type of greens and added meatballs or sausage to her red sauce. The party wound down around four o'clock, as my parents retired early most evenings so they'd be ready for work promptly the next morning.

My parents became especially close with the Calcagnos, a

family they met through their Club Paesano connections. Joe Calcagno was of Italian descent but born in the United States, and his wife, Adalgisa, came straight from my homeland. The story of their arranged marriage was remarkable.

Over the years, Joe had peddled produce from his Uncle Louie's farm and delivered to all the local grocery stores in Portland. At one grocery stop, he'd always visit the bakery for a loaf of freshly baked bread before heading home. Dorinda Bonaduce, the gal behind the bakery counter, loved visiting with Joe when he stopped in.

One day she studied him a little more than usual. She handed him his loaf of bread and said, "Ya know, I've got a cousin in Italy made just for you."

Joe thought it was nice of her to have such concern for his well-being, but he didn't respond, thinking it was better to just take his bread and go home.

But Dorinda couldn't get over it; her cousin Adalgisa Foglia was just the girl for him, and she reiterated this sentiment to Joe every time he stopped at her market. Finally it got Joe thinking, and he decided to mention this lady's words to his father.

"Maybe this is somethin', Joe. Maybe you should find out who this girl is," Joe's dad told him. "Why don't you go meet her? I'll tell you what. Go ahead and propose. If you're worried when you get there, check in with the local priest. He'll know everything. If he says she's a good girl, marry her."

And that was it. They notified the Foglia family in Italy of Joe's proposal, and the marriage was arranged. Joe would need to get himself to Italy, meet his betrothed, get married, and then return home with his new bride.

Unfortunately, it did not turn out to be that simple. Joe did check in with the local priest upon arrival, asking for full disclosure on his prospective mate.

"*Non troverai mai una donna megliore*," the priest told Joe. He'd never find a better woman. It was a done deal.

The priest performed the wedding, and Joe and his new bride went to the local consulate to file paperwork to get Adalgisa (Algi), to the U.S. The local consulate sized up Joe and made it quite clear his wife's paperwork was not going through without a payoff.

As the proceedings dragged on, Joe began to worry about Uncle Louie; he had to get back to help his uncle plant the crops on his farm. Having no choice but to leave his new bride to fend for herself, Joe left for the States. Algi's family decided to concede to this man's extortion with a special delivery of six live chickens to his home one night. Lo and behold, the next day, Algi's paperwork had cleared, and she was free to join her husband in Portland, Oregon.

Over the next two weeks, Algi went from ship to train, nearly starving to death for lack of language and money. When she finally arrived and reunited with her husband, she had to rebuild her health. Eventually they built a home on Uncle Louie's land, which spanned twenty-five acres on Columbia Boulevard.

Uncle Louie lived in the old farmhouse surrounded by an abundance of fig trees and camellias. Joe lived in the newly built home with his bride, and they farmed the land. Joe was a workhorse and highly skilled at his craft; his produce rivaled what we harvested on our land in Italy, and Joe's farm transported me back in time. My parents began spending nearly every weekend during harvest time on the farm.

Joe and Algi Calcagno on their wedding day in Italy.

"*Andiamo!*" my mother yelled up the stairs at six o'clock on Saturday mornings. "*Aiutiamo Joe!*" It was time to help Joe.

I'd groggily drag myself downstairs, dunk a day-old donut into my coffee, and the three of us would head off for Columbia Boulevard, leaving my brother and sister at home to sleep. I had been set apart from the "kids" and categorized as an adult since the day I was reunited with my family.

We'd work all day on the farm doing whatever Joe needed

done: picking, washing, and boxing vegetables. When Joe had a particularly large order to fill, first thing in the morning he'd say, "Let's go see if any bums want to earn some money today."

I'd hop in Joe's truck, and we'd ride downtown to Burnside Street near the shelter. Joe would offer twenty dollars cash to anyone on the street for a hard day's work, load them in the truck, and return them at the end of the day. A win-win situation.

Algi and my mom always had a meal ready for the crew at precisely one o'clock. They would work on the farm until it was time to cook, then the two compact Italian women, each approximately four foot nine, headed for the house, side by side, talking a blue streak, neither one having time to listen to the other.

We'd break at one and always start our lunch in Joe's basement with his favorite, minestrone, followed by whichever produce happened to be in season, and we never went without bread, pasta, or the treasured jug of red wine.

We always had meat at these meals, too. Joe would often slaughter a homegrown cow or an elk or deer killed on a hunting trip. It was a familiar scene: just like when Grandpa Giuseppe had raised a pig in Italy, the family gathered around for the butchering, knives flying—the meat to be shared.

After lunch, it was either straight back to work or, if we happened to be done for the day, Joe would take my dad and me fishing. When Joe's children got big enough to help, they were in on the harvest too; Joey, Howard, and the youngest, Joanna, known as "Tootsie" to her dad, were told by Joe, "You work on the farm 'til lunchtime, then maybe we can go fishin'." They'd do whatever it took to earn that afternoon fishing trip.

My parents would never think of accepting money for their

Joe and Algi Calcagno with their children Joey, Howard, and Joanna on their farm.

work on the farm, but we always went home with whatever goods Joe could stuff into the trunk of our car.

It is not unusual for Italian families to be discordant, clashing due to regional differences or status levels, but the Calcagnos paralleled the Russos in all ways Italian and became intertwined in each other's lives as family, having the same work ethic and standing for the same beliefs and values, supporting one another through the good, the bad, and the outrageous.

CHAPTER SEVENTEEN

Mr. Turkey

In June, when the closing bell announced our dismissal from another year of school, I was aware that time was running out for me to accomplish my wrestling goals. I knew next year would be it—my senior year. My last chance.

The impact of my shoulder injury and the devastating end to my season lingered for weeks. Having Mike still living with my family helped put some bounce back in my step and gave me something else to focus on. My first instinct about him had been right; he was smart, acing most classes seemingly without effort, and he was nice enough to help me with my studies. After his graduation, Mike moved in with his older brother in Portland. I was sad to see him go but happy to put a lid on the year. I was ready to move on.

That first weekend of summer, while working at the Azlins' house, I asked Leonard if he knew of any summer jobs available. He told me they needed help at the Brooklyn Diner and that I could come work with him there. Leonard and his wife Flo had sold their restaurant, and Leonard had become the head chef at the Brooklyn Diner on SE 17th and Holgate.

When I arrived home, I announced to my parents, "I have a job with Leonard at the Brooklyn Diner."

"*Bene, bene.*" My mom and dad agreed this was a good thing.

"*Sì, va bene.* I need money for a car," I said, mentioning the car in English; I wasn't sure if they understood me.

"*Sì, ci serve un'altra macchina in famiglia,*" my father answered. He had understood perfectly. As the only one in the house who could drive, my father thought it would be nice to have another car in the family with two of us who could handle driving duties.

I got my driver's license early that summer using my father's car, which at the time was a 1957 Chevy. I borrowed it whenever I could to get myself to work, but many times I had to catch a ride with Leonard and then wait for my father to pick me up. I had a couple of paychecks under my belt, but they always went straight to my mother, so my pockets were empty. Luckily, my father decided it was time. He knew it would be easier if we had two vehicles, so we went out together, and he purchased a 1950 Ford. It was by all accounts my car, and even though it was a dingy gray color and eight years old, I loved it and couldn't wait to prime it to my specifications.

My '50 Ford was reliable and accomplished the task of getting me to and from the Brooklyn Diner. Leonard had me working as a combination sous chef and janitor all summer, peeling potatoes, prepping vegetables, doing dishes, and mopping floors— pretty much anything he needed done, I did. The money wasn't great, one dollar and a quarter per hour, but it was steady, and as the paychecks rolled in every two weeks, my mother was happy to take them off my hands.

"*Lavori duro!*" my mother would sing out, reaching up to grab my face. She appreciated how hard I worked. "*Che bravo mio figlio.*" I was such a good son.

My mother's dramatics were over the top, but this validated my promise to myself that my life was going to change after my near-jail experience that fateful night at The Grove.

With my new car and the newfound freedom that came with it, I often drove to the high school and ran the stadium steps after my shift at the diner. I also frequented the PAL (Police Activities League) club, where a gymnast friend of mine had invited me to work out. In lieu of dues, I was a sparring partner for the boxers, getting my head handed to me on a regular basis. I didn't care. My intentions were clear: I wanted to play varsity football and win an individual state title in wrestling. Hershell Green was still the only David Douglas wrestler to attain the title of state champion, and I knew that's what I wanted. I was going to start the school year in shape and ready to perform.

My parents continued with their noses to the grindstone during the week, but on the weekends, our home was infused with the pungent smell of garlic and onions, the kitchen a madhouse, pots bubbling with tomato sauce and steam rising from the frying pans searing fish or meat and spitting olive oil. The house became even more of a battle zone as we had several new cousins added to the mix: Michael, born to Uncle Tony and Aunt Gladys, and Maria and Mike, Aunt Lucia and Uncle Felice's children. My mother stuck to her mantra that all of the children should "go play in the street," which we gladly did on most occasions.

A corner of our detached garage had been transformed into my father's winery, as he and Uncle Tony wanted to make *il vino* in the old style, like they had done in Italy. They went in as partners to purchase grapes, mostly Zinfandel, which would be delivered and stacked in crates in my father's driveway; my dad had also bought several barrels and a makeshift crusher with a motor and a belt, along with a presser. After putting the grapes through the crusher, it was then pressed to extract the juice. We'd dump the juice mixture into an open barrel until it was filled to the top. My father would then cover the barrel with a blanket, *per fermentare*, and begin the process of daily stirring. Before and after work he'd go into the garage and agitate the bubbling mixture, punching it down.

About this time, thousands of fruit flies began to swarm the barrel, but when I would mention it to my dad, he'd always tell me, "*Non fanno niente le mosche.*" Don't worry about the flies.

"Okay, okay," I'd reply, as I'd watch him push down the bubbles and then cover the barrel back up with the blanket to continue the process, the air around him thick with flies circling their coveted fruit. About a week or so in, my dad would ready one of the other huge barrels, big enough for me to fit inside, to house his wine. He'd fill it with water, tighten the metal rings to make sure there weren't any leaks, and place it on a sturdy platform.

When he was satisfied that his barrel was ready and his brew had stopped bubbling, the slushy concoction went through a strainer. Pure wine came out, and we'd place a funnel into the bunghole of the barrel to make the transfer.

"Bring the funnel," my dad would sing out, as he'd carry a bucket over for dumping. It was my job to hold the funnel while he dumped in the wine.

There was a spigot about four inches from the bottom of the

barrel, just high enough so impurities and sediment would settle below it, and when ready, clean, pure red wine would flow from the spigot.

Every time my mother went into the garage to fill her glass wine bottle, she'd sing out the same thing: *"Bellissimo! Molto buono!"*

No matter what, the wine was always beautiful, and it was always *molto buono*—very good.

Having started the school year in top physical condition from my workouts over the summer, and with my new attitude about the way I was going to live my life, things started to play out for me in a positive way. I was invited to join the Letterman's Club, and some of my friends had convinced me to run for student body vice president. I was truly astounded when I won the election.

I found myself running with a different crowd of people, and my days at David Douglas High School were hitting an all-time high. I played varsity football in the fall as left linebacker. Coach Hiebert was the assistant varsity coach that season, and he helped keep me motivated and focused on my goals. My father attended his first school function at the end of football season when I convinced him to come to our awards banquet.

He lit up when he realized I was being recognized in a video clip and introduced as part of the 1958 Oregon All-Star team.

At school, I was not looking for popularity or recognition, but it seemed to find me as I stood front and center in the gymnasium at David Douglas High School. I had taken a leading role in organizing trucks to collect for the canned food drive, which the senior class had won hands-down.

With an audience composed of the entire student body before me, I wore a paper crown adorned with golden glitter. All eyes were on me as I awaited the presentation of my award. I had been named "Mr. Thanksgiving" by the senior class, and this was my coronation. I stood with my hands clasped behind my back as my principal, Mr. Horner, wrapped up his speech about how well we had done with the food drive this year (especially the senior class, which had out-canned everyone else), and how much it was going to help those in need.

"And now, without further ado," he announced, "I'd like to present this year's 'Mr. Thanksgiving' award to senior class vice president, Tony Russo!" He reached down and retrieved my coveted prize within its prison walls. Grabbing a huge crate, he held out and presented to me my trophy: a twenty-pound dirt-brown Thanksgiving turkey, live as could be and notably pissed off.

My prize writhed and stretched its neck through the crate, trying to peck at my flesh with its beak. As we made the transfer, the gym erupted when my trophy, as if aware of his mocking presence, hit the bull's-eye with a splattering of turkey droppings dead center on my foot.

My brother, now part of the freshman class, was amidst the hysterically laughing group, and I laughed along with them, thinking, *I hope this isn't a sign of things to come.* In Italy, getting pooped on by a bird is generally thought of as good luck, but I had no idea if that extended to turkeys.

My "Mr. Thanksgiving" coronation.

During the Thanksgiving holiday, my "trophy," although not the star attraction nor as highly revered as my mother's lasagna, did sit in the middle of our table. Needless to say, turkey did not make its way onto my plate that holiday. Unlike when I had killed that bird back in Italy as a child, at least this time I could choose whether I wanted to eat it or not.

With football season wrapped up, every chance I got I was still trying to convince my brother, Pete, that he needed to wrestle. He kept professing to be a baseball player.

"That's okay," I'd tell him, "you can wrestle and play baseball." They were in different seasons, after all. And, although Pete only weighed somewhere in the eighty-pound range, Hiebert was expecting him to be our 98-pounder. I told my father this, and he began to work on him also. Between my father and me, in all fairness, my brother didn't stand a chance—he would have to wrestle.

Pete reluctantly went out for the team his freshman year, the fall of 1958, and at the time of my "Mr. Thanksgiving" crowning, he had three weeks of practice under his belt. He was holding his own with the kids in his weight class. I knew he could be a talented wrestler and would love the sport once he had a real match and started winning. I took it upon myself to facilitate his wrestling skills by trying to toughen him up at home.

Our mother hated to climb the steep stairs that led to our private lair up in the attic; it took an act of God to get her anywhere near them, so we used this knowledge to our advantage. When our father wasn't around, showing my brother some of my favorite wrestling moves was a frequent occurrence, and this resulted in numerous roughhousing sessions that got my mother seething mad.

"*Madonna mia! Figli disraziati!*" she'd yell up the stairs to her unruly sons.

We were throwing each other around one day, and I tossed

my brother a little too hard (not difficult to do, considering his compact build). He rolled across his bed and slammed his foot right through the sheetrock.

My mother heard the commotion from downstairs and started screaming, "*Che successo?*" wanting to know what had happened.

Seeing the hole in the wall, we both panicked, and I quickly grabbed a poster-sized bracket from a wrestling tournament I had won the previous year and pinned it to the wall. *Please God, don't let this be the time she braves the stairs*, I prayed.

"If she sees this, she'll kill us both," my brother said, with a true look of fear in his eyes.

"It's okay," I reassured him. "She won't come up, and if she does, she won't move the bracket." I looked at the bracket hanging askew in the most conspicuous location, low on the wall just above my brother's bed, and thought, *She'll never question it.*

The day finally came when my mother's patience ran out. While roughhousing and throwing each other around, we broke my brother's bed. The mattress fell through the frame and made an enormous thud as if it were going straight through the floor. We stopped, still breathing hard but not moving, trying to evaluate our options.

"*Madonna mia!*" We heard our mother's scream shoot up the stairs like a bullet. Then we heard the most frightening sound of all, the soft shuffle of her feet making their way up the stairs.

"*Figli disgraziati! Siete pazzi!*" she muttered under her breath. *We're not that bad*, I thought.

At this point, we knew there'd be no reasoning with her, so we decided our best line of defense would be to hide under the blankets on my brother's bed and maybe she wouldn't notice the damages. We hunkered down, holding the blankets over our heads for more protection, and then we felt it, the whack of her wooden spoon, blow by blow, from my head to my brother's.

"Ma, stop!" I yelled through the blankets.

"*State zitto! Vi ammazzo!*" she screamed as she whaled on us. Be quiet! I'll kill you!

Then the unthinkable happened.

I felt a whack and heard a cracking sound at the same time—and it wasn't my head. My mother's wooden spoon had broken in half.

She was seething even deeper. "*Dio mio! My-a God!*" she wailed to the heavens, but the blows ceased, and then we heard her feet slowly descending the stairs, both coming to rest on each step as she made her way down.

When we could no longer hear her footsteps, we pulled our heads out from under the blankets and looked at each other. My brother glanced over at the wrestling bracket covering the hole in the wall near the floor and said, "At least she didn't notice the bracket," with a puzzled look on his face. At that, we both burst out laughing, and I threw my brother into a front headlock for good measure.

It wouldn't be the last time my mother would scream at the top of her lungs for us to stop wrestling around, but she never again made the mistake of wasting one of her good wooden spoons on our heads.

Our first wrestling match of the season was finally upon us—David Douglas against the Newberg Tigers. My brother was in the varsity lineup at the 98-pound weight class. He had some good workouts in the wrestling room under his belt and was revved up and ready to go. We had faced off with our opponents one by one during introductions, and now the match was about to kick off with Pete as the opening act.

Coach gave him advice as he jumped up and down, shaking out his arms and legs to warm himself up. In his wrestling uniform, my brother looked so tiny, like we'd just snatched him off the playground from a local primary school. The referee went to the center of the mat and called out both wrestlers. Pete was fired up and sprinted toward the center to shake his opponent's hand. As he got halfway there, the tip of his toe caught on the canvas, and he did a face-plant before the entire audience.

A collective gasp rose from the crowd, and then Hiebert's voice called out sharply, "Let's go, Pete! Get after it!"

My brother got up and shook his opponent's hand, and then, on the whistle, took him down, turned him to his back, and pinned him before the end of the round to win the first official match of his wrestling career. He was hooked.

I also wrestled my Newberg opponent to a pin, and we beat the Tigers handily. Our lineup was tough, with two and sometimes three high-caliber wrestlers at each weight class. Hiebert knew that if he played his cards right, David Douglas could win the state title this season.

Back in the classroom, I was hanging in there, not excelling but bringing in Bs and Cs. I was also working on my car whenever I got the chance. My friend Don Dell's dad owned an auto shop on Union Avenue, on the east side of the Willamette River, and Don had been helping me spruce it up. I now had a shiny purple 1950 "King of the Road" Ford, and it was the center of attention in the high school parking lot. I fondly called it the "Purple People Eater" after the 1958 Sheb Wooley song that was so popular around that time.

Meanwhile, my previous hoodlum antics were being replaced with harmless hijinks, like the Letterman's Club senior prank. We'd decided that one day we would all come to school in costumes and park our cars haphazardly in the school lot. I knew exactly what I'd be wearing, thinking back to that cap gun and holster Grandpa Beard had presented to me when I'd first arrived in Portland. It had also served as my first trick-or-treating outfit. "A real cowboy," Grandpa Beard had said. From then on, any chance I'd had to dress up, I was always a cowboy, and I had also acquired a hat, boots, and a pair of chaps.

I was in full dress as I pulled into the parking lot driving the Purple People Eater. Looking to take up as many spots as I could, I parked diagonally, crossing about three lines, and the lot quickly filled up with cars all being parked at different angles.

We greeted each other like a bunch of goofballs and then entered the school looking for kicks. Kids were laughing at us, and teachers were smirking and shaking their heads. During first period I received a handwritten note: "Tony Russo, please report to Mr. Horner's office."

Horner's pissed, I thought.

When I got to the main office, my fellow Letterman's Club members were already in Horner's office standing around his desk. The secretary pointed. "They're waiting, Tony."

"Thanks," I said as I meandered in, joining my friends.

"You're here to set an example!" Mr. Horner spewed, his eyebrows raised to his hairline. Standing there in our ridiculous getups, we all stared at the floor.

"This is disgraceful and not fitting for members of the Letterman's Club!" He said it with a questioning inflection, as if we should've already known that. "You look like a bunch of idiots!" he continued, shaking his head and pointing at each of us. "I want you all to go home, change your clothes, and then come back and park your cars like civil human beings!"

And that's what we did. It was the beginning and the end of our one and only senior prank, but it marked a major milestone for me—it was a long way from siphoning gas, illegal duck hunting, and looking for fights on the weekends. I called it progress.

CHAPTER EIGHTEEN

State Tourney

In the wrestling room, our team was a unified machine. Hiebert had us revved up and motivated for each match, and we hadn't lost yet that season. We were also looking to repeat for the league title. I had an untarnished record, and the state championship felt within my grasp more than ever.

The week before the district tournament, Hiebert called me into his office and told me he'd decided the best chance for our team to win a state title would be to enter myself and my teammate Bob Baker into the district tournament at the 148-pound weight class. I was surprised to hear it, since I had handled every wrestler I'd matched up with at 141, my primary weight class all season. I felt 141 would have been the natural place for me and my best chance for a state title.

I didn't argue with him, though. If Hiebert felt 148 was the best place for me to give our team a shot at the title, then that's how it would be. Coach Hiebert always constructed his lineup with the team as a whole in mind. He had even wrestled me at 157 during a dual against Clackamas, and although I won the match by points, I went home that night with a swollen face, having physically taken a beating—I was nearly twenty pounds lighter than my opponent.

I didn't think the district tournament would be a problem, but at the state level, the 148-pound weight class had a returning state champion that I had never matched up with, Chuck Seal from Redmond. Because of previous years in which I'd missed the state tournament, I would not be seeded in the competition. This meant I could meet up with the returning state champ at any point in time during the tournament instead of meeting him head-to-head in the finals.

Once the district tournament got underway, I confidently made my way to the finals. I knew all along there was a good possibility I'd face my own teammate once I got there, and I did. I had trouble stepping on the mat with a killer instinct knowing I was wrestling a teammate and a friend, but Bob flew onto the mat like a madman, and before I knew it, he had scored on me. I realized he wasn't going to make this easy. He didn't care that we were both David Douglas Scotsmen; he was out to win. I had to block out my feelings and crank up the pressure, which led me to claim the victory and the title of district champion at the 148-pound weight division.

David Douglas did repeat for the league title as a team. The crowd was on fire, and it was catching; fans and wrestlers alike were a mob on the gym floor, and Hiebert threw his arms up in victory as the screams erupted when the championship trophy was awarded. We had a number of wrestlers going on to the state tournament, and although my brother had a fairly successful season as an 85-pounder in the 98-pound weight division, unfortunately, he wasn't one of them. This would be the one and only time in his high school career, however.

Oregon State University in Corvallis housed the hundreds of wrestlers that would be competing in the state tournament. From the start, David Douglas was near the top of the scorecard. Although I'd never been to the state tournament before, I knew I was performing on a completely different platform; the level of competition was intimidating, but I was feeling good. My matches started out tough, but they ended in my favor by a solid point spread. Even though my brother wasn't wrestling, he had come along to watch the tournament and was keeping an eye on the returning state champ, my most dangerous opponent. At this point, we knew I'd be meeting up with him in the semifinals.

"He's huge!" Pete reported back to me. "He must cut some serious weight to make 148! I remember when he pinned Loomis at the David Douglas tournament—twisted him up like a pretzel!"

I didn't remember that, and those kinds of scouting reports were not helpful.

I was nervous about meeting up with this guy but confident in my own abilities; I could take him if I wrestled smart. I felt unstoppable after the two matches on Thursday and one on Friday morning. *Nobody can beat me if I continue to wrestle like this,* I thought.

On Friday evening the gym was set up with a spotlight on the semifinal round.

Showtime.

I knew my fate either way: if I won the match, I'd go on to wrestle one more time in the state championship finals for first or second place. If I lost, I'd have to make my way through the back door, wrestling two more matches to place either third or fourth in the tournament.

I had been running and jumping rope trying to sweat out my nerves, and I had more than the usual light sweat going before the match. I was drenched. Hiebert was rubbing my shoulders and reassuring me. "Wrestle your match and you can take this guy, Tony."

I couldn't drown the nerves, but I was excited, and Hiebert kept up his mantra as I shook out my legs and rolled my head from side to side.

The 141-pound wrestlers finished, and we were on.

The referee clapped his hands, and I ran to the center of the mat, ready to go. My brother was right—this guy was huge, not just broad-shouldered and thick-thighed but also tall. I quickly ran through my strategy; I need to get that first takedown.

We shook hands, the whistle blew, and before I had time to blink, I was taken to the mat.

"Two, takedown!" the ref yelled. I was shaken up and knew I needed to reverse him. I could feel his strength. His height really had me tied down, and his riding skills were phenomenal. Working hard from the bottom position, I knew I had to match his two points—not just escape, but reverse him. I finally broke through and came out on top.

"Two, reversal," spat the ref just before blowing his whistle to signify the end of the round.

At the start of the second round, my opponent was placed in

the bottom position. I put one hand just above his elbow and my other arm around his belly with the intention of breaking him down to the mat and then turning him to his back. The ref's arm went up in sync with the whistle, and I applied all my weight with as much force as I could to break him down. I couldn't seem to turn him, but he hadn't gotten away, either. I decided if I can't turn him, at least I'll ride him out to the end of the round.

I was able to hold on for about sixty seconds, to the middle of the round, and then in a burst, he was up and out, facing me.

"One point, escape!" I heard.

Three to two, his favor. We danced around the mat, both nervous to take a shot, to finish out the second round.

Going into the third round, I knew my game plan: escape for one and then take him down for two. That would put me up five to three, but to tie it up, I knew all I had to do was get away. On the whistle, I tried to spring to my feet. I felt a blow to the back of my skull and then the sting of my face slamming into the mat. I worked my way back up to my base and got to my knees, trying to get one foot out and break free from his grip. I had never been controlled and held in the bottom position for an entire round. I kept trying to free myself from his stronghold.

I knew my two-minute time frame was slipping away, and I began to panic when the timekeeper stood up to warn the ref at the ten-second countdown. I gave it one last shot, trying to scramble, and then I heard the whistle. Over. I had lost the match.

The crowd roared for my opponent. I couldn't believe that was the end; my chance to be a state champion was gone. I shook my opponent's hand in disbelief, and it took all my strength not to throw something. As I grabbed my gear, Hiebert patted me on the back, and I could feel the sting of tears as I began to jog my way to the upper section of Gill Coliseum. I took a seat, wrapped my arms around my knees, and hung my head.

I couldn't figure it out; this was not the outcome I had pictured. My chance had slipped away. I hadn't reached my goal, and I would not be standing at the top of the podium. My best placing at this point could only be third. That was not good enough. I wanted to go home and tell my father I was *il campione*, the champion. Again, a tornado in my head was spiraling out of control with questions about what I could have done differently. Why couldn't I at least tie up that match? All I had to do was get away. For the life of me I could not figure it out.

After an hour or so, I made my way out of the balcony to find my coach. He knew I was devastated.

"Hey, it's tough, but you gotta move on," Hiebert said as soon as I found him. "You've got some of your toughest matches yet to come if you want to get a third place finish in this tournament. The third-place finisher wrestles the toughest tournament of anyone in this gym." He threw his arm in a half circle, pointing out the scattering of athletes to make his point clear.

"Okay," I said, all the while still thinking, *I don't want third.*

After the semifinals were over, we returned to our hotel. I didn't sleep all night. To punish myself, I incessantly replayed the match, going over and over everything in my head.

The next morning, as we walked into the gym for another round of wrestling, I felt a renewed sense of motivation. I was called to the staging area for my next match, and as soon as I spotted my opponent, instinct kicked in. I was ready. It was a tough match, but I came out the victor, unleashing all of my frustrations out on the mat. I now had only one more match to wrestle for the determination of third and fourth place.

"Don't take this kid for granted, Tony," Hiebert told me as I warmed up. I nodded my head in agreement. That statement didn't help my nerves, and I continued jumping up and down to keep a sweat going before stepping onto the mat.

The ref ran to the center. Hiebert grabbed me. "You ready?"

"Yes," I answered.

He slapped me on the side of the head. "Okay, let's go!"

I ran onto the mat, and the whistle blew. We were both cautious, circling and going for halfway shots. I got in on a double leg, but the takedown ended up out of bounds.

"No points!" shouted the ref.

Round one ended 0–0. It was my turn for the bottom position in the second round. I'd had this game plan before. I needed to escape for one and then go for my takedown. It didn't happen. Although I didn't get away, he couldn't turn me, either, and it was the end of round two, still 0–0.

This was a bad scenario going into the third round. My opponent would be in the bottom position, and if he escaped and I was unable to take him down, then he'd win 1–0. After my semifinal match, there was no way I was going to let that happen. I made up my mind to go for the pin. I had to turn him. My opponent took his position on the mat, and I grabbed his arm just above the elbow and wrapped my opposing arm around his belly, ready to squeeze the life out of him upon the sound of the whistle.

The ref's arm went up; I squeezed my opponent tighter than in any other match I'd wrestled before, breaking him down to the mat. He pulled his arms into his chest, making it difficult for me to get in a half nelson or run an arm bar. I worked two on one, using both of my hands to control one of his wrists, and got his arm free. Then he got back to his base and put one knee up and his head down.

"Near cradle!" Hiebert yelled. I hooked one arm around his knee and one around his head, cinched it up, and stacked him up onto his shoulders.

My opponent was flailing around, kicking his free leg and squirming hard. This was it. I knew the round was winding down.

"Tighten it up!" Hiebert yelled. I cinched him up even tighter, but the flailing continued. I looked up and saw the timekeeper get out of her seat. She hit the ref with a towel, and the whistle blew. I had no idea if it had been enough to earn back points. My opponent relaxed and lay flat on his back with both hands over his face, and I looked to the ref for an answer. He raised his hand with three fingers extended.

"Three, near fall!" he shouted, looking toward the scoring table.

The points went up, my hand was raised, and I smiled and breathed a sigh of relief. I ran to my corner, and Hiebert hugged me. "Way to go!" he congratulated me.

I had just scored the final points and won the last match of my high school wrestling career.

Hiebert was right, third place was no easy task, and I was proud of my third-place finish in the OSAA State Wrestling Tournament of 1959. David Douglas took second place in the state that year, and something clicked in my head as awards were handed out. This was not going to be the end for me.

Somehow, I knew this was only the beginning.

CHAPTER NINETEEN

Graduation

When I arrived home from the state tournament on Sunday afternoon, I walked in the front door into what felt like a garlic-infused sauna. My mother began to howl, "*Sei tornato!*" You're back! She grabbed my face and pulled me down to kiss my cheeks, overly dramatic as usual. My brother behind me got the same treatment.

"Jeez, Ma," Patty chimed in, shuffling her feet across the kitchen floor. "They've only been gone for three days."

"*Hai vinto?*" my mother piped up again, smiling and laughing. She wanted to know if I had won.

"*Sì,*" I answered, holding up my bronze medal. "*Sono vinto terzo.*" I explained I had come in third and lost only one match.

"No!" my father threw out from behind his wine glass while sitting at the kitchen table. "*Tu sei il migliore!*" You are the best! Third place wasn't okay to my father.

"*Sì,*" I answered under my breath, knowing what he was thinking—that no matter who I was up against, there was never a reason for me to lose.

"*Va bene!*" my mother argued. It's all right! She threw her arms out across the table and looked at my father in disgust.

"*Bene, bene,*" my father conceded.

My mother drained the pasta, and we filled our bowls with lightly sauced rigatoni. Then she took the large, triangular hunk of hard *Parmigiano* cheese from the cutting board and sliced paper-thin shavings to top it off.

It was good to be home, and I was ready to get back to school and finish out my senior year.

I had taken metal shop all four years at David Douglas, and it continued to be my favorite class and one of the best marks on my report card. As I was finishing the golf putter I had made, Mr. Crisp grabbed it, held it straight out from his face, then looking down his long, thin nose, gave it a once-over inspection. He was impressed and pushed me to enter it in a high school art show in Portland.

"I don't know if it's any good, though," I said, laughing and shaking my head.

"No, it's good, Tony. Let's give it a shot."

For the final touches, I needed help working on the lathe to smooth out the nub on the back end of the putter's head. Mr. Crisp helped me out; he told me to be patient and work it a little bit at a time instead of trying to do it all in one shot.

This resonated with me from my experiences in wrestling, having started with the fundamentals and worked my way up to where I was, one day at a time.

When I was satisfied with the final touches on my putter, Mr. Crisp sent it off to the art show. After a week or so, I walked into metals class, and right away Mr. Crisp called me over to his desk.

"Hey, you won a second-place ribbon. Check this out." He held out a large red ribbon with gold lettering and a plaque with my name on it.

"Wow," I replied as I took my putter back from him. "I can't believe it."

"I also met a guy at the show that liked your putter so much he wants to buy it, if you'd be willing to sell it."

"Really?" I didn't know what to think. "Sure, I guess so."

Mr. Crisp handed me seven bucks and took the putter back out of my hands.

"Thanks," I said. I couldn't help but wonder who had purchased my putter. I was always suspicious it may have been Mr. Crisp himself. It was no secret that he was an avid golfer.

As the school year wound down, the weather was changing in Portland. We finally had daylight past four thirty in the afternoon, and we were getting our typical intermittent sunny days. My friend John Dukart was excited that his family had gotten a new speedboat; it was all he could talk about, and he was dying to take it out on the river.

"Let's skip school and go," he suggested. "We can take a couple of gals and go water skiing."

I agreed it was a good idea.

"This is what we'll do: we'll write our own notes for the office and then wait until my parents leave for work to get the boat out of the garage. No one will know."

Although I had agreed, I was still unsure about it. Academics were not my forte, but I never skipped school because being there was much better than being at home or work. But with the sun beginning to shine, it was hard for me to pass up a day on the river. I wrote a note stating that I had a doctor's appointment— in English—and then signed it "Aniello Russo." This would turn out to be mistake number one. We took our notes to the office early in the school day, and then met the girls in the parking lot and headed off to pick up John's boat.

I'd asked Sue, a girl I'd been dating off and on, and John convinced a girl he'd had a crush on all year by impressing her with news of his new boat. We headed for the 42nd Street boat ramp off Marine Drive. It couldn't have been a more beautiful day on the Columbia River, the sun glittering off the clean, cold water, the kind of day that makes you feel sorry for anyone who's never experienced the undeniable splendor of this terrain. We spent a glorious day on the river, the girls laughed and skied, and John and I showed off our skills as speedboat captains flying across the river.

John was a varsity tennis player, and he didn't want to miss practice, so at 2:30 we gathered up our stuff, stashed the boat back in John's garage, and headed straight for the high school. Mistake number two. We'd been quite impressed with our covert operation, thinking our parents and the office would be none the wiser. When John went off to tennis practice, the girls went on their way, and I figured I'd get a workout in and made my way to the weight room.

Athletes filled the room, all working out and lifting, weights clanking and making my ears ring. I decided to pick up a jump rope to get myself warmed up. The rope was whizzing past my head, and I was on a roll, two rotations per jump, when in walked Mr. Daggett, my freshman football coach. He was now one of the vice principals at David Douglas. He pointed over at me and ordered, "Russo, get over here!"

My rope hit the floor one more time. I stopped jumping, doubled up the rope, and put it around my neck like a scarf. Grasping each end of the rope, I held on tight and walked across the room toward Mr. Daggett. I couldn't imagine what was up.

He held out the note I had written in one hand, and pointed at it repeatedly with the other. "Tell me about this," he demanded.

"I had a doctor's appointment?" I replied, as if asking him if this were the right answer.

"Russo, first of all," his spit sprayed my face, "by now you know I know your dad doesn't even speak English, let alone write it! Second of all, this is obviously your handwriting. No question!"

I looked at the floor. "Yeah," I stammered. "Dukart and I went skiing."

"I knew it! Where's Dukart?" Mr. Daggett barked.

"At tennis practice," I answered.

"What the hell? He can't practice if he wasn't at school! Get outta here. I'll take care of Dukart. Don't pull this crap again or next time I'm gonna have to do something about it!"

"Okay." I threw my rope back in the weight room and walked down the hall toward the exit. I found my way to the parking lot, sulked myself into the Purple People Eater, and headed for home. As I was driving, I started thinking about my high school graduation. It was just around the corner, and I couldn't let anything get in the way of that. My school days would soon be over, and I needed to get a job, something that had potential to lead into a solid career.

It was time to start contributing full-time to the welfare of our household; my parents put every penny they earned into paying off the house, and I wanted to help out too. I had fallen in love with the sport of wrestling over the past four years and never felt I belonged anywhere more than in the wrestling room. I felt slighted that it was over; I didn't know what I was going to do with myself if I couldn't wrestle.

Graduation day arrived, and by this point, my parents had come to understand that to get ahead in this country, school was important. I would be the first person on either side of the family to get a high school diploma, and they were proud. The ceremony was held in the David Douglas High School gymnasium, and the entire family dressed up for the occasion. As I walked in with my classmates and looked up in the stands to see my family, it hit me—this was all coming to an end.

We took our seats, and I listened to the principal and administrators hand out awards. As proud as I was of my accomplishments, I also wondered if I could have done better. Could I have gotten better grades and received an award like some of my classmates? Could I have done well enough to have gone on to college? It was too late for all of that now, and I had to come to terms with that.

When I walked across the stage and shook hands with the vice principals, I paused for a second at Mr. Daggett, the man who had given me a pair of cleats on the first day of football practice. It was unbelievable to me that I was standing there.

Barely able to read my native tongue at the age of ten when I arrived in New York, I was in a completely different world from where I'd started. When Mr. Horner handed me my diploma, I realized I really had accomplished something. I had acquired survival skills at each step along my journey, and whether it was asking teachers for extra help or picking my friends' brains to help me complete my homework, those skills, honed through facing many challenges and difficulties, helped me earn my high school diploma.

My graduation from David Douglas High School, 1959.

When we arrived home from graduation, the house began to fill up with family and friends. Among the crowd were Uncle Tony, Aunt Gladys, Joey (now a handsome young boy of six), and his sister Susan, my goddaughter, talking a blue streak and running circles around everyone. Also in tow was their new baby boy, Michael, born in January. The house was crowded and so loud I could barely hear when Grandma Beard congratulated me on my graduation and asked me about my future.

"I don't know yet," I told her.

"Well, you've come a long way. I'm proud of you."

"Thanks," I said as she squeezed the air out of my lungs.

In the midst of the chaos, one guest in particular struck a chord: Bobby DeFrancisco. He was still skin and bones and still wore the same Coke-bottle glasses he'd worn eight years before when he stood with me before I boarded my plane from New York, telling me we'd meet again in Portland someday.

Recently, he'd found a deal in which a rental car in New York was going to be sold at auction in Portland, and that was his ticket. Bobby had rolled up in front of our house with not much more than the clothes on his back about six months before, and here he was now, shaking my hand on the day of my high school graduation.

When the family party was over, it was time for a night of fun for the David Douglas graduates. We were having a spaghetti dinner at the high school, then going bowling and swimming at the YMCA. I was off for the final hurrah of my high school career.

CHAPTER TWENTY

Loprinzi's

It was a sad day when Grandma Nappi's funeral prayer card arrived in the mail. Since we'd been in our Portland home, we had received an occasional letter and some phone calls from my mom's younger brother Aniello, who had married my father's sister Antonietta. They lived in Rocca in the same home where I had been born, and Aniello kept us abreast of how everyone was doing in Italy. When the prayer card arrived for Grandma Nappi, my dad was shaken up, and I couldn't help reliving my memories with her, so tiny and tough, carrying bundles of sticks down from the hills. She impacted my life greatly. We all sat quietly together around the kitchen table, drinking wine and being quiet for Grandma Nappi.

That wasn't the only loss my family had endured in the recent years. Since my stay with Uncle Mike in New York, he had kept in touch sporadically over the years. He had enlisted in the U.S. Army shortly after arriving in the country; like my mother, he, Uncle Tony, and Aunt Marie all had dual citizenship, all born during the short period of migrant work my grandparents had done in Pennsylvania.

At some point during Uncle Mike's service in the U.S. Army, he had contracted tuberculosis. During one of my summers with Uncle Tony and Aunt Gladys, upon hearing the news of his brother's illness, Uncle Tony loaded us up in the car, and we drove nearly 1,500 miles to Tucson to visit him in the hospital.

"*Come stai?*" From his hospital bed, Uncle Mike asked how I was.

"*Bene.*" Good, I answered.

"*Quando mi sento meglio ti vengo a trovare a Portland,*" he said.

He told me he was going to visit me in Portland when he was better, and he did. He showed up at Uncle Tony's front door on 115th Street and took me out to dinner. He ordered his favorite jumbo prawns, and over prawns, burgers, and Cokes, we talked, both remembering our time together in New York.

"*Tu eri così piccolo ma adesso sei tutto cresciuto,*" he said, noting how small I had been when I'd gotten off the ship and that he couldn't believe how much I'd grown.

I sensed he felt bad for not being able to take care of me. He stayed with us on a pullout couch in the living room for a couple of days; I remember the whispers from Aunt Gladys and Uncle Tony about how skinny and pale my uncle looked.

One day, during Christmas break of my senior year, I returned home from wrestling practice to find Uncle Tony, Aunt Gladys, Uncle Felice, and Aunt Lucia all sitting around the kitchen table with my parents. They were red-faced and drinking wine, not too out of the ordinary, but the room felt dark. They told me that Uncle Mike had passed away, and they were discussing his burial. They said they had decided to fly him out from Tucson to have him laid to rest in Portland. He was to be buried at a place for veterans, Willamette National Cemetery.

My Uncle Tony shook his head. "*He's-a too-a young!*" he yelled out.

Uncle Mike was one year younger than my mother, so that made him forty-one at the time of his death. I never asked how he died, but since his stay in the hospital, over the years I'd heard murmurs from the adults of his failing health. Uncle Mike was buried four days after Christmas, 1958.

Uncle Tony and Uncle Mike when Uncle Mike came to visit in Portland. Uncle Tony is enjoying one of his favorite cigars.

Post-graduation, summer was underway, but I hadn't acted on anything regarding my future. Throughout the spring of my senior year of high school, while struggling with the career choice that would define the rest of my life, I checked out the bulletin boards in the counseling office at school. One notice that always stood out to me was a butcher apprenticeship at Selling's Fine Foods, a small grocery store at 152nd and Division. I read and reread it, thinking back to my time chopping up that pig in the piazza of Grandpa Giuseppe's home in Cicciano. At least it would be somewhat familiar. While I thought about the butcher apprenticeship every day, I still couldn't bring myself to make a decision.

Around that time, my friend Chuck Pyle invited me to be the best man in his wedding to his high school sweetheart. Chuck had lived around the corner from us on 116th, but his family moved away during the summer after our junior year. They originally moved to Bend and ran a motel, but that was short-lived, and they ended up moving from Bend to the coast, where his family owned and operated Otter Rock, a beach resort in Newport.

Many of my friends got married around the same time, and I seemed to be everybody's best man. Chuck was the first, and I decided that I'd forget about my future long enough to enjoy myself at the wedding, and when it was over, I would make my final decision.

I hopped a bus to Newport to stand up for my friend, and

during the reception, after my toast to the bride and groom, Chuck sought me out.

"Thanks for being here," he said.

"Sure, nice wedding," I told him.

The ceremony had been short and quiet, nothing like the Italian Catholic ceremonies I was used to. He told me that after his honeymoon he was moving to Seattle.

"I'm in with Boeing Aircraft," he said. "I'm gonna be building missiles."

"Wow, missiles?"

"Yeah," he said. "The pay is outstanding, and it's a great company. Hey, you should think about coming along; we're renting a home up there, and I've got a tent trailer you could stay in."

"I don't know. You think they'd hire me?"

"All I had to do was pass a test." He shrugged. "It's nothin' really."

"I'll think about it," I told him. I wasn't sure building missiles was the job for me, but from the sounds of it, with the pay and career potential, maybe it was something I shouldn't pass up.

On the bus ride home, I mulled things over in my mind. I was still feeling a void over the end of my wrestling career, but I knew it was time to get on with my life and make some serious decisions about my future. Maybe Seattle would be a good idea. Only a five-hour drive from Portland meant I could go home on weekends to be with my family and hand my paycheck over to my mother.

When I walked into the house, my father was pacing the kitchen, throwing his arms to the ceiling and yelling in Italian at the top of his lungs. He was so infuriated he didn't even notice me walk in. He kept repeating himself, something about boys calling the house. My mother sat on the couch with my sister, consoling her.

Patty was supposed to be entering David Douglas High School as a freshman the following year, but because of her sporadic schooling, I didn't know if she would be. Since arriving in the U.S., she had not had an easy time assimilating, and she still hadn't adjusted to school. She despised going; just getting her there was a battle in itself. Unfortunately, when she was there, she was never able to catch on academically, and as she grew older and developed a taste for my father's wine, the free-flowing nature of it in our home did not help the situation. I went upstairs and found my brother lying on his bed, thumbing through a pack of baseball cards.

"What's going on down there?" I asked Pete.

"Boys have been calling the house like crazy. *Papà's* been throwing things."

I shook my head. "Man, she needs to be careful about that."

"I know, but she won't listen, and half the time she's leaving the house drunk to go meet her friends."

"Damn it!" I said. I didn't know what to think. When my sister smiled, she could light up a room, but she was angry most of the time. Catching a glimpse of her smiling was like finding an agate among river rocks—beautiful but rare.

I ran back downstairs. My father was in the garden putting stakes in the ground for his young tomato plants. I helped him tie up the tomatoes, wanting to get his mind off my sister. I told him I'd heard about a good job.

My sister and me on the day of her confirmation.

"It's in Seattle, working on airplanes," I told him.

"*Sì?*" he answered.

"*Sì,*" I said, knowing his mind was still preoccupied. I decided to leave it at that. By the time we finished staking the tomatoes in silence, I had made up my mind. I was moving to Seattle.

When the phone call came from Chuck that he and his wife had moved into their rental house in Seattle and he had started working at Boeing, I packed up the car and headed north, promising my parents I'd be home on the weekends. I was now driving my father's 1957 Chevy. He'd purchased a 1958 Chevy for himself, so we had three cars at home. Pete got his hands on the Purple People Eater.

Chuck and his wife had a tiny home, and in their backyard was a two-person tent trailer. How I was going to fit into this equation was beyond me. I had a gut-wrenching feeling I was out of my element. I set up camp in Chuck's trailer and was being put to the test by Boeing. The testing went on for about two weeks, and having to eat out of cans and go into Chuck's house to use the restroom was inconvenient to say the least. At the end of the two-week period, I was told I had scored well and was offered an entry-level position with Boeing.

I called home to give my parents the good news, and I mentioned the less-than-accommodating amenities of my new living quarters. My dad reminded me that Uncle Tony's good friends Frank and Nancy Spaccarotelli lived in Seattle. Frank was a distributor for the Oberto Sausage Co., and my father instructed me to get in touch with him.

I called the Spaccarotellis, and they were more than happy to offer up their basement. Actually, Frank wouldn't take no for an answer. "You stay with us!" he yelled through the phone. Frank and my uncle were such close friends that Frank had named one of his sons after Uncle Tony, which meant we shared a name. That night I thanked Chuck and let him know I'd be leaving, no hard feelings. The relief was mutual.

I felt at home with the Spaccarotellis; Frank even made my lunch, fried sausage and onion sandwiches, and Nancy cooked dinner every night. But each time I drove into the Boeing lot, instinct told me I was not supposed to be there. The crowded lot and hectic pace did not feel right. I talked to Frank about it one night, and he encouraged me to follow my gut. I made the decision to put in my notice at Boeing and, thanking the Spaccarotellis for their hospitality, made my way back to Portland.

I pulled into our driveway and opened the metal gate that led to our yard. Lucky ambushed me. If nothing else, the dog was happy to have me home. This was Lucky number two, a lovable wire-haired terrier mutt. My sister's first Lucky had an affinity for chasing cars, and even after breaking his leg during a maniacal chase, he continued his favorite pastime to his own demise.

There was a comfort level in returning home, and I was ready to move back into the attic with my brother. As I was unpacking, I noticed the poster-sized wrestling bracket hanging low on the wall and chuckled to myself that my parents still hadn't discovered the hole. It was entirely possible they never would.

I didn't waste any time. The very next day I drove over to Selling's Fine Foods to see if the butcher apprenticeship was still available. It was a small grocery store with the meat department in the back. They had actually given it to another kid, but Bob Gilbert, the journeyman meat cutter, said he'd give us both a shot. For the first few days, the two of us showed up, and then for some reason, my competition disappeared. I was on my own.

After a few weeks, Bob had me breaking down sides of beef, boning, and making hamburger. I was also learning to cut T-bone steaks.

"You're catching on quickly, Russo," Bob told me almost daily, and I felt at home in this environment. The pay was nothing, but there was potential for a long-term, solid career and a decent salary in the future.

About a month into my apprenticeship, Bob decided to leave Selling's to work at a small grocery store down on 21st and Division. He asked if I'd like to continue working with him at the new location, and I agreed. This store was even smaller than Selling's, and the meat department was pretty much a one-man operation. Tony Brugato, the store owner, liked me, and I worked hard to learn the trade and bring in whatever money I could. The hours were not enough, though. I was only getting about fifteen to twenty a week, so I did what I could to put in extra time.

Next to the grocery store was a large meat market called Ladd Wholesale Meat Co. The owner came in now and again to make deliveries, and I could tell he was watching me, but he never said anything until one day when I was cleaning the counters. He was short, round, and balding on top, with salt and pepper hair cut in a U-shape around his bare spot. He wore a white butcher's coat and could have passed as a doctor except for the bloodied apron tied around his middle. Chewing on a cigar, he commented on how hard I was working to keep the area clean.

"I've been watching you. You're shining the hell out of that counter. What's your name, son?"

I stopped cleaning. "Tony Russo."

"Well, if that's not Italian, I don't know what is," he shot back, pulling his pants up around his belly underneath his coat.

"Yep, I'm from Naples," I told him.

He shook my hand. "Well, I'll be! A goddamned Neapolitan!" He looked at me for a moment and then continued. "Sam Galluzzo. How'd you like to come to work for me next door at Ladd Wholesale?"

His question caught me off guard, but I knew I needed to jump on the opportunity.

"Sure, that'd be great," I told him.

"Alright then, come in at eight-thirty tomorrow morning. I'll introduce you to my partner and the guys."

I found Bob in the back room digging through the freezer and explained to him what was going on. "On the fast track, eh?" he said without looking up from his frozen meat.

"I don't know about that," I said, "but I really need the extra hours."

I couldn't wait to finish up that day to get home and tell my parents the good news. I explained to them I'd be working at a big meat company, having been hired by Sam Galluzzo.

"*È Italiano!*" I added. They were thrilled.

"*È un buon lavoro,*" my mom said, smacking her wooden spoon on the side of a boiling pot. She knew this was a good job for me.

"*Sì.*" My father nodded in approval. Then he ranted on in Italian, making it clear that I needed to work hard for these people.

"I do work hard!" I said in my defense. "That's why they want to hire me!"

I pulled into the parking lot at Ladd Wholesale around eight o'clock the next morning, wanting to make a good impression. I sat in my car until people began to arrive closer to eight-thirty, and as soon as the front door swung open, I decided to brave the day.

I walked in, and the familiar smell of raw meat put me at ease, if only for a moment. As the crew began to arrive, I sensed I was being sized up from every direction, and luckily, Sam Galluzzo quickly burst onto the scene from a nearby hallway.

"Hey, you made it, Russo. Let's go meet my partner, the other Sam." Sam Conchuratt, as I would soon find out.

He took me to an office area where a man sat at a desk with his back to the door writing up orders. He wasn't tall, but even sitting down, it was apparent he was taller than Galluzzo, with a full head of wavy reddish hair. He didn't bother to look up at us.

"Hey, Conchuratt, you crazy bohunk! I've got someone here I want you to meet!" Galluzzo announced to the back of his head.

"What the hell, Galluzzo? I'm busy." He looked back at me, unimpressed.

"This is Tony Russo." He slapped me on the shoulder. "We could use him on the patty machine."

"Oh yeah? Is he a hard worker?"

Galluzzo threw his arms in the air. "You're damned right he is. He's *Italiano*!"

"What the hell, you goofy dago? The rest of us are gonna be outnumbered," Conchuratt said, laughing.

Even though they bantered this way with one another, they seemed to carry a mutual respect. I didn't say a word.

"Go ahead, give him a try." Conchuratt finally gave his blessing, cracking a half-smile and wasting no time getting back to his paperwork.

Sam Galluzzo then gave me a tour of the place. He jerked hard on a huge steel lever to open the heavy door to the meat cooler.

"This is where we hang the sides of beef," he said as he walked in. I could see my breath as we walked down the aisles between the enormous carcasses, halved and hanging from beams across the ceiling.

"Beautiful," Sam said, slapping some of the carcasses as he

walked by. Grandpa Giuseppe's admiration of the dead pig flashed through my mind. "Leanest stuff you can get," Sam continued.

As he admired the huge slabs of meat, I zeroed in on the glistening, thin layer of white fat encasing the dark-red flesh. We continued the tour, and I took it all in until we finally ended up at the hamburger patty machine.

"This will be your station," Sam told me. "Making patties."

He explained that the local restaurants ordered different sized hamburger patties, and we had molds and presses to fit each size, from an eighth of a pound on up. Over the next few years, I would make patties by the thousands.

By the end of that week, my coworkers had been introduced to me one by one, and they all had their own specific jobs—and personalities to match.

Warner Oster stood at the sausage machine and spoke with a thick German accent; Sid Su, a slick butcher in the form of a petite Chinese gentleman, was stationed in the center of the room at one end of the huge butcher block; Ken Swenson, a.k.a. "Swing," a tall, slender, highly skilled Texan, was stationed in the middle of the butcher table; and the person closest to me in age, Sam Simich, a tall, dark, and handsome Yugoslavian (although I thought he looked more Italian), another excellent butcher, was stationed straight across the table from Sid.

The first month or so I didn't say much to anyone as I was getting acclimated and observing the inner workings and dynamics of the place. I stayed close to the patty machine, pumping out patties by the dozens as the orders came in from the local diners. I also helped load and unload the delivery vans.

My favorite times of the day were the ten o'clock coffee break and noon—lunchtime.

Every morning, Sam Conchuratt brought in a box of butterhorns, and religiously at ten o'clock we stood around the box soaking up coffee, the pastries a perfect sponge for the creamy, sweet beverage. I would head back to the patty machine, coffee in tow, and when lunchtime rolled around, Sam Simich and I gravitated toward one another, being closest in age and both interested in sports. We ate in my car, usually talking baseball and listening to music, then headed over to nearby Cleveland High School to throw the ball and play home run derby.

Halfway through the summer, I noticed two of Sam Galluzzo's sons putting in some time at Ladd's. Sam's second son, Greg, was a year younger than me and would be a senior at Jesuit High School in the fall. We began to talk when he'd come in to work and were becoming fast friends. He confided in me that after high school he was going to enter the seminary and become a Jesuit priest.

"Wow, that's excellent," I told him.

"Yep, my mind's been made up for a while now," he said.

I was more than impressed, although at this point he was just a regular boy, and he changed the subject from his future priesthood quickly.

"Hey," he said. "I belong to a gym down the street called Loprinzi's where I lift weights. You should join, and we could work out together."

I didn't know how to answer. I knew my mom would not be happy if I spent my hard-earned cash on gym fees. I told him I'd go with him to check it out but couldn't guarantee I'd join.

"Great," he said. "You're gonna love it. A bunch of real body-builders work out there!"

The next day after work, Greg and I headed off to Loprinzi's Gym; it was a sight to behold—men glistening with sweat, grunting and pumping iron, building muscles on top of muscles. The room was crammed with dumbbells and more machines than I could count, and a slew of pictures on the walls boasted professional wrestlers and champion ironmen in flexed poses. I was starstruck; I recognized some of these faces from professional wrestling on television.

Sitting behind the front desk was a dark-haired, short-statured muscle man.

"This is the owner of the gym," Greg said.

The man stood up and chimed in, "Hi, Sam Loprinzi," shaking my hand.

"Tony Russo."

"What brings you in?" Loprinzi asked.

I didn't want to tell him I couldn't really afford to join his gym, or mostly that my mother wouldn't allow me to, so I mentioned that I liked all the weights and would love to work out there, but what I was really interested in was wrestling.

His face lit up, and he looked me up and down and then asked, "Have you wrestled before?"

"Yeah, I wrestled at David Douglas High School. I placed third in state last year." I didn't want to brag but wanted him to know I was competent in my sport.

"Are you headed off to school to wrestle?" His question stung.

"Nah, I've just started at Ladd Wholesale, cutting meat," I told him. "I'm working my way up the ladder to become a full-fledged journeyman, but I really miss wrestling."

"You know what?" Sam went on. "My brother Joe is one of the fitness instructors over at the MAC club downtown. They have a pretty good wrestling team, and if you're any good, they might let you be a workout partner. It's mostly guys who have graduated from college and are thinking about participating in international tournaments, or guys who are trying to get their grades up so they can wrestle at the universities."

"I'd love to check it out," I told Sam.

"Great, I'll give you my brother's card, and he'll get you in to see the coach, but only if you promise to come back here and work out."

"I'll make sure of it," Greg said, laughing.

I promised them I'd be back, and Sam handed me his brother's card: *Joe Loprinzi – Fitness Instructor – Multnomah Athletic Club – Portland, Oregon.*

I was smart enough this time not to mention anything about wrestling to my parents. I knew my mom would still find reason to protest. I kept Joe's card in my pocket for about a week, and then one morning I decided to pack up my workout gear before I headed to the meat market. That evening, when I clocked out, I took Sam's advice and drove downtown to check out the Multnomah Athletic Club.

I walked in and flashed Joe's card to one of the employees. He took me straight to find Joe downstairs in his weight room, and on our way through I noticed the place had more of an upscale feel than Loprinzi's. Joe was nearly a mirror image of his brother, although maybe slightly taller, with the same dark hair and hard-bodied build. *Man, these guys are serious about their training,* I thought. I had my bag of gear slung over my shoulder, and Joe asked me what he could help me with.

"Your brother Sam over at Loprinzi's gave me your card," I told him.

"Ahhh, you know Sam, huh?"

"Yeah, I just met him, and we got to talking about wrestling. He said you have a team here at the MAC and that I might be able to be a workout partner."

He asked me my name and about my wrestling background, and then, realizing I was serious, he said, "Heck, let's go meet the coach."

We headed upstairs, where practice was in session. The smell brought me back to the high school wrestling room, which it could've been except for the size—it was much bigger, and these wrestlers weren't boys. They were men. The coach directed practice from the back of the room. He was thin, in his mid-fifties, and wore dark slacks with a white button-down shirt finished off with a red bow tie—the best dressed wrestling coach I'd ever seen.

"Cy, I've got a kid here who wants to wrestle," Joe shouted above the scrambling feet and grunting brawls that were taking place.

He led me across the mats, and as we got closer, I noticed this man's face, weathered and tough, and his mangled ears—the sign of a true mat warrior.

I hid slightly behind Joe as he introduced me. "Tony Russo, this is Cy Mitchell. He's our head wrestling coach." We shook hands. "Tony wrestled in high school, and he'd like to be a workout partner."

"Oh yeah?" Cy looked me over. "What are ya, about 140?" he asked.

"Somewhere in there," I answered.

"Well, get yourself dressed down," he said. "Let's see what you can do."

I sprinted out of the locker room, ready to go. I hadn't wrestled since last school year, but I was still in somewhat decent shape—or so I thought. Cy matched me up with a wrestler near my weight named Lee Allen. Although he was a bit before my time, I'd heard this guy's name. He was a legend at Sandy High School, winning the state title all four years.

Coach blew his whistle, we squared off, and it was full speed from there. I pulled out all the stops, using every move I knew, but every shot and each maneuver was countered. Lee was cleaning the mats up one side and down the other with my face—and every inch of my body for that matter. During a break in the action, I knew Lee was thinking I was some kind of a wuss, a fish flopping all over the mat. He thought I was going to hit the showers.

"Let's go," I said. "I want to keep going."

Lee shook his head. "Okay, I guess," he replied in a sympathetic tone. "But if you want to keep going, you need to wrestle freestyle."

I'd never wrestled freestyle before in my life.

"It's different than the collegiate style you're used to," Lee explained. "If you expose your back to the mat, you give up points, and if you even touch your back for a split second, you're pinned."

That was drastically different than what I was used to, as a pin in high school wrestling required both shoulders to be firmly pressed against the mat, the offensive wrestler having to prove his point by holding his opponent flat.

With this brief description of the new rules, Lee and I went at it again. Although I didn't come close to scoring on him, it was an entirely different match.

Lee was impressed, and I was exhilarated, having found my way back to the sport of wrestling.

CHAPTER TWENTY-ONE

The MAC

The Multnomah Athletic Club housed some of the greatest athletes of all time, many of whom would go on to become national and international champions; some even went on to become Olympians. Unbeknownst to me, when Joe Loprinzi directed me to Cy Mitchell, the wrestling room was stacked, and it started with my workout partner.

Lee Allen was a national Greco-Roman champion in 1954 and went on to become a two-time Olympian, and here I was, scrapping with this guy every night after my shift at Ladd's. I was in the midst of some serious talent but had no idea at the time: Rick Sanders, Sandor Szabo, Gary Hoagland, Mike and Pat Clock, Marlin Grahn, Joe Casale, Autry Ehler, Ron Calhoun, Fritz Fabian, Lon Allen (Lee's brother), and Garry Stensland—to name a few.

Lee and I were the same weight, so I didn't have any false hopes of breaking into the lineup. I was sweating hard, happy to be in the room, and once again, I had an outlet for my demons.

As winter set in, I was on a roll at Ladd's, honing my butchering skills and still brawling with Lee every night at the MAC. Meanwhile, my brother's wrestling career was going strong in his second season at David Douglas High School. He had grown over the course of the year, so this season he could actually claim to weigh the ninety-eight pounds his weight class stipulated.

It was around this time my mother decided it was about time I find myself a good Italian girl—enough with those skinny-boned blonds who were gracing our home on occasion. When I had company, she would give me the death stare as she shuffled by us in her slippers, or worse yet, the slit-throat gesture if she was really pissed. As I'd walk my female "friends" out of our home, I'd hear the yelling start up: *"Madonna mia!"* followed by a splattering of spaghetti hitting the inside of the kitchen door as we left.

My mother had made up her mind. She was concerned for my future and had decided to call on expert advice, Bobby DeFrancisco. He had made his way to Portland a single man, was serious about finding a wife, and had started mingling with an Italian singles club.

While sitting at our kitchen table drinking wine one day, Bobby told my mother he had found me a beautiful Italian woman. *"Ho trovato una bella donna Italiana!"* he said.

"Sì?" Her radar was on full force.

"Sì," Bobby said. "She is a little bit older than Tony. *Perfetta!"*

I overheard the conversation and wasn't having anything to do with it. "No way!" I said.

My mother snapped at me across the kitchen from her chair. *"You no knows-a nothing!"* she said in disgust.

"Tony, c'mon, let me set you two up on a date," Bobby pleaded. "You never know."

"Alright, I don't care." I was surprised at how easily I'd given in, but as Bobby had stated, you never know.

That Saturday night around five o'clock, I anxiously watched out our kitchen window, dressed in my only pair of slacks with a white shirt and a skinny black tie, as a car rolled into the driveway. From behind the wheel stepped a short, stocky Italian man with a round face. From the passenger's side, a young, svelte, olive-skinned beauty emerged. *Perfect for my mother,* I thought. The rest of the family climbed out of the car as well. Standing at our door when my mother opened it was the Bausilio family.

My dad poured wine all around as the two families talked. Mr. Bausilio, a painter, already had my mother signed on as a client, while his daughter Maria, knowing full well why she was there, looked at me with her big brown eyes and whispered in my ear that she liked to dance—my least favorite thing. Even so, we left the families to their wine and headed off in the Chevy for our first date, at a dance hall, where the twist was raging on the floor. Maria cut up the dance floor with some highly technical moves while I bumbled my way through and was more than ready to sit down to pizza and finish out the night.

Her family liked me, my family liked her, we liked each other, and Bobby DeFrancisco was proud, but I was finding it difficult to allow myself to become too attached. We did continue to date, though, and Mr. Bausilio was thrilled whenever I'd come to their home for dinner; his daughter would cook his favorite sauce with mushrooms and spicy meatballs.

The new year came and went, and we were now approaching the start of another summer. My brother had a third place finish under his belt from the state wrestling tournament at ninety-eight pounds, and nobody was more excited about it than my father. I had completed my own season at the MAC and was still focused on wrestling, escaping to the mat to pour it all out every day after work. My parents couldn't figure me out. I had everything I needed, they thought; I didn't need wrestling. It was a distraction and could potentially interfere with my work if I were to be injured.

"*Non paga, non paga niente*," my mom would yell at me, rubbing her thumb and first two fingers together. Wrestling didn't pay, so it didn't make any sense to them. I didn't care.

One night at the MAC wrestling room, my main workout partner was nowhere to be seen. I didn't think much of it, but right away Cy Mitchell called me over and wanted to chat.

"Hey," he said. "Lee got called up to Fort Lewis for duty."

"What?" I didn't know what to make of it.

"Yeah, they're calling everyone in for the Berlin crisis."

I knew Lee was in the National Guard, and there were times he was off at training, but I had no idea he'd be called into action. Cy told me Lee would be in a holding pattern at Fort Lewis until his unit might be needed.

"That makes you our 137-pounder," Cy announced, hitting me on the shoulder. I had officially made the lineup, the precise weight class being 136.5.

Cy had been wrestling me in some competitions when there was an opening in the lineup at 145.5 or even at 136.5, if Lee was out for his National Guard training, and I'd had a successful season with the team, but this was big. Cy put me in the lineup at 136.5, and I amped up my workouts even more, motivated to be a full-fledged member of the MAC wrestling team.

Wrestling had once again become the focal point in my life. The team was a cohesive unit, and I was taken under the wings of many of the older, more experienced wrestlers. I had gained their respect during my days as Lee Allen's workout partner, and they taught me every day about the true nature of competition—what it takes to go hard for a full six minutes in an all-out brawl no matter how bad it hurts. When I took my lumps, and I did, I had an attitude—controlling my anger once it was on a roll was no easy task. After one particular beating I had taken, my teammate Joe Casale sought me out during my brooding fest and pulled me aside.

"Hey! There is no need for that," he told me. "Never put your head down." His statement was straightforward and to the point, and as simple as it was, it hit a nerve. I knew he was right.

Sometimes my experiences with these guys were just plain funny. Garry Stensland, our heavyweight, used to hand me his false teeth before a match. The first time he pulled them out and handed me his two front teeth he said, "Hold these, would ya, Russo?" Then he laughed his ass off before lumbering his behemoth body out onto the mat and beating his opponent to a pulp. Knowing better than to do anything other than hold his teeth for the entire match, I waited until he sought me out when he was done; then he took them from me and popped them right back into his face.

Sandor Szabo, a balding, short, stocky 119-pounder made of pure gristle and with ears set at nearly a 90-degree angle, was another teammate and friend. He was a Hungarian refugee and had defected to the U.S. a few years earlier; he was a complete nut about the game of soccer. He cornered me after practice one day.

"Hey, you eye-talli-uns know soccer, right?" he asked, grabbing me by the shoulder.

"Uh, I guess," was the best reply I could muster.

"I play on a team. We have games on the weekends. You don't need to practice. Just come to the games, and you will be on my team," he said, slapping himself on the pecs with both hands.

Sandor was not a person you could say no to. Sure enough, I played on his soccer team, and as soon as the ball came my way I got rid of it, passing it off to Szabo as quickly as I could. These were the only soccer games I'd ever played in where the players took smoke breaks. When they were called out for substitutions or had a break for the half, they'd light up and smoke like chimneys. Then they'd snuff their cigarettes out in the grass and head back onto the field without missing a beat.

At the MAC, we had been training for an upcoming tournament in Seattle, the Pacific Northwest AAU Wrestling Tournament. Since Lee had left the MAC and been stationed at Fort Lewis, he had managed to get a wrestling team going on the base, and they came to Portland for a dual—a teammate one

The soccer team that Sandor Szabo, my teammate from the MAC, convinced me to play for. Sandor is second from the left in the front row. I'm at the far right of the front row.

minute, opponent the next. I matched up against Lee in our dual against Fort Lewis, and it was embarrassing. I vowed never to feel that way again, thinking it highly likely that we'd meet in the upcoming Seattle tournament.

Sure enough, Lee was entered in the tournament at 136.5 pounds, and I had to make my way to the finals to get my shot at wrestling him again. As I began my matches, I noticed Frank Spaccarotelli, the close friend of Uncle Tony's that I stayed with while working at Boeing, sitting up in the stands.

I rarely had an audience member, and this cranked me up. Frank stood up and cheered every time my hand was raised, and I made it all the way to the finals for a rematch with Lee. I had already devised my strategy. Lee was phenomenal with his legs, so I knew I couldn't get caught in the bottom position and let him get his legs in on me. My plan was to go a hundred miles an hour from the whistle to the end and set a pace he couldn't sustain.

The whistle blew. Frank was screaming, and I went berserk. I took Lee down, he reversed me, I got away, he took me down, I reversed him—the score was tight, but at that point I thought I was up by one. The match continued at this psychotic pace, and it was hard for me to know where I was at; my match management skills had gone out the window, but I didn't stop.

At the start of the third round, I was in the bottom position, and I knew this was a dangerous place to be, so why I did what I did next is beyond me.

I made a vital mistake. I slowed down. Instead of going in a frenzy on the whistle, I hesitated, Lee got his legs in, and by the end of the third round, he had scored points on a tilt, turning me over enough to get back points but not flat enough to pin. Lee won by one point.

I was disappointed my hand would not be raised to the crowd for Frank to see, but I couldn't believe how close I'd come to winning that match.

When it was all over, Lee came to find me while I was talking with Frank before he went home. I introduced Lee to my Italian friend, and he confided in me that if I'd kept up the pace I'd started with, he never would have beat me.

"I knew it!" Frank said, and I couldn't help but laugh.

"Why don't you think about going to school?" Lee blurted out unexpectedly. "You should think about the University of Oregon or Oregon State."

Lee had wrestled for the U of O, but there was no way I could go to school. First of all, I didn't have the grades, and second, I wasn't sure I could keep up with Division I wrestlers.

"Nah," I said, shrugging it off.

I took my second place trophy, shoved it into my gym bag, and headed back to Portland.

CHAPTER TWENTY-TWO

Word On The Street

For about the last year, my mother and Uncle Felice had been conspiring about opening an Italian restaurant, and they had finally found a location in the Montavilla district of Portland. It was to be called The Naples, and my mother took a leave from ShedRain Umbrella so that she could cook. Before I knew it, Sam Galluzzo was taking the crew from Ladd's for my mom's pizza at lunchtime. Sam loved how she put the sliced tomatoes on fresh, after the pizza had been baked.

When they'd finished their first helpings, my mother would come out from the kitchen and slap more food onto their plates.

"*Mangia!*" she'd yell.

"No, no," they'd all say, waving their hands furiously, they couldn't possibly eat another bite, but they loved it.

"Ma, stay in the kitchen, would ya?" I'd tell her.

"*Noooo, you-a stai zitto!*" She'd throw her hand toward me in disgust, in front of the group, telling me to be quiet.

"Okay," I'd laugh and then shut my mouth. It was a perfect

alliance: my mom and uncle bought meat from Ladd's, and in return, Galluzzo frequented The Naples and indulged in my mother's pizza.

An ad placed in The Oregonian in June of 1961 for The Naples Restaurant.

Even though the food was amazing, my mother's restaurant had a short lifespan. It was meant to be a family affair, but everyone was too busy. My mother and uncle sold The Naples, split their earnings, and then my mother headed straight back to her piecework at ShedRain Umbrella.

They were ecstatic upon her return, as she was their only employee to come to work with her needles already having been threaded in order to out-sew (as she saw it) her competition. If anyone beat her out on umbrella production, we paid for it at home with a full-scale Italian tongue-lashing.

She'd pull out a dollar bill, hold it up for all to see, and sing out, "*Il mio sangue!*" My blood! Then she'd continue on in Italian, her dramatics impressive as always, "If you squeeze this dollar bill, you will see my blood pour out!"

*Uncle Felice and my mother during their stint as restaurant owners.
The food at The Naples was outstanding, especially the pizza.*

We got the point. She worked hard, and the least we could do was help her thread the needles.

Another fall was upon us, and with it came wrestling season for me at the MAC and for my brother at David Douglas. Early one Saturday evening, there was a knock at the door, and there stood Pete's wrestling coach, Bob Majors. Bob had taken over the program Pete's sophomore year when Coach Hiebert became the head football coach. My parents invited Coach Majors in, and my father immediately offered him a glass of wine. He cordially accepted, sat down at the kitchen table, and began to talk to my mom and dad about Pete's potential in the sport of wrestling. I helped translate along the way.

"Your boy is talented," Majors told them. "So talented, I think he can get a scholarship to go to a major university if he continues on this track." I jumped in to make them understand, translating Majors' words.

My dad's face was fire engine-red from his wine consumption, and he was excited, smiling and nodding, loving every minute of this conversation. He continued to refill Bob's glass. My parents were always offended if anyone refused their hospitality, and being the polite guest that he was, Coach Majors couldn't refuse.

"There's one thing, though," Bob went on. "I know he's growing, but I need him to stay at the lowest weight class possible."

"*Pete deve rimanere piccolo,*" I said, doing my part, and I could tell they were getting it.

"*Sì, sì!*" my dad continued, agreeing and nodding with every comment.

"At the 106-pound weight class, I really think your son can win it!" Coach Majors continued, and I translated again.

"*My-a son,*" my father said, hitting himself in the chest, "*è un campione!*" he added, pointing at Majors.

Coach Majors had enjoyed several glasses of wine to this point, and upon hearing my dad's words and feeling his enthusiasm, he stood up and shouted, "Yes!" He knocked the table back a few inches, thus thrusting my father out of his seat, and the two of them leaned across the table toward one another, pumping fists and yelling in unison, "*Sì!*"

We escorted Coach Majors out to his car, said our goodbyes, and as he drove away, my brother and I tried to explain to our father, "Don't give wine to the Americans when they come over! They can't handle it!"

He looked at us like we were a couple of idiots, and then angrily under his breath, in a slurred mumble, he said, "*Bull-a shit-a! Fa bene il vino!*" It's good for them.

My brother was somewhat distraught over the conversation that had just occurred at our kitchen table; he was definitely growing, and 106 pounds was tough for him to make. That night up in the attic he confided in me that he didn't think he could get down to 106 all season long.

"Don't worry about it," I told him. "Majors will wrestle you up for most of the season, and then you'll only have to make the weight at district and state. It's your best shot for a medal."

"I guess," my brother agreed, but I knew he was not convinced.

Between my history in the sport of wrestling, my reputation at David Douglas, my brother's record on the mat, and his inborn, deep-seated mean streak, the Russo boys had begun to make a local name for themselves. Adding to our notoriety was the fact that my father attended all of my brother's matches *after* he'd had his evening wine. Everyone knew he was there, including the opposing spectators and referees. If Uncle Tony and Joey decided to come along, it became an even more boisterous event. Joey was now eight years old, and I had shown him a few moves. He loved the excitement of wrestling matches. Even on nights his dad couldn't attend, he'd call and ask if he could still join us; many times it was my dad, Joey, and me in the stands rooting for my brother. Since I had graduated, I became the one in charge of getting my father to and from all of Pete's wrestling matches and tournaments. We didn't miss a contest.

Pete and I still looked so much alike, we could have been twins: short black hair, dark eyes, compact build, identical stride. Now that Pete had grown, the resemblance was undeniable. My brother clinched our title as "the boys from Italy you don't want to mess with" when Moses Lake, the previous year's state championship team from Washington, came to duel it out with the state championship team from Oregon, David Douglas. The two teams had been matched up as a goodwill event, a show, and the outcome was predicted to be close. Word on the street regarding Moses Lake, though, was that they couldn't be beat.

They strutted into the gym, each wrestler chiseled out of stone and looking to weigh ten pounds more than his weight class. The Scots were scared. The Moses Lake wrestlers had been allowed to weigh in at home, and Coach Majors was suspicious, to say the least. The crowd that appeared for the show in the David Douglas High School gymnasium was colossal—standing room only— and sure enough, the Scots began to get picked off right and left.

Pete was wrestling up at the 115-pound weight class, and someone had forgotten to get word to my brother that these guys were unbeatable. When he stepped onto the mat, he wasn't planning on showing his Moses Lake guest a good time. Pete was a highly skilled wrestler overall, outstanding from all positions, and when the whistle blew, my brother took his Washington opponent to the mat instantly. The crowd erupted, and my dad went crazy. The match went back and forth, Pete pummeling his opponent through it all. When they raised my brother's hand at the end of the match, the Moses Lake coaches were irate, and Pete had just made a statement to everyone in the local wrestling community. He would be the only wrestler on his team to win that night.

As the season progressed, Pete was a machine, winning every

single time he stepped on the mat. One evening, when I'd just walked in the door from my practice at the MAC, the phone rang as the family was sitting down to dinner. I answered it, and on the other end I heard a boy's voice saying, "Who is this? Let me talk to Pete."

"This is Tony, who's this?" I answered.

"This is your worst nightmare," the caller said. "Let me talk to Pete."

"You can talk to me!" I told the guy.

"Tell your brother," the caller continued, "I'm gonna kick his ass in his own gym next week."

"What the hell?" I said. "Who the hell is this?"

"When I'm done with your brother next week, they're gonna have to use what's left of him to mop up the mat."

Pete and my dad had taken notice, and my dad started yelling in Italian, "Who is it? What is wrong?" Pete had gotten up from the table and was standing next to me, trying to decipher the conversation. I put my hand up to motion that I had it under control, and by now I knew the caller must be my brother's opponent in his upcoming match against Parkrose.

I said into the phone in as badass a voice as I could muster, "Hey, my brother is gonna kick the shit out of you next week, and when he's done, make sure you stick around—I'm gonna kick the shit out of you too!"

"We'll see about that," the caller said, and then click, he hung up.

I was irate. My dad was out of his mind, words and arms flying, and Pete was still standing next to me. I put my finger in his face and said, "You better kick the shit out of that Parkrose kid next week."

"Yeah? Was that him?"

"Yes, that was him. He says he's gonna kick your ass!"

My brother looked at me with a confused look and asked, "How'd he get our number?"

"Don't worry about that. All I know is that you better be ready to kill this kid next week!"

The night of the match, we were all fired up. I couldn't tell if this Parkrose kid's psych-out tactics had gotten under my brother's skin or not. I stopped to pick up Uncle Tony on our way to the match, and I was hoping for a fast pin because I knew what kind of circus could erupt.

No such luck. The match ended up to be a barnburner.

It was going back and forth with the ref throwing points out equally to both wrestlers. Coach Majors was yelling, I was yelling, and my dad was red in the face and yelling in Italian along with Uncle Tony. Then a voice rose above the rest from the Parkrose stands.

"Go back to Rome, Russo!"

The well-crafted rebuttal shot back from the David Douglas stands: "He's not from Rome, you idiot! He's from Naples!"

When my brother's hand was raised at the end of the match, the grandstand exploded, and it was purely gratifying.

By the district tournament, when Pete had to make the scratch weight of 106 pounds, he was worn out and starving. Pissed off, he made his way through districts easily and was the favorite to win the 106-pound weight class at state. On the way down to Oregon State University for the tournament, though, Pete confessed he didn't think he could make the weight.

"What are you talking about?" I asked. I couldn't believe it.

My brother, Pete, wrestling his opponent to a pin.

"You only have to make 106 one more time, then the next day you get a one-pound allowance to 107. That's easy! You've come this far, you can't give it up now!"

Pete ran every ounce of water weight out of his body the night before weigh-ins. He was sucked down to nothing. He made the weight and won his way through the first day of the state tournament.

That night he came to me before we left the gym and said, "I quit!"

"You what?" I said incredulously.

"I quit. I'm done. I can't make the weight. I'm done!"

"Quit? Like hell! Get your ass in the car!"

I put my brother in the car and drove him to the hotel where we were staying in Corvallis. When we got there, I filled the tub about a third of the way with steaming hot water and pulled the curtain shut to hold in the steam.

"Get in there!" I said.

"No," Pete started whining. "I quit. I told you."

"Like hell you quit. Get in there and do sit-ups until I tell you to stop."

"Noooo," my brother wailed.

"You do sit-ups until I say stop. If you don't hear me say stop, then you keep goin'!" I pulled the curtain back, and my brother stepped into the tub.

"Ouch! It's too hot," he cried.

"It's not hot. Get in."

My brother started doing sit-ups, and I drilled him for another fifteen minutes. All of a sudden, he jumped up, pulled the curtain back, and stepped out of the tub.

"It hurts! I can't do it," he complained.

"Get back in there, and don't get out again until I say so."

That night when we went to check Pete's weight, he was right on—107 precisely.

Pete won the state title at 106 pounds that year, 1961, making him the second individual state champion in David Douglas history. Watching him on the podium, I remembered Hershell Green and the impression he made on me back in my early days in the sport, and here was my brother being awarded the prize I had set my sights on.

At home, we were all proud of Pete. After cutting all that weight, he was ready to start enjoying his favorite foods again. When he came down the stairs that next day, my mother didn't miss a beat, getting right back into loading up his plate.

The following year, Coach Majors wrestled Pete at the 115-pound weight class, and there would be no cutting involved, as this had become my brother's natural weight. He won his second state title, and sure enough, Coach Majors was right:

the scholarship offers started rolling in. One offer in particular stood out above the rest.

Bob Majors had done his secondary schooling at Cornell College, a small private school in Iowa. The wrestling team at the time was outstanding; not too long before, they had surprised the wrestling world by winning the national championship, and many of Bob's teammates were considered some of the best wrestlers in the nation.

Two of these wrestlers were Dale Thomas and Ted Bredehoft. Dale Thomas took the head wrestling coach position at Oregon State University. He was fiercely passionate about the sport of wrestling, and he became the central driving force that began to raise the quality of wrestling in the state of Oregon. Anyone who was anybody in the sport knew Dale, and he convinced some of his teammates to make their way to Oregon along with him. Bob Majors was one such person, and he had landed the head coaching position at David Douglas High School.

Ted Bredehoft followed Dale out west as well; he coached at the University of Washington and became the head coach at Arizona State University—and this was to be Pete's best offer, nearly a full ride. He'd have to work for food and laundry money, but his tuition and housing would be covered.

Arizona State had wrestling in the form of a club when Ted Bredehoft took over, and his job was to get a program off the ground as a varsity sport. He was trying to recruit a team that could immediately compete with anyone in the nation. Bob Majors knew this and had made a phone call to his friend from Cornell College about my brother. That call resulted in Pete heading off to wrestle for Arizona State University in the fall of 1962.

CHAPTER TWENTY-THREE

Unlikely Devil

In late August, Pete hopped a train to Tempe to begin his career as an Arizona State Sun Devil. A black shroud enveloped our home after my brother left, as my sister, was beginning to make herself known, and her troubles were escalating. A counselor from the school district had visited our home the year before and tried to explain to my parents that Patty needed to go to school. My parents took the advice seriously, enrolling Patty as a freshman at David Douglas High School for the 1961–62 school year, Pete's senior year. By her age, Patty should've been a junior, but because she had missed so much schooling up to that point and was so far behind, this was their best attempt. That was like putting a bandage on a gushing wound: it would never stick.

Patty had a vise grip on our home; she was there all the time, not working, drinking, and messing with boys—to my father's complete horror. My sister was slender and tiny, tough yet somehow fragile, and my parents had sheltered her from the world her entire life. She had never learned survival skills or academic skills, and being introverted and shy, worst of all she'd never learned social skills. Now she was an angry young woman out to make a statement.

"Patty, you're beautiful. You could do anything you want to," I tried to tell her. "You need to quit drinking and smoking, and don't mess around with these idiot boys. They're no good!"

"I know. You're right. I'm gonna stop," she'd promise, but the next day she'd be right back to the same destructive patterns. I couldn't understand it. My parents yelled and screamed, but Patty never yelled back—she just continued on her self-imposed path of depravation.

Things got darker yet when I showed up at Ladd's one day, and Sam Galluzzo called me into his office. Over the previous three and a half years, I had climbed the ladder to journeyman status as a butcher and had joined the union, earning benefits and making a decent salary.

"We're not doing well financially, Tony," Sam said as I walked into his office and sat down.

"Okay …" I said, bracing for the big blow.

"We can't afford to keep you on as a journeyman." And there it was. "Please understand me—you are not being fired," Sam quickly explained. "I will call you to work anytime I can, and now that you're a journeyman, you can go to work anywhere. Safeway and Albertson's are always looking for butchers."

I was disheartened. I finished out my two weeks, all the while working up the courage to give my mother the news. She was angry and didn't understand it. I tried to explain I hadn't been fired and that I'd be able to work anywhere now. It didn't matter how much explaining I did; she was not happy.

"*Non va bene!*" she screamed repeatedly. Not good at all.

"It's okay," I'd reassure her, but she wouldn't hear it.

I began to fill in at grocery stores, and Sam called me to work when they had big orders to fill, but I also started helping Joe Calcagno more frequently on the farm. Not for the money—I would never accept cash from the Calcagnos, but I felt a connection with the land, getting my hands dirty pulling up parsnips, cutting lettuce, or helping Joe with his produce deliveries. I was at home. Over the years, Joe had become a confidant. We talked about everything—his kids, the weather, fishing, and wrestling. Joe would always ask me, "How's the wrestlin' goin'?"

"Great," I'd tell him.

Wrestling at the MAC was the one thing that always seemed to be going well. Although we had lost a few outstanding wrestlers, we gained excellent new recruits to fill their spots. It was still my escape from reality. My mother had begun questioning whether my time in the wrestling room had interfered with my job at Ladd's, and it was a lost cause to try and assure her it hadn't. I tried anyway. I wrestled hard for myself with no concrete benefit in sight, but it didn't matter.

During the Christmas holiday, Pete came home to be with the family. Patty, who loved to make popcorn strands for the tree, was sitting at the kitchen table eating and stringing when my brother called me up to the attic. "Tony, get up here," he hollered.

I found him going through some of his old things, and when I hit the top step, my brother launched into a well-thought-out speech about the splendors of Arizona.

"I like Arizona a lot," he said. "It's sunny all the time."

"Oh yeah?" I answered, half-listening.

"Yeah, you'd really like it there," he continued.

"Nah, it's too hot for me."

"Not in the winter. The weather's amazing. You'd love it, I guarantee it." Pete spoke like a well-trained salesman. "Hey, I talked to my coach about you," he threw in, quickly gaining my full attention.

"What the hell? Are you kidding me? What'd you do that for?" I asked.

"I'm not kidding. I talked to Coach Bredehoft about you. He remembers you. He said he remembered your match against Lee Allen in Seattle."

"Oh yeah?" I said, laughing.

"Yeah, I told Coach my brother could kick butt on all these guys he has in the room at 137 pounds."

"What?" I said. "Are you crazy?"

"Why don't you come down and try to make the team?"

"You're kidding me, right? I can't go to school. I don't know the first thing about college. I barely made it through high school."

"It's not that hard. All you have to do is go to class, get your reading done, and then pass the tests. You could do it." My brother was dead serious, and he had it all figured out.

"No way," I told him.

There was a heightened energy in the house with my brother home for the holidays, but he had to get back to campus; it was midseason, and they practiced daily. Pete's words had sent me into a spiral. *What if?* I thought. I knew I couldn't go to school, so that should have ended it for me, but I couldn't stop thinking about what he'd told me. If nothing else, it was flattering that Coach Bredehoft remembered me.

About a week into the new year, I received a letter in the mail from the Office of Athletics and Activities at Arizona State University. My heart started pumping. I opened the letter, and it was from none other than Coach Ted Bredehoft. Pete had told him about how well my wrestling career was going at the Multnomah Athletic Club, and he wrote that he remembered my match against Lee Allen. He finished the letter by stating he'd like to see me come to Arizona State and find out if I might be able to hold my own against the guys on his team. For someone who didn't talk much, my brother must have really done a number on Coach Bredehoft. I put the letter next to my bed and headed across the street for a run.

The field where I had run the dogs and played baseball so many times was now the portal for my plunge into a reflection of my life. I had to run full speed. I needed a gut check—how hard could I go? Every single demon I'd encountered in my life was now playing tug of war inside my head. The only way I knew to defeat them was to drive them into the ground as hard as I could through sheer physical exercise. I ran until my lungs were on the verge of exploding and I was dripping with sweat, but I kept going—I couldn't stop.

I'm nearly twenty-three years old, I thought. *These guys in the room are fresh out of high school, just out of their state tournaments, most of them probably two- and three-time state champs. And as far as the classroom goes, I have no clue.* It was like trying to look through a concrete wall; I couldn't see any possible way for this thing to work out.

The next day, I was completely exhausted but also had a sense of relief and lightheadedness that felt like a tingling in my brain, probably from the pounding headache that had finally gone away. But I took it as a sign. The demons were gone—for now. That afternoon I told Joe about the letter while we were loading his truck for a delivery.

"You know, that sounds like it might be a good idea," he told me.

"Yeah, I don't know ..."

Indecision put me right back where I started, so I talked to Uncle Tony and Aunt Gladys.

"*Go-a, go!*" Uncle Tony started yelling. "*Now-a you can-a be a dottore!*"

Aunt Gladys chuckled. "That's really something, Tony. You need to give that some serious thought."

Again, right back where I started.

Lying in the attic that night, a ton of bricks hit me square between the eyes: *I have nothing to lose. I'm a full-fledged journeyman meat cutter; that's something I can do at any time. If this thing doesn't work out, Albertson's and Safeway aren't going anywhere.* I'd made my decision.

The next day, I took out the letter and translated it for my parents. Up to that point, I hadn't told them a thing about it, so I explained that Pete's coach wanted me to come to Arizona and try to make the wrestling team.

"*Nooooo! Madonna mia!*" my mother wailed. "*Non è buono!*" Not good! Then she finished me off with, "*Tu fai o' chianchiere, ti sposi!*" You become a butcher, you get married!

"*No, Mamma, adesso no. Non è tempo per quelle cose.*" It's not time for that yet. I tried to be as clear as I possibly could.

My father kept quiet through the entire conversation; he seemed sad.

I gave myself enough time to say my goodbyes, but once I'd made my decision, that was it. I purchased a plane ticket to Phoenix to leave in two days. I still needed to have a conversation with Maria, whom I'd been seeing since Bobby DeFrancisco had set us up, and I tried to soften the blow by telling her I was just going to see what would happen.

"You need to give me a ring before you leave," she blurted. Then, backtracking, she added, "It doesn't have to be an engagement ring, just a promise ring." She'd put me on the spot.

I knew what I had to say, and it was hard. "It's very difficult for me to do that right now," I told her, and tried to explain to her that this was an opportunity for me, something I had to do. I also didn't know how long I'd be gone. Maybe it wouldn't work out and I'd be back in a month or two, but I had to give it a try. My decision did not sit well with her and her family.

I couldn't sleep the night before I left, so while it was still dark, I got up and began packing. I didn't need much—some clothes, workout gear, and my wrestling shoes, and it all fit in one suitcase.

As morning approached, it was still dark outside with the recent cloud coverage and deluge of rain. I heard the door open downstairs, then my cousin Joey's voice. When he was old enough, Joey had taken over the same neighborhood paper route my brother had when we first arrived in Portland. Joey could always tell the days that my mother had been baking bread; she got up before dawn on baking days, and the smell would envelop the neighborhood. On those days, Joey made our house his last stop and came in for a hunk of fresh, hot bread with butter. My mother hadn't been baking this morning, though. He was there to say goodbye, and there he was, sitting at the kitchen table, eating a piece of my mother's day-old bread toasted with warm melted butter.

"Hey, Tony. I hope you like Arizona," he said.

"Thanks. I'll be sure to call," I answered.

"Okay. Maybe you could get me a shirt with a Sun Devil on it?"

"Sure," I told him, and then too quickly I watched him head back out to his bicycle.

My cousins in Portland. Left to right: my goddaughter Susan, Joey, and Michael.

I sat at our kitchen table waiting for Joe and Algi; they were coming with us to the airport. Joe would be driving, and I couldn't wait for them to arrive because I couldn't take any more of my mother's wailing. My parents were heartbroken. They were ready for me to settle down and move into a house down the street. It was beyond their comprehension why I needed to do this. When Joe and Algi arrived, Algi handed me a wrapped gift—a gold watch engraved with my name and the date: Tony Russo, 1963.

"So you won't be late for class," Joe explained.

"That's great," I said. "Thank you."

Kisses followed all around. My mother wiped her eyes repeatedly, and Algi took on the job of consoling her. "*Tutto andrà bene Teresa. È meglio così,*" Algi said as she held on to my mother on our way to the car. She explained that she thought I was making the best decision and told her everything would be fine.

The five of us drove to the airport, and the goodbyes were not easy. I was glad Joe and Algi would be with my parents after I left. The flight to Phoenix was short, and the only regret I had was that I hadn't told anyone from the MAC I was leaving. I had no idea if this thing was going to work out, so I didn't see the point in telling them. If I was back in a week, they'd never know the difference.

I stepped onto the plane in Portland in a complete spectrum of grays and stepped off in Phoenix into the brightest hues of blue I'd ever seen. My brother hadn't exaggerated about the sun. Pete greeted me the minute I stepped off the plane, and by his side was Coach Ted Bredehoft.

Bredehoft was a handsome young man, small in stature with

short, light-colored hair. He was dressed in a suit and tie and had a smart, slick way about him. There was no doubt in my mind that in his day, he had been a swift marvel on the mat.

"Nice to meet you, T," Coach Bredehoft said, shaking my hand vigorously, not waiting for an introduction. From that point on, he never referred to me as anything other than "T."

"Nice to meet you too," I answered. "Thank you for having me."

"Let's get you settled, and then this afternoon we'll see what you can do," Bredehoft went on.

"Sounds good." This guy wasn't wasting any time. We drove to an apartment complex just off campus on Apache Boulevard in Tempe. Pete lived across the street in a dorm, Hayden Hall, which he'd told me about at Christmas.

"Since it's the middle of the school year, there aren't any dorms available right now," Bredehoft said as we climbed the steps to the apartment. "So I've hooked you up with Buzz and Manuel. Buzz is from Oregon." He knocked on the door.

On the other side was a thick-bodied middleweight with light-brown hair cut nearly to his scalp, a squared-off face, and eyebrows thicker than any of the Italians I knew, and that was saying something.

"Hey, Buzz, this is Tony Russo," Bredehoft said. We shook hands, and I noticed standing off behind Buzz was a short Hispanic wrestler.

"Get over here, Manuel," Bredehoft barked. Manuel jogged the short distance toward me.

"Hi, nice to meet you," he said as we shook hands.

Buzz Hayes wrestled for the Sun Devils at 157 pounds, and

Manuel Aragon was in the lineup at 125. These were to be my new roommates, and the introductions were amiable. As Bredehoft headed out the door, he said, "Take care of him, guys. Why don't you show T around campus before heading to practice?"

As I unpacked, Buzz and Manuel began to bombard me with information about Arizona State. They were making it sound like a carnival.

"Grab your wrestling shoes," Buzz said. "We'll show you around campus and then hit the wrestling room."

I threw my gym bag together and slung it over my shoulder. On the way to the apartment I had noticed a large butte, void of any trees, with an enormous letter A imprinted on the side of it. When we got outside, it was the first thing I asked about, and talking over the top of one another, they explained, "Oh, don't worry. You'll get to see that A up close and personal—we run that mountain all the time."

During my guided tour across campus, the first building to impress me was Old Main, a large brick building. "The oldest surviving building on campus from which Arizona State has grown," Manuel rattled off like an encyclopedia. Old Main was at the center of a meticulously landscaped courtyard; in fact, all of the campus grounds seemed to be impeccably landscaped and pristinely clean. After that, there were so many things named *verde*, green, that it was hard to keep them all straight. As we continued across campus, we ended up at a long walkway lined with skyscraping palm trees on each side.

"This is Palm Walk," they said with pride. I couldn't help but be impressed by the perfectly lined-up trees, so narrow and top-heavy I had no idea how they were standing upright. When we reached the end, they pointed out the Memorial Union.

"The MU is where the athletes eat," Buzz told me. "They have excellent Mexican food."

"That's great. I love Mexican food," I said, remembering the only Mexican food I'd ever eaten, Aunt Gladys's tacos. I looked up and noticed a clock above the MU—no numbers, but in place of each number was a letter, and when you read it clockwise, the letters spelled out ARIZONA STATE, as if to remind me of my place in time.

We took a left at the clock, and I realized my tour was over when we entered an activities building. Inside, the guys directed me to a checkout counter where I was issued burgundy shorts and a gray T-shirt. Dressing down, I tied up my wrestling shoes and followed them into what looked like a dance studio. The floor was covered with mats and had one full-length wall of mirrors from floor to ceiling with a waist-high wooden bar going across it.

Bredehoft started us off with some light running, and as we circled the mats, the swift sound of shoes hitting canvas began to drone on. I looked at my brother, confident and running in stride with the group, and my mind drifted off, questioning what in the world I had gotten myself into.

Bredehoft's whistle broke the trance. "On the wall!" he snapped.

The entire team hit the wall, sitting down with their backs against the mirror, facing the mats. Bredehoft started to call guys out two by two for full-speed wrestling. We hadn't done any drilling yet, but the next thing I knew, he'd called out my name.

"T, get out here! Oklahoma, let's go!" he yelled.

This is it, I thought. *Showtime.*

Oklahoma and I started going at it. I knew I couldn't mess around.

I was pummeling this guy hard, and even though there were other matches going on in the room, I felt Bredehoft's eyes zeroed in on me. As we continued to wrestle with no round breaks and no one keeping score, a welling of emotion started to build up in the room. It didn't take me long to figure out it was directed against me. Everyone was cheering on my opponent. An uprising of anger swelled inside of me. I didn't even want to let the guy breathe, and I tried like hell to finish him off. About eight minutes later, Coach's whistle sounded.

"Take a seat!" he yelled.

In my mind, I was sure I'd just whipped this guy, but Bredehoft said nothing. I sat down against the mirror, sweat pouring off every inch of my body, and watched while Coach Bredehoft continued to run full-speed matches.

Not five minutes later I heard him yell, "T, you're up! Pennsylvania, hit it!"

I headed back out to wrestle my next opponent, and the animosity toward me was now palpable. I realized what was happening; if I did well, it meant one of these guys was going to lose a spot in the lineup. They didn't like it, and I didn't care. I was in that room for only one reason. Nobody was keeping score, but I was keeping track in my head. We must've been out there for ten minutes this time, and the way I saw it, the match was going in my favor hands down. Bredehoft still didn't say a thing.

His whistle cut through the room again. "Time!" he bellowed.

I sank back down against the mirror, my face leaking like a

faucet. As I wrung out my T-shirt onto the floor in front of me, I made eye contact with my brother from across the room; he knew exactly what was going on, and he looked away quickly.

I sat there watching the action for a bit, wondering if I might be done, and then Coach barked again, "T, hit the mat! Arizona, get out here!"

Exhausted, I pulled out everything I had left to sprint out onto the mat. The whistle blew, and *crack*! Arizona and I slammed our heads together so hard blood started flying. Nobody stopped the match.

This guy did not want to lose to me, and the blood fired up his teammates even more. I was dizzy from the head-cracking, but my rage was so focused I knew this guy didn't stand a chance. I wanted to inflict pain. When the whistle blew to end the match, my opponent was irate, and the room went quiet. I sat back down against the mirror, hoping for a sign from Bredehoft. Nothing.

I hadn't counted on the fact that these guys were already teammates, having bonded before I arrived. The last thing they wanted was some intruder coming in and taking one of their spots. Practice ended with some sprints. As the group disassembled with still no word from Bredehoft, I took off for the locker room.

"T, come back here," Bredehoft yelled across the room just as I'd approached the door. I turned around and walked back across the mats toward him. He waited until no one was left within earshot, and then, "Can you come to my house tonight?" he asked in a near whisper.

"Sure, Coach," I said, truly surprised when he handed me a small piece of paper with his address on it.

"Good, we're gonna talk scholarship," he added.

My insides screamed. *Maybe I stand a sliver of a chance here,* I thought. But outwardly I quietly thanked my new coach and hit the showers.

On the mat at ASU.

CHAPTER TWENTY-FOUR

The Interrogation

At Bredehoft's home, he introduced me to his wife, Susan, and his son, a toddler named T.C., and we sat down to a dinner of Kentucky Fried Chicken. I reached for a drumstick and began to gnaw my way around the leg when I noticed Bredehoft was eating his piece in a sophisticated manner, with a knife and fork. Susan saw my expression and, understanding I was wondering if I was supposed to follow suit, shot me a don't-worry-about-it expression that put me at ease. I felt an immediate connection with the Bredehoft family, an unspoken bond that made me feel like I'd known them for years.

Bredehoft got quickly to his point. "We're gonna get you tuition, fees, and housing, T," he stated matter-of-factly. "You're gonna need to work to cover food and books, but that's nothing. I've got you hooked up for a job in the dining hall at the MU."

"Thank you, I appreciate that," I said to both Coach and his wife. It felt insufficient, but I was at a loss for words. "I can't thank you enough," I added.

"Hey, T," he piped up across the table. "It's okay. You're gonna wrestle for the Sun Devils. We need you!"

"Wow," I said, beaming.

Bredehoft continued, "I want you to go see this academic counselor." He handed me a piece of paper with a name on it. "And then I want you to go to arena scheduling with Buzz and Manuel."

"Okay," I said, still at a loss for words, and then, "Thank you." I had to say it one more time as I left their home. I so badly wanted to call my parents and give them the good news. I kept playing a scene in my head in which they were ecstatic for me, yet I knew that was not how it would play out.

Next thing I knew, I found myself signed on for sixteen credit hours, sitting in classrooms in which I was pretty sure the professors spoke something other than English. It transported me right back to my first days in an American school when I literally didn't speak the language. This wasn't as extreme, but it was just as confusing.

About three weeks into the semester, I was battling daily in the practice room but still completely in the dark as far as my academics were concerned. Bredehoft called me into his office as we broke from practice one day.

"Have a seat, T," he said as I walked into his office. "The admissions people are trying to figure you out. They wanna know where you came from."

"What do you mean?" I asked.

"In the last four years, have you ever attended a university?" Bredehoft asked me with a slightly worried tone.

"No," I said. "I tried to take one night class after high school, but it didn't work out. I dropped it."

"Okay … Yeah, I knew that. I knew that," Coach repeated himself. "Here, you need to go see this guy." He pointed to a name on a piece of paper. "He's the assistant dean of students, and he wants to ask you some questions. Just answer every single question honestly, and everything will be fine."

"Okay, Coach, I will," I told him, not liking the sound of that.

Later that day a nice secretary escorted me into the dean's office. The dean, tall and tightly dressed from head to toe, stood up to shake my hand.

"Nice to meet you, Mr. Russo," he said, and then, looking at a piece of paper on his desk, he sat back down, straightened his jacket, and began grilling me.

"So I hear you're a wrestler?" he started.

"Yes, I've been wrestling since high school," I answered, thinking, *I hope that's honest enough.*

"And," he paused, "what have you been doing for the past four years since high school, Mr. Russo?"

I nervously launched into an explanation about my internship at Selling's and then moving on to Ladd Wholesale and how I had become a full-fledged journeyman meat cutter. Then I told him about Loprinzi's Gym and wrestling at the MAC. I didn't want to leave anything out.

He looked at me funny and said, "Yes, I see, but where did you go to school?"

"I haven't gone to school," I told him, my stomach in knots. "Except for one night class that I didn't finish."

He continued to stare at me, and then, clasping his hands together as if he were praying and looking down at the paperwork on his desk, he muttered under his breath, "I don't know what Bredehoft is trying to pull. Tell you what," he continued, "we're going to do some checking, and then we'll get back to you."

"Can I keep wrestling?" I was afraid to ask.

"For now, Mr. Russo, you may keep wrestling." Then, standing up, he walked to the door and led me out. "Thank you for stopping by. I'll be in touch."

"Thanks," I said, feeling nauseated and guilty—for exactly what, I didn't know.

Bredehoft informed me that the admissions people had launched a full-scale investigation. In the meantime, I continued to drown in the classroom, feeling confused and out of place; I couldn't wait to punish people for it when I got into the wrestling room. After about a week, Bredehoft finally called me back into his office. I knew the verdict had arrived.

"T, here's the deal," he said. "I have to tell you there's some bad news. You are currently ineligible to wrestle, and the dean has put you on academic probation."

"Oh man," I said quietly. In my head, I felt an iron curtain close on my life.

Bredehoft continued. "The admissions people checked out your high school transcripts from David Douglas, and they're fine, but right now you're only pulling about a 1.9 GPA in your current classes. They're skeptical about whether or not you can make it here."

"I'm sorry, Coach," I told him, feeling like I'd really let him down. "When do I leave?"

"What?" he said. "You're not going anywhere." I listened to him as he explained the next sequence of events. "First of all, let me see your schedule."

He went over my schedule, shaving off four credit hours, and said, "From now on, I'm your counselor. Before you go to arena scheduling, you come see me first. Understand?"

"Yes," I replied.

"Next, they want to do some testing on you. It's gonna take about two days, but you'll be fine. Just go in and do what they tell you."

"Okay," I answered, but I knew I had to admit something to him. "Uh, Coach ... if I can't wrestle to earn my scholarship, I can't afford to stay in school."

He looked at me for a moment in silence, and then he put his elbow up on his desk. He pointed at me hard with each word. "You know what, T? Don't worry about that. You're keeping your scholarship, and I'm gonna wrestle you all over, in every open tournament I can get you entered into, but you need to know one thing."

"What's that?"

"You must keep a 2.0 GPA to be eligible to wrestle next semester. You're gonna need to S-E-U!" he said.

"Yes, Coach," I answered, fired up but having no idea what he meant by SEU. "I can do it!"

I later found out from Buzz and Manuel that SEU was Bredehoft's abbreviation for "suck 'em up." Why Bredehoft was so generous and willing to take a chance on me, I didn't know, but I had never been more appreciative of any gift from another human being in my life.

Interestingly enough, not being eligible had an upside; it alleviated the tensions in the wrestling room as my new teammates realized I wouldn't be knocking any of them out of the lineup. Not yet, anyway.

The testing they put me through revealed two things: my

reading comprehension skills were devastatingly low, but I was gifted in the area of communications. I had to produce a writing piece for my inquisitors; I chose fishing as my subject, and although my spelling was atrocious, they were captivated by my story.

I finished out my year at Arizona State, wrestling in every open tournament Bredehoft could find for me. I wrestled all over Arizona and traveled to California and Wyoming. I was winning tournaments while working to finish out the semester with that magic number 2.0 printed on my transcript—and I did it.

When my brother and I arrived home for the summer, my mom handed me a sealed envelope that had been delivered while I was away at school. It was a letter informing my parents their son was on academic probation and would be ineligible to wrestle for the semester. The dean's message had fallen short, and having already redeemed myself, I was glad my parents would be none the wiser.

I got to work straight away at Albertson's. Roy McCormick was the meat department manager; he appreciated my skills and used me to cover the vacation time of all of his employees. When he ran out of vacation time for me, he checked in with the other local grocery stores, and I filled in for employees all over Portland. It kept me working the entire summer. Roy told me, "Always check in with me first when you're home for the summer. I'll put you to work." And he did.

Meanwhile, that summer my sister dropped a bomb on my parents, deciding to move out of our home into her own apartment with a boy she'd met, Randy Delaney. Against my parents' wishes, I helped her move, but we were all worried about what was going to happen now that she would be away from the family.

My brother threw a twist into our summer as well by surprising us with the news that he was getting married to his high school sweetheart, Dorothy Fox. On August 3, 1963, they were married at Saint Peter's Catholic Church on Foster Road; I stood in as best man.

Although I was happy for Pete, I started to realize when he began looking for a full-time job that he was contemplating not returning to Arizona State. This concerned me, but I bit my tongue and helped him find work with Gunderson Brothers Inc.

George Okeson, who had been head foreman there and Uncle Tony's good friend, had a son Glen, who I'd developed a friendship with over the years.

Our connection had been contrived by his parents and my aunt and uncle back when I was fresh from my turbulent time in New York. They'd plan sleepovers for us after an evening of socializing; it was easiest if I stayed at Glen's house because he was diabetic and needed an insulin shot every morning. I'd go over, but Glen and I didn't quite know what to make of each other, and we didn't interact much. Over time though, even with Glen attending Roosevelt High School while I was at David Douglas, our friendship began to grow.

With Glen's parents still part of Aunt Gladys and Uncle Tony's social circle, we realized we shared some of the same interests: sandlot football (or any kind of ball) and fishing. Glen also loved to listen to music—we simultaneously went through a Buddy Holly kick, and Glen knew a local radio disc jockey who'd play our Buddy Holly requests on demand. Diabetes never interfered with Glen's doing anything; except for his morning stabs of insulin, I wouldn't have known he had an illness.

One day, we had been out playing a game of sandlot football and were both sweating and breathing hard by the end. On the way home, Glen was driving his new little Volvo when the car began veering across the road. I looked over at Glen; he was trembling and shaking.

"What's wrong?" I asked, but there was no response. His eyes glazed over and were beginning to roll back into his head. He had dropped the steering wheel, and he was slumping down in his seat when I realized I needed to act quickly. I grabbed the wheel and pulled the car toward the curb; the car hit the curb immediately, killing the engine. I opened the door and started yelling for George.

"What's going on?" he demanded, flying out their front door.

"Something's wrong with Glen!" I yelled.

George ran back into the house, grabbed some kind of a drink, ran to the car, and forced the liquid down Glen's throat. I watched, terrified. George decided to take Glen to the emergency room. He would be fine, but from then on, I was always acutely aware of his condition, and I was so thankful we were close to Glen's house when he'd gotten sick that day.

We carved out time for our friendship for years to come, and now, thanks to Glen, my brother would be starting a new career working the swing shift building boxcars, and I'd be heading back to Arizona alone. It was what my brother wanted, but as far as I was concerned, he had not heard the last of it from me.

CHAPTER TWENTY-FIVE

Outstanding Wrestler

In the fall semester of 1963, I found myself living in a trailer near campus with a new recruit from Oklahoma who had made his way to Arizona in a 1952 Chevrolet, a shiny red coupe. He was so short he had to cut the top half of the steering wheel off and sit on a pillow just so he could see to drive. Glenn McMinn was to be my new training partner. We got right to it, wrestling every day, either on campus or at the nearby Wristlock Club. Because he was a transfer student, Glenn would need to train during this school year, with his eligibility starting the following season.

"I've got a brother back in Portland who would be a great workout partner for you," I told Glenn one day.

"Oh yeah? Why the hell ain't he here then?" he asked in his eloquent manner. I launched into the story of my brother's scholarship, how he'd convinced me to come down and try to make the team and then decided to get married and stay home with his wife in Portland.

"Gettin' married's one thing, but giving up your wrestlin' career, that's another thing altogether," Glenn stated, as if he knew my brother's best interest. That night I decided to make a phone call to tell Pete about how he was missing out and needed to come back to school.

"You can be married in Arizona just as easily as in Oregon." I tried to reason with him over the phone.

"What about Dorothy's job at the phone company?" he asked. His wife had landed an excellent job with the phone company, and they were reluctant to give that up.

"I don't know, but Coach wants you back." Bredehoft did want him back; he'd told me to stop at nothing to lure Pete back to Arizona.

My classwork was going fairly well; I was keeping my head above water at least, and Bredehoft had helped me to decipher my schedule, putting me into a major called Professional Activities.

"You're gonna be a coach," he told me.

"Okay," I answered, secretly just hoping to make the grades to be eligible to wrestle and not thinking much beyond that. As our dual meets started and I began my official career as a Sun Devil, I felt invincible, and Bredehoft was animated about my performances.

"Keep it up, T! You're on fire!" he said to me after one of our home duals.

Our first tournament of the season was approaching at the Naval Training Center in San Diego, California. Bredehoft had us sitting in a group on the mat as he reviewed his strategic plans for the upcoming battle.

Our 1963-64 lineup. I'm in the middle. Manuel Aragon is the wrestler to the far left, and Buzz Hayes is directly to my right. They were my roommates upon my arrival at ASU.

"This is an open tournament," he said. "Guys from all over the nation will be there, but we can win it as a team if we play our cards right. We're gonna need a few of you in the finals, so get out on the mat and attack with pure aggression. Everything you've got! S-E-U!" Then he looked directly at me. "T, you've got the big gun your very first match."

I raised my eyebrows, thinking, *Who's the big gun?*

Before I could even ask, Bredehoft continued. "You drew Lee Allen right out of the chute."

You've got to be kidding me, I thought. *My first match?* All I said was "Okay." I couldn't believe it. My thoughts flashed back to the last time we wrestled in Seattle and he outscored me by one point.

Coach then talked to the team about how 1964 was an Olympic year; he felt we had some guys talented enough to think about going to the trials qualifier.

"Every wrestler out there with Olympic aspirations is gonna be at this tournament in San Diego," he said. "For those of you interested, the qualifier is held in May in Cheyenne, Wyoming. If you win it, you earn the honor to wrestle at the Olympic Trials in Queens, New York, during the World's Fair." Bredehoft clapped his hands to get us up. "Let's hear it!" he barked. "Devils on three. One, two, three!"

"DEVILS!" We shouted back so loudly I thought the pure force of it was going to knock Coach's head clean off his shoulders.

I stayed after practice. "Hey, Coach B," I said after the room had begun to clear. "I want to train for the trials qualifier. I want to go to the trials."

"That's great, T. You're on, but get home and get some rest. You need to focus on what lies ahead of you tomorrow."

Coach was right, but sleeping was not going to happen that night. For one, I had to hop a plane the next day, which made me nervous, and two, how could I sleep when he'd just told me I was matched up with Lee Allen right off the bat for my first official tournament as a Sun Devil? I went for a run, needing to cut about three pounds, and recounted my last two matchups with Lee. The first time, there had been no competition for him; the second time, I'd relaxed near the end of the match, not keeping the pace I had set for myself. He'd admitted that had I kept that pace, it would've gone my way. So that was the plan again—only this time I would not let up.

The next day, after we unloaded our stuff into the barracks at the Naval Training Center where we were staying, I went to check my weight. *Perfect,* I thought. I was right at 138, only a pound and a half over. All I had to do was go for a run that night to sweat off as much as I could, and then overnight I'd float about a pound or more, which would put me just under 136.5.

I weighed in the next morning, and everything had gone according to plan except that I was now on my second night of no sleep because the barracks weren't conducive to actual sleeping. We were right next to the military police headquarters, and all night long we lay on our spring-loaded bunks listening to sirens blaring and the sound of feet pounding the pavement in unison; we were also blinded by the swinging movement of a spotlight that flashed across our faces intermittently until sunrise, which had all of us pissed off enough by morning to put Bredehoft's plan of pure aggression into motion.

As I warmed up for my first match, I thought about what I needed to do at the sound of the whistle: stay on my feet, don't let him get his legs in on me, go like hell for six minutes—and pray to God I'd wind up on top. That's exactly what happened. I pulled it out by a point. My coach was out of his mind, my hand was raised, and my friend and I embraced, Lee smiling through the entire scene. I couldn't believe that four years before, I was barely worthy of being this guy's workout partner, and now, here I was, in my first collegiate tournament, prevailing over Lee Allen to move forward in my bracket.

Through the rest of that day, I continued my winning streak, which put me into the next round of competition the following day. Upon checking my weight before bed, I weighed exactly

137.5 and knew that I'd float about a pound off overnight, putting me right at 136.5 in the morning. I took a small swig of soda and decided to hit the barracks for some sleep, but I knew it would be my third night in a row of staring at the ceiling.

I don't know if it was the lack of sleep or my body hitting a set point, but whatever it was, when I stepped on the scale that next morning, it hadn't budged—137.5. I was shocked. I'd never encountered this before. I knew my body's inner workings, and this threw me.

"I didn't float any weight!" I yelled over to Coach.

"What in the world?" Bredehoft said, running over to the scale and zeroing in on the number. He kept lightly tapping the metal bar, thinking he could will it down. But that was it. The scale had made its decision, and when Bredehoft realized this, he panicked.

He ran over to a phone bolted to a post in the middle of the room, a direct line to the military police. "Hey, where's your closest workout facility with a sauna?" he shouted into the receiver. "What do you mean about a mile away? We don't have time for that!" Bredehoft grabbed my arm. "Let's go!"

As we ran outside to a parked MP vehicle, I realized it was already eight thirty. Weigh-ins closed at nine, giving me thirty minutes to drop a pound and get back in time to make the official weight. Coach shoved me into the back seat of the jeep, and the driver pulled away, going at a nice, steady pace toward what I assumed would be the closest sauna.

"Can't this thing go any faster?" Bredehoft demanded, drumming nervously on the dash. "This guy needs to lose a pound, and fast!"

The driver looked suspiciously at me in his rearview mirror, squinting hard as if trying to read the fine print on my face. Saying nothing, he turned on his siren with the red light flashing, put the pedal to the floor, and sped us across the grounds.

When we arrived at the gym, Bredehoft told the driver, "Wait here, and leave the motor running. We'll be right back."

We ran in and spotted an old silver whirlpool. Coach began to fill it to the top with boiling water and told me to get in.

I sat on the white belt that kept your butt from touching the water. Bredehoft had found a camouflage plastic rain poncho that he put over my head, choked around my neck, and spread out over the whirlpool to keep the steam and heat in, creating a makeshift sauna. Sweat began running out through the top of my head like water through a sieve, and Bredehoft cooked me for twenty minutes or so. *Payback,* I thought, *for when I had Pete doing all those sit-ups in the tub at his state tournament.*

When Coach was satisfied I was done, I got out and redressed, and he covered my head again with the poncho and wrapped it tightly around my body. We ran back out and jumped into the running vehicle.

"Step on it!" Coach yelled at the driver as he leaned forward to hold on to the dash. The driver peeled off toward the sporting complex, and again, he looked in his rearview mirror as I sat there in the back seat, hooded up like a troll. This time I think he felt sorry for me and, sensing our urgency, hit the gas even harder, lights and siren at full blast all the way back.

I stepped on the scale at 8:55. The weigh-in official tapped it ever so lightly.

"136 even," he yelled.

"Nice work, T," Bredehoft remarked with a smile.

I'd lost a pound and a half of sweat in that whirlpool, leaving me shriveled up, lethargic, and just angry enough to want to rip people apart.

In the semifinal round I had to wrestle one of my own teammates. The last time I'd wrestled this guy in a match was my very first day on campus when Bredehoft was putting me through my paces—and Arizona and I cracked skulls.

After that, Arizona admittedly hated to work out with me; he was a finesse guy, and I was a brawler, so he didn't like the bruises or blood that came as part of the equation.

Before the match, Coach walked over to me and whispered something under his breath without looking me in the eye. "You're gonna have to pin him, T."

I felt bad, but I knew what he was thinking; I couldn't afford to get any black marks. Black marks were points accumulated against each wrestler during their contests, and the only way to avoid any black marks was to acquire a clean pin.

There was no blood this time, but when I threw Arizona onto his back, he looked up at me and said, "You're not gonna pin me, Russo."

I looked away and increased my arm tension around his throat until I heard the slap of the mat. As I left the mat, Bredehoft nodded. I had done what I had to do, and I'd made the finals.

Coach had predicted it would take a couple of us for Arizona State to win it, and it had come down to two: my old roommate Buzz Hayes and me. Bredehoft had calculated the points and figured either Buzz or I would have to pin one of our guys in the round-robin finals to cinch the team title for Arizona State.

"I don't care what you do out there," he said, pacing back and forth in front of me and Buzz, stopping only to point a finger in our faces. "But one of you has got to get a pin," he ordered, his voice cracking. We nodded in unison.

Warming up, I psyched myself up so hard that when I stepped onto the mat, nothing could permeate me. I went in for a throw against my opponent, and he landed flat across his shoulders. The ref slapped the mat so fast it shocked me. Bredehoft came unhinged. Not only was I the 136.5-pound NTC champion, I had also helped give Bredehoft what he wanted, and Arizona State went home with the team title.

Getting ready to throw my opponent.

Buzz had also won his matches in the finals, although not by pin, and he was an NTC champion that day, too. He was also given the Outstanding Wrestler award of the tournament.

Buzz and I posed for a photo with Bredehoft holding his plaque for the team title. I looked over at Buzz with his Outstanding Wrestler award and thought, *What more could I have done?*

After winning the NTC Tournament. Bredehoft is in the middle with his team plaque. I'm to the left, and Buzz is to the right with his added award of Outstanding Wrestler.

Returning to campus, I unwound and got back into the swing of things. Many of my teammates and I were working the odd jobs Coach had set up for us. Going up and down the steps inside Sun Devil Stadium picking up trash was one such job, and we'd usually scrape up enough fallen cash to head over to the local greasy spoon, Pete's Fish-n-Chips, to order their signature dish.

When Coach had first sent me to work upon arriving in Arizona, scraping slop from the trays in the MU had been my entry-level position and my weekday meal ticket. I continued to work for my meals at the MU, but this year I had been promoted from the hog line to the kitchen. It was a much more dignified position, and the round, compact Mexican lady who acted as my boss was always impressed with my intuitive culinary skills. She couldn't figure it out.

"You just know what to do, Tino," she called me, reminding me of home. "And you work much harder than these other kids I have to deal with."

"Thanks," I replied, deciding not to enlighten her on my previous experiences.

Bredehoft was always conscious of our need to earn spending cash, hooking us up with whatever he could find, and one day after practice, he called me and Buzz over. "Hey, I've got a great job lined up for you two," he said.

"Oh yeah?" Buzz answered.

"Yeah, go on over to the art building during studio hours, and tell them Coach Bredehoft sent you."

We wondered what was in store for us as we headed to the art building and checked in with the secretary in the office.

"Yes, the students are expecting you," she said, getting up from behind her desk and walking us into the studio.

"Your models are here," she announced as we followed her through the door.

Models? What the hell?

The room was filled with tall easels, each connected to the arm of a coed, and empty stools were placed around the room.

"Great, come on over," the teaching assistant called out to us. "We're ready for the figure drawings," he said to the students. Then, looking at Buzz and me, he continued, "Go ahead and strip down. You can each take one of these stools."

Buzz grinned from ear to ear. He couldn't wait. He stripped off his clothes and stood up on the stool, posing in a flexed form showing off every muscle he had.

"I'll have to wear my wrestling singlet," I announced to the TA.

"But we're sketching the human form, so we need to see the entire body," he retorted.

"Nah, I can't do that," I told him again, looking at Buzz's valiant grin as he stood there buck naked, loving every minute of it.

"Okay, tell you what, you can lower the straps of your singlet and get into a seated pose. I guess that'll have to work," he said, shrugging his shoulders.

I was relieved he was willing to be accommodating, and as I sat there for what turned out to be much longer than my attention span could handle, I went over my plan for talking to my brother when I got home for Christmas. Bredehoft was still on me about getting Pete back to Arizona, and I was pretty sure I could convince him.

When the budding artists skimmed their canvasses with their final strokes, I checked out the accomplished works, impressed with what I observed.

I then took the cash for my first and last modeling session and walked away with no aspirations of a regular paycheck in that line of work.

CHAPTER TWENTY-SIX

The Ides Of March

When I returned to Portland for the holidays, the garlic and red wine were at optimum aroma levels, but there was a void in our home. Pete and Patty were both married and gone, and Patty was pregnant with her first child, due in February. They did frequent the house, though, which gave me an opportunity to work my persuasive powers on Pete.

He'd been thinking about going back to Arizona for months now, and even though I was ready to hit him with a hardcore speech, by the time I started in on him, it didn't take much.

"Coach will set you up. You need to come back." I tried to convince him the first chance I got.

"Yeah?" was all he had to say in response. This let me know I could get to him quickly, which I did, and Bredehoft did set him up. He found Pete and his wife an apartment in Scottsdale, where they lived rent-free in return for managing the complex. Pete was reissued his scholarship, and we began wrestling for Arizona

State together again in January of 1964. Pete and Glenn McMinn hit it off as workout partners, and they would both begin their eligibility that fall, so there was ample time for Pete to work his way back into condition.

My brother (left) and me on the mat at ASU.

My studies continued to be oppressive, but somehow my grades were staying afloat just above the line to keep me wrestling; Bredehoft helped me out in the classroom, too.

By now I had learned he was masterful at working an angle in just about any circumstance. I was enrolled in a four-credit zoology class, my most difficult to date, and Bredehoft knew I'd been struggling to understand the coursework. To make matters worse, the four-hour lab conflicted with wrestling practice and in many cases with our dual meets.

"Hey, T, I got you some help in that zoology class of yours," Bredehoft told me after practice one day.

"That's great," I said. "I really need it." I had been worried for a while that I wasn't going to pass the class.

"Here's what you need to do," he said. "The lab TA is a judo guy, and he's training for a big tournament. He hasn't been able to win one yet, and he needs some tough competition to get ready."

I wondered what Coach was concocting.

"You just need to stay after practice a few days a week until his tournament to work out with this guy," he continued, like it was nothing. "In return, he's gonna tutor you in zoology. It's a great deal."

"Sure, sounds good," I said. I was willing to do whatever it took to make it through that class.

The first time the guy showed up, I stayed after practice to work out with him and asked Bredehoft how I should go about it.

"Just wrestle the guy; it's pretty much the same thing," he told me.

I watched this guy practicing some shadow drills, dressed in a Judogi with a black belt tied around his waist. Bredehoft called him over, and we faced off, each of us getting into our respective stance. I stood with my feet shoulder-width apart, knees slightly bent, back rounded with arms tucked in tightly to my sides, and my hands relaxed, reaching toward my opponent. His stance had his legs nearly straddled, knees bent slightly and pointing out, back straight, and arms up near his face, hands clenched into fists.

"Ready ... wrestle!" Bredehoft shouted.

I went in for a takedown on his legs, which were completely unprotected. He grabbed onto my shirt and tried to throw me, but I cinched up his legs and took him to the mat. I noticed Bredehoft watching with a smirk. "Nice," he said under his breath as I continued to pummel the guy in hopes I was giving him what he wanted for his tournament preparation.

Then all of a sudden, my judo partner squealed, "Time, time!"

"Break," Bredehoft called. "What's up?"

"I need to work on some specific moves," he whined to Coach. "He's not letting me get any of my holds in on him."

"Okay, T, you gotta let him practice his holds," Coach said, widening his eyes as if to tell me we better give this guy what he wants.

"Alright, I can do that," I said. We continued to work out, and I became his drilling dummy for the next few weeks; in return, he made sure I understood zoology. Coach Bredehoft had worked his magic once again.

The 1964 season was approaching an end. We had one dual left before the conference championships, and I was still planning to wrestle in the Olympic Trials qualifier in May. Our final dual meet was against our archrivals, the University of Arizona Wildcats, and Bredehoft had a new recruit on campus, Curley Culp. Curley stood like a Black giant, although if you were to actually measure him, he'd only come up to about six feet. His 285 pounds and lightning speed put him in the running for a combination football and wrestling scholarship. Bredehoft had given me the task of making sure Curley fell in love with Arizona State.

Curley may have been large, but he had a softness about him; his rounded face and little boy's smile could light up a room, and Coach wanted to sign him badly. Bredehoft turned up his enchanting powers to full tilt. He'd decided that the dual against the University of Arizona would be an outside show. He wanted standing room only in the crowd, and even though the event was on the last day of February, Coach found a way to drum up some drama. He had posters made and plastered around campus that stated:

"THE IDES OF MARCH ARE COMING! COME TO THE DUAL IN THE SUN, AND WATCH THE WILDCATS MEET THEIR DOOM."

He set the mats up right near the end of Palm Walk, making sure the Sun Devil wrestlers' chairs would be in the shade of some nearby trees. The Wildcats' chairs were positioned along the side of the mat with no trace of shade; they were getting full rays. It was springtime, so the Valley of the Sun hadn't hit fry-an-egg-on-the-sidewalk status just yet, but the mercury had been moving up to about eighty degrees. At three thirty in the afternoon, with no wind and the mat lying directly on concrete, it was hot.

The Wildcats' coach was out of his mind. He couldn't believe the antics Bredehoft was pulling. His guys were overheating, the mat was scalding, and, as far as he was concerned, we were cheating.

"Shady Brady!" quipped the opposing spectators more than once during the competition. I still had Curley by my side, and he was thoroughly enjoying himself amidst the mass humanity of the crowd, the battle between the Wildcats and the Devils intensifying with every match. He was loving every minute of it. I wanted to impress Curley with a pin, and I knew it would be possible against my opponent.

When I got ready to step out onto the mat, though, Bredehoft motioned me to move back and called one of my teammates out to wrestle my match. *What the hell?* I thought. The Wildcats' coach looked questioningly in my direction as I stepped back, wondering what was happening.

After the match got underway, Bredehoft called me over. "T, get ready. You're wrestling the next match," he said, keeping his eyes glued to the contest currently developing on the mat. "We need to beat this guy at 147, and I need you to do it."

I never questioned my coach, but this was ludicrous. I'd already cut hard to get down to 136, and why he wanted to switch things up at the last minute, I didn't know. ASU prevailed over the Wildcat opponent at 136, and I stood off to the side as the Arizona coach sent his 147-pound wrestler to the center of the mat.

"Get out there, T!" Bredehoft yelled.

When the U of A coach saw me run onto the mat, he lost it.

"Time-out!" he called, motioning to the refs with his hands.

The refs huddled around the Wildcats' coach. He was red-faced and spouting off, his suit jacket swinging back and forth with his arm motions, and all the while Coach Bredehoft just stood back, a cool character with his hands on his hips, taking it all in.

I waited for my turn to wrestle. My nerves were ratcheting up; I knew the guy was tough. He was the prior year's conference champion, not to mention ten pounds heavier than me, and I had an audience to impress today. Curley needed to see his mentor beat this Wildcat.

The refs got the Arizona coach settled back into his corner, and the whistle blew for the start of my match. As we faced off, my opponent reached across to my head with his hand, and instead of the common head tap and takedown attempt, he locked his elbow as if to hold my head still and keep me from executing an offensive move. The mat, softened to a marshmallow consistency by the sun, made it difficult to stay light on my toes, and when I tried to move, my feet sank straight to the concrete.

"Come on, T, let's see that takedown!" Bredehoft yelled.

Over the course of my time at Arizona State, Coach had named the takedown done in my specific style the "T Take-down." It was set up with an arm drag and then an inside trip, finishing as a double leg, and Coach got worked up every time I pulled it off. I was not about to let this guy control me by locking in on my head, so I threw my arm hard at his elbow to knock his hand off, then squeezed his tricep, cinching him in close and tripping him to the mat.

"There it is!" Coach yelled, clapping his hands wildly as my opponent fell to the ground. In an attempt to avoid back points, he turned in midair. Immediately, I heard the impact as his head blew straight through the inch and a half of soft canvas to the concrete.

I felt my fury unleash. This guy thought he could control me. I threw my forearm across the back of his head, pressing his face hard into the mat, inflicting as much legal pain as I could. The match carried on, a brawl, the scalding canvas like hot oil melting my skin, and in the end, the point spread was not wide but in my favor. When my arm was raised, I saw Curley stand up and cheer. I shook hands with the Wildcat across from me and noticed he had a nasty mat burn, his skin welted and crimson red, spanning his entire forehead.

My opponent turned, dejected, to meet a pissed-off Arizona coach in the Wildcats' corner. I turned to meet my coach in the Sun Devil corner, but he was already charging toward me. He was so excited he body-locked me around the middle and lifted me off the ground, above his head.

"Yes! You did it, T!" he yelled. "You did it!"

He'd caught me off guard, but I took in the moment, pumping my fists toward the screaming fans. As Coach set me back onto the mat, I grabbed him tightly around the neck—an embrace of gratitude for much more than just his confidence in me that day.

The Sun Devils prevailed over the Wildcats, and Bredehoft pulled off a spectacle unlike anything the collegiate wrestling world had seen to date. It would be the last time The Ides of March would be showcased in an open arena at Arizona State. Needless to say, Curley was hooked. He signed with the Devils in both football and wrestling, beginning a highly successful dual career. He was an All-American in both sports, an accomplish-

Starting in the down position against my Arizona Wildcat opponent during the Dual in the Sun. I was sucked down to 136 pounds, but Bredehoft wrestled me up at 147 pounds at the last minute.

An embrace from Coach Bredehoft after pulling off a win against a highly ranked opponent during the Dual in the Sun.

ment nearly unheard of on the collegiate stage, and went on to have a career in the NFL.

After the intensity of the Dual in the Sun, Bredehoft called me up. "T, we need to cook up some of your spaghetti," he said. "Get a hold of the guys and come on over. Susan will let us use the kitchen."

I went over to Coach's house before my teammates arrived and put my culinary skills to work in their kitchen. I'm sure Susan, Bredehoft's wife, was overjoyed. Her angelic face, petite frame, and white-blond hair were a one-eighty from the motley crew that would soon fill their home.

We all lit up with stories, each of us trying to top the next guy, all the while stuffing our faces with spaghetti and meatballs. This group had become my family away from home.

CHAPTER TWENTY-SEVEN

Olympic Trials

The Dual in the Sun marked the end of our regular wrestling season, but it was just the beginning of what was to come—a complete whirlwind in my life. Back in Portland, my sister had given birth to her first child, Anthony, and he became known in the family as "Little Tony." I was touched that Patty named him for her big brother, but I felt detached from the happenings at home and continued to focus on my post-season tournaments.

The Western Athletic Conference (WAC) Championships would be first, and they were held exactly two weeks after my battle against the Wildcats. At the conference championships in Laramie, Wyoming, I brawled my way through the 136-pound bracket and came out the 1964 WAC Champion; Buzz did the same at 147. We would be the only two Sun Devils to move on to the national tournament at Cornell University in Ithaca, New York, two weeks later at the end of March.

Buzz, Bredehoft, and I boarded a plane bound for Ithaca, and soon after we arrived, we found the wrestling room at Cornell.

With Bredehoft watching, Buzz and I rolled around, Buzz stuffed up like a rag doll trying to sweat off about two pounds.

"Hey," Coach yelled. "T, go do some sit-ups. I'll work with Buzz for a while."

I went to the wall to do some crunches. Coach weighed about 125 to Buzz's 150. I assumed Buzz would know to take it a little bit easy on Coach, but about twenty crunches in, I heard a crack, loud enough that it echoed off the wrestling room walls. I jumped up from my sit-ups to see Coach looking stunned.

"Ahhhhh!" he yelled, grabbing his eye.

"Oh man, I'm sorry," Buzz said in his Neanderthal way.

Coach was pissed, and I felt bad, but something about the whole scene was comical. Buzz and I had trouble not laughing every time we saw Bredehoft's blackened face for the remainder of that trip.

After winning my first match in the national tournament, I injured my clavicle in my second. When the match started, I took my opponent down and was hanging onto his legs trying to gain riding time points—points given for controlling your opponent on the mat for at least one minute. He suddenly fell flat to his stomach and got away with one leg. I held tight onto his other leg, which was a mistake. I should've let him go and taken him down because he suddenly mule kicked me in the collarbone, and I heard it crack. Coach stopped the match immediately, which ended up a loss for me as an injury default. I headed off to get an X-ray and my opponent, who wrestled for the Army, lost in the next round. Had he won, it would've given me a chance to return to the tournament, but because he lost, the rules at that time put me out.

I should have placed.

Buzz did well, coming just one match from placing. But there we sat on the plane flying back to campus, the three of us, beat-up.

Back at school, I focused on my studies to finish out the school year. I also worked on healing up my body. The Olympic Trials qualifier was in May, which gave me about a month and a half to recuperate. I needed to take first in my weight class at the qualifier to move on to the trials.

My brother was still working out hard with Glenn McMinn on a daily basis. McMinn was also planning on wrestling in the qualifier, and I knew when they both hit the lineup next season the Devils were going to be a force. Pete caught up with me before practice one day, frantic.

"Hey Tony, you need to call Ma!" he said.

"Why, what's going on?" I asked.

"I don't know, she just called the apartment screaming something about getting a letter and me being drafted," he went on nervously.

"What?" I questioned. "Okay, don't worry about it. Let me call her."

I'd told Pete not to worry, but I wasn't heeding my own advice. I knew of the United States' involvement in Vietnam, and it made me nervous.

I dialed home. "*Pronto!*" my dad answered on the other end.

"*Ciao! Sono Tony,*" I said through the line.

"*Ayeeee, Tony, che cosa vuoi?*" He asked what I wanted.

I got to the point. "*Pete mi ha detto che è arrivata una lettera a casa?*" Pete said a letter had arrived at the house.

"*Sì, sì, una lettera dall'Italia,*" he told me.

What, from Italy? I couldn't figure it out. "*Cosa dice?*" I wanted to know what it said.

"*Pete deve entrare nell'Esercito Italiano!*" he boomed into the phone. Pete has to go into the Italian army!

How can that be? I thought. With further explanation, I realized my brother had been drafted, not by the U.S. military, but by the Italian army. I couldn't believe it. I didn't know he hadn't become a U.S. citizen yet, and I had no idea what to do.

If there was one person who could sort this out and keep my brother from being deported to Italy, it was Coach Bredehoft. The man could figure out a way to take care of anything. It took much translating, a trip to the Italian government offices in Phoenix, and some letter writing by Bredehoft, but eventually, my brother was deferred from his obligation.

A newspaper article was printed in *The Arizona Republic* about my brother being drafted into the Italian army, and he is quoted as saying, "I hope to become an American soon." To that point, my mother and I were still the only ones in our family to have American citizenship. My brother and dad did gain theirs shortly after that incident, but I'm not sure if my sister ever did.

A group of us wrestlers hoped to win the upcoming Olympic trials qualifier, and Bredehoft was fully supportive of our endeavors. We flew to Wyoming, and the tournament was overwhelmingly tough, but I managed to win my way through, coming in first. Three of my teammates did also, and four of us moved on to the trials: Buzz Hayes, Glenn McMinn, me in freestyle, and Art Martori in Greco-Roman, a style of wrestling that consists of only upper body throws.

Bredehoft worked every angle to get financial backing for us to make the trip to Queens, New York. We'd be wrestling outdoors in the Singer Bowl Stadium, right smack-dab in the middle of the 1964 World's Fair. Dr. Frerichs, a local ear, nose, and throat guy, sponsored me directly, and the Tempe Touchdown Club also put money toward our trip.

Bredehoft had several more tricks up his sleeve to bring in money, including convincing the university to allow a stunt during a baseball game at Tempe Stadium. Bredehoft's plan was that his four Olympic hopefuls would be introduced before the game, and then we'd spend time mingling with spectators. The stunt? Three skydivers would jump from a plane just as it crossed over the field, attempting to hit the bull's-eye—the pitcher's mound.

As the stadium filled up, Coach called the four of us to the pitcher's mound, and there we stood, Bredehoft with a microphone in hand.

"I'd like to introduce four Sun Devil wrestlers who will be representing Arizona State University in the 1964 Olympic Trials!" he blasted to the crowd.

He listed our accomplishments from the previous season, and I listened to my teammates' glory—Buzz had something like forty-one consecutive wins this past season—but I was overwhelmed when Bredehoft got to me.

"This is Tony Russo," he said, putting his hand on my shoulder. "I like to call him 'T.'"

I smiled, and the crowd gave a chuckle. As he read my stats, which I'd never seen listed on paper before, I realized that except for the nationals in which I'd injured my clavicle, as a Sun Devil wrestler I'd won every single tournament to date. Coach emphasized my standing as a WAC champion, and it started to sink in that maybe I'd really accomplished something this season.

"These young men put in a lot of hard work," Bredehoft continued, with the rapt attention of the crowd, "wresting every night and nearly every weekend. And we'd like to encourage you to donate to their efforts and become a part of helping these outstanding young athletes reach their full potential. And now, look to the sky. We've got a great show for you!"

We left the mound and watched as the plane flew overhead, and sure enough, out jumped three skydivers. They pulled their chutes, but there was a rare wind that day in Tempe. Two of the skydivers barely hit the outfield, nowhere near the pitcher's mound, and the third skydiver missed the field entirely. Regardless of the botched stunt, Bredehoft still brought in a sizable amount of donations that day.

The semester had come to a close, and when grades came in, I was still above the 2.0 line, but, in the words of my own mother, you could squeeze my blood out of every single mark on that transcript. It was not easy. The four of us were training daily, and I could only go to Portland for a short time during the summer of 1964. It would be the first time in years I wouldn't be spending my summer in a meat market. I met the new addition in our family, my sister's firstborn son with whom I shared a name, but to my great disappointment, my sister was pale and had deep, dark circles under her eyes. She was still struggling.

After my quick week of catching up with friends and family in Portland, I returned to Arizona to complete my training. Glenn McMinn, my trailer-mate from the prior school year, had gotten married, so when I returned for the rest of my training before the trials that summer, Bredehoft had found a fraternity house for me to live in. Once it started, our training was all-consuming: at 6 a.m., a three- to five mile run; at 1 p.m., two hours of hard wrestling; and at midnight, another three- to five-mile run. We didn't do much weight training, if any, but we were in the best cardiovascular condition of our lives.

The fall semester started at the end of August, and we had to be pardoned from our coursework by the dean to be able to compete in the trials. Finally, just after classes got underway, three of us boarded a plane to New York. Art Martori, who would be competing in the Greco-Roman tournament, which started after ours, had decided to drive himself. Coach Bredehoft would not be with us, but he said he'd call every day for status reports and wire money if necessary.

Once the plane landed in New York, we were ushered onto a helicopter and flown to another airport. Whether we went from LaGuardia to JFK or JFK to LaGuardia I'm not sure, but after being jolted all over my fellow teammates en route, I was just thankful to have gotten off that helicopter with my life. We then boarded a tram to the Hotel Diplomat on West 43rd Street, and because the trials were sanctioned by the Amateur Athletic Union (AAU), we were grouped with other wrestlers from all over the nation and crammed into one hotel room. I quickly realized I'd be carving out a place on the floor.

The up-and-coming space age was the focus of the World's

Fair, with signs of that theme every way you turned, but the main focal point was a huge steel globe, the Unisphere, which stood out impressively above everything else. The Singer Bowl, where we'd be wrestling, was in Flushing Meadows, a venue for entertainment—again, like the Dual in the Sun, we'd be wrestling in an open arena. My weight class was loaded, and I didn't know how far I could go, but my plans were to go all the way.

The sights and sounds of New York started to stir up memories of my days there as a child. I felt a deep longing to reconnect with my relatives who had taken me in back in 1951. My revised plan was to win the trials and then sneak in a few days to seek out my family before the Olympic training camp began.

As wrestling got started, the mats were a familiar mush. It was overcast but humid, and to make matters worse, a fine layer of grime covered the canvas. Regardless, we were all in the same conditions, and as I wrestled each match coachless, not even my teammates there to cheer me on (they had their own matches to get through), my mechanics were clicking. At the end of the day, I found myself to be untouchable.

My teammates hadn't fared so well. The only other person left in the freestyle tournament was Buzz, but he hadn't made it through the day unscathed. Bredehoft called the hotel to check on us.

"I'm gonna wire you some more spending cash," he told us over the phone. "But only for the guys still winning."

Sure enough, he sent a hundred dollars to the Hotel Diplomat with a telegram reading "Buzz, $40.00; Tony, $60.00," and he added a message: "All the way now, tiger!" Bredehoft was big on rewarding a little bit more to those of us who were winning. It was just his way.

The telegram Bredehoft wired to the Diplomat Hotel during the Olympic Trials. I was awarded an extra $20 because I hadn't lost a match.

In scouting out the competition for my second day of wrestling, I realized there was a wrestler named Bobby Douglas winning his way through the bracket in my weight class. I'd seen him here and there at different tournaments, but we'd never matched up. My most immediate concern, though, was a wrestler who had recently finished well in my weight class at the national tournament in Ithaca. I knew if I made it to the semis, I wouldn't be expected to beat this guy. I didn't care.

With ten seconds left in the third round, the score was 0–0, and my opponent went in for a desperation throw. He'd gotten sloppy, and it gave me an opportunity to return the favor. I threw him to his back, one of his shoulders hitting inside the boundary line and the other just crossing over. I looked to the ref for his answer to my throw. No points. Just when I figured the match was going to end in a tie, the ref sitting off to the side acting as mat judge held up two fingers. I looked up to see the head official at the last second deciding to concur with the mat judge.

"That's two!" he yelled, and there I stood, the winner of my semifinal match in the Olympic Trials.

Between the semis and the finals, I took the opportunity to call Aunt Marie from the hotel.

"When I'm done wrestling, you need to come to the World's Fair. *La Pietà di Michelangelo è qui,*" I said in Italian for emphasis. "It's locked down behind glass, but you can see it. We could go together."

"*Costa troppo,*" was her reply. It's too expensive.

"We'll see." It was all I could think of to say.

Warming up for my final match, I met Charlie Tribble, a young man who would also be competing in the finals.

He came over to me and shook my hand. "Hey, Bredehoft's recruiting me," he said as I was trying to gain my focus.

"That's great," I told him. "You're gonna love Arizona State." I knew if we added Tribble to the lineup, with Curley signed on and my brother and McMinn rejoining the team, things were going to go well for the Devils.

I was having trouble focusing, and my mind was spinning; the demons were getting the best of me. My opponent was unfamiliar, my family couldn't afford to see the World's Fair, my coach was a million miles away. One disconnected thought after another.

As we squared off, I looked across at my opponent, Bobby Douglas: ferocious, angry, and chiseled from stone. At the whistle, I made an attempt at the "T Takedown," and in a whoosh I felt myself fly through the air, and smack, my head drilled right through the mat. The next six minutes were a blur. This guy was slick and monstrously strong, his brute force absolute. He was tearing me up.

At the whistle, signifying the end of the third round, my Olympic dreams came to an abrupt halt. I stood there, arms to my sides, blood dripping off my face, sweat and grime ground into every inch of my skin, and I came to the realization that I would not be representing the United States in Tokyo for the 1964 Summer Olympic Games.

While cleaning myself up and tending to my wounds, I thought about the phone call with my aunt and what she had told me. They couldn't afford the tickets to get into the World's Fair. I made a decision. I asked Art Martori, who still had his Greco-Roman matches yet to wrestle, if I could hitch a ride back to school with him when he was done. He was more than happy to oblige, so I cashed in my plane ticket and decided to bring my aunt and her family to the fair.

Aunt Marie and my now grown-up cousins came to experience the 1964 World's Fair with me, and we did see Michelangelo's *Pietà* while riding a conveyor belt as it sat in lockdown behind glass walls. Even so, it was awe-inspiring.

They were grateful to experience the fair, and in saying our

*Enjoying the World's Fair in Queens, NY, with my aunt Marie
and cousin Connie after my final match in the trials.*

*Posing in front of the Unisphere at the World's Fair
with my aunt Marie and Cousin Connie.*

goodbyes, I sent Aunt Marie home with some of the cash left over from my ticket exchange.

Shortly after Bobby DeFrancisco had made his way to Portland my senior year in high school, so did his mother Lucia, whose fried egg sandwiches had made such an impression on me during the tornado that defined my first year in this country. Uncle Mike had since passed away, so this left only one more family member still in town for me to reconnect with, and that was Pasquale Mozzariello. My time with him in New York had been the shortest stay of all, but I can still picture myself on that stool, head enveloped in steam as I washed pots and pans in the kitchen of his father's Brooklyn restaurant.

Now, sitting on the patio of Pasquale's new home, I thought about my parents in Portland and how far we'd come since leaving Italy. As we barbecued steaks and drank red wine, raising our glasses in a toast, I realized I had come full circle.

Pasquale Mozzariello and his wife.
I was able to meet up with him during the Olympic
Trials. I hadn't seen him since my short stay with
the Mozzariellos when I first arrived in the States.

CHAPTER TWENTY-EIGHT

The Mission

The demons caught up with me when I returned home from the Olympic Trials, and I fell into a deep depression. The letdown was tremendous, not only from my loss in the finals, which was devastating, but also from the high of my 1964 season to my reentry into the classroom. I was overwhelmingly behind, even with the dean's pardon.

A realization of the lack of direction in my life hit me. Combined with hearing from my parents of the troubles at home with my sister, I couldn't make sense of anything. For the first time in my life, I was lackadaisical in the wrestling room, not caring if I worked hard or not. I was completely unfocused and couldn't put my finger on why. And for some reason, I couldn't shake it.

I packed my bags, ready to head back to Portland. And I was going to just up and leave. No need for goodbyes.

Somehow, Coach Bredehoft caught word of my decision and knocked on my dorm room door at 6:30 a.m. the day I was planning to take off.

"Come get some coffee with me, T," he said, glancing at my bags, packed and against the wall.

"Sure," I replied quietly. I could never say no to my coach.

We sat together at a counter in the diner at the Sands Motel, Coach studying me. We were the only two people there.

"I know you're hurting, T," he said, "but let's put this in perspective. All this you're experiencing is nothin' compared to what you've persevered through up to now."

I answered him with a nod of my head, realizing he didn't even know how right he was.

"I tell you what," Bredehoft continued. "You are gonna be my first recruit in this program to earn a degree. I'm gonna make sure of it!" He hit the table hard with his index finger.

"I don't know," I said, shaking my head.

"Well, I do know. And I've already told you, you're gonna be a coach. You will make an excellent coach," he said, looking me square in the face.

Coach Bredehoft believed in me and further showed his faith by making me team captain the following season. Even when I was down, he stuck with me, and when I needed extra time over the summers to get my coursework completed, he made sure it happened. When I took kinesiology and physiology, Bredehoft told me outright, "The only way to pass those classes is to memorize the material, T. That's it." And that's what I did.

I lived up to Coach B's expectations and pulled myself together, reevaluating my goals, and for the next three years continued as an integral part of the Sun Devil wrestling team.

There was only one time when Bredehoft was not happy with me. He never once yelled at me, and almost every match I wrestled ended with a hug or at least a handshake from my coach.

HEADED FOR THE TOP — *Looking like strong contenders for this year's No. 1 NCAA ranking, coach Ted Bredehoft and his undefeated grapplers are geared for a rough schedule ahead. Pictured left to right, kneeling, Tony Russo and Glenn McMinn; standing, Charlie Tribble, Coach Bredehoft, and Curley Culp. The four wrestlers are all defending WAC champs in their divisions.*

Heading into my 1965 season.

There was one dual meet on the road when I was having trouble making weight, and I made the dim-witted decision the night before to take laxatives to help shed the extra two pounds. My body didn't respond. I just figured the stuff didn't work for me.

The next day, literally a minute before my match, my stomach started to gurgle. I was completely panicked, knowing there was not enough time to make it to the restroom and back. The ref couldn't have started my match quick enough, and all I could think of was ending it. I went in for a throw, and my opponent went flying. I cinched him up and heard the slap of the mat.

After my hand was raised, I flew by Bredehoft, not stopping for our ritual hug, and I could see the look on his face. He was hurt. The next day, just as we boarded our plane back to Phoenix, Bredehoft motioned to me. "T, come over here for a minute," he said.

I headed in Bredehoft's direction and looked at my coach questioningly, although I knew what he was about to say.

"We aren't gonna do that anymore," he said sternly. He'd somehow found out about my idiotic weight-loss plan.

"Yes, Coach," I promised. And although I did have some crazy weight-cutting strategies over the years, I never pulled that stunt again.

Sure enough, I did become Coach Bredehoft's first recruit to wrestle four full seasons and earn a degree. I graduated with a Bachelor of Arts in Physical Education and Health, and Bredehoft set me up with a student teaching gig at a private school called Phoenix Country Day School. They'd never had a wrestling program; I taught PE and headed up their brand-new wrestling team.

Coach Bredehoft's Dream Team, 1965 Western Athletic Conference champions. Back row, left to right: Glenn McMinn, Pete Russo, Buzz Hayes, Tony Russo, Coach Bredehoft. Front row: Art Martori, Lloyd Ek, Charlie Tribble, Curley Culp.

Dr. Frerichs, who had sponsored me during my Olympic endeavors, had two sons at the school, and he was gung-ho to have them excel in the sport, so much that he wanted us to travel far and wide as a team to get as much experience as possible, and we did. We slowly started winning matches.

At this time in Portland, my sister's life was still going in the wrong direction. Patty had given birth to her second child, Johnny, who was now a toddler, and she was unable to care for him. My parents had taken on Little Tony, her firstborn, but they couldn't handle the two boys, and I made a trip to Portland to pick Johnny up.

During my 1963–64 season at Arizona State, amidst the whirlwind of wrestling, our team trainer somehow set me up on a blind date with his girlfriend's friend who had just moved to Arizona.

"She's Italian," he said. "She just moved here from Connecticut."

Constance Kathryn Caserta (a.k.a. Connie) was a quiet, sweet-hearted, beautiful young woman. She was perfect, but the blind date was a disaster. I ate all the pizza, my chivalrous manners not anywhere near being fine-tuned. Somehow she saw past the deficits in my social graces, and after three years of dating we were married at St. Joseph's Catholic Church in Phoenix.

Connie and me on our wedding day.

Our first child, Tonya, was born in 1968. We named her after me—Tony with an "a." When she was born, we were still caring for my sister's son Johnny. He had a gentle demeanor and enjoyed playing, especially outside in the Arizona sun. He now had a tricycle we purchased used that my in-laws helped us paint a shiny red, and he liked to ride around in the front driveway. He fit right in and looked as if he could be our child with his olive skin and jet-black hair. He was very attached to us, although I could sense that he deeply missed his mother. I wished things were better for Patty so that he could be with her. Taking care of Johnny resonated with me, and I would do anything to help my family, just like Uncle Tony and Aunt Gladys did for me.

To complicate matters even more, I also had a Weimaraner pup by the name of Rocky. He was, of course, named for the great boxer Rocky Marciano. One of my wrestlers came to me after practice one day and said, "Hey Coach, my dog had puppies! You can have one for free."

His mom was a Weimaraner breeder, and she wasn't sure if these pups were purebreds, so she was giving this litter away. "You can have the pick of the litter," she told me when I showed up to "look" at the puppies. I've always had an affinity for dogs, and I couldn't say no.

Needless to say, things were hoppin' in our home, and unfortunately, Phoenix Country Day School was barely paying the bills. We were eating dinner at my in-laws' home on most weekends, and we filled our fruit basket from the orange tree in their yard. We didn't have health insurance, and my wife was left exactly $800 when her grandmother passed, which paid the hospital bill for Tonya's birth.

Dr. Frerichs had become a true friend along the way and supported us when we needed it most. One night the baby woke up screaming, and my wife and I ran into her room to find a nightmare scene with blood spread all over her face and her crib. She was teething and had bitten a chunk out of her tongue. I called Dr. Frerichs immediately, and even though it was the middle of the night, he had me bring her over, and he cauterized her tongue right then and there at his home.

Even though money was tight, I was enjoying my job, and we were starting to gain momentum as a team. We were headed into the last dual meet of the season, and if we won it, we would become the private school league champions. The match was a showdown, and it came down to the final matchup. I had taught all of my athletes the "T Takedown," and sure enough, my wrestler went in for a shot, took his opponent to the mat, turned him over, and pinned him.

It was exhilarating. In two years, the squad at Phoenix Country Day School went from zero to league champs.

As the school year was winding down, one of my students stayed after class and announced, "My dad wants you to come over for dinner."

I knew his dad was of Italian descent, had played football for ASU, and had recently opened a physical therapy clinic near St. Joseph's Hospital. My wife and I took the kids to my in-laws and went for dinner. Over bread and lasagna, he asked me to work for him.

"It's a great career," he said and mentioned that it would pay at least triple what teaching and coaching paid.

I was intrigued and took the time to research it; the pay would have been excellent, and I was surprised to find out that because

... In a Coach's Life

TONY RUSSO of Phoenix Country Day School displays almost as much activity from the sidelines as does his young wrestlers on the mat. With all this enthusiasm, he should have won the tourney—but PCDS finished dead last. (SUNfotos by Eric Lundberg)

*Coaching for Phoenix Country Day School.
In spite of losing this tourney, we won several
dual meets. The very next year we won almost
every dual and were crowned league champs.*

I had passed kinesiology and physiology, I only needed a few more classes at ASU to get certified. But I could not budge my inner drive to continue as a coach in the sport of wrestling, and for me, somehow all roads led back to Portland.

I still yearned to be with my family; my brother was already there coaching at Newberg High School, and he had already won a state championship. I wanted to join the ranks of those coaches, so I reached out to Coach Hiebert, my coach from

David Douglas High School, and he started putting the feelers out for me. I received a job offer at a high school in a town on the Oregon coast called Warrenton. I asked them for twenty-four hours to think about it. My gut told me it wouldn't be a good fit for my young wife, and we now had a new baby boy as well, Pete, named for my brother.

My squad at Phoenix Country Day School.

The next afternoon, I got a call from Hillsboro High School. Hillsboro is in the Portland metro area, and I accepted right away. I'd be coaching freshman football and freshman/sophomore wrestling. Those students were in a different building across town from the juniors and seniors—it was something new they were trying, and they called it a mid-high school.

We made plans for the move. I was to drive my wife's Mustang with Johnny and my dog Rocky, and my wife would fly with our young children, Tonya and Pete.

The drive did not go well, to say the least. Johnny slept most of the way but still needed attention, and Rocky needed to run. After driving all day in the Arizona heat, the belts on the car started squeaking, and we broke down in a small town at dusk. I was trying to transport the weights I used for working out, and that was not a good idea, as it put a huge strain on the car. Luckily, there was a service station still open with a mechanic who was able to replace the broken belts and get us back on the road.

Eventually, we rolled into the driveway at my parents' house on 118th Street in Portland. The house was bustling, and the

Our home in SE Portland. My parents would live here for fifty-plus years.

smell of red wine and garlic was familiar. My mom was at the stove as usual, and my dad was enjoying a glass of his favorite red wine at the table. We were all together again in Portland.

At this point, I was driven, and I had set out on a mission—a mission to give back to the sport of wrestling. I wanted to help kids who might be struggling in life like I had—kids who might not be cutting it in the classroom. I wanted to help those kids excel.

I knew if I could sell them on the sport of wrestling, if they were willing to work hard, and if they were willing to develop the mindset of a champion, great things could happen.

CHAPTER TWENTY-NINE

The Return

Nearly thirty years since the day I stepped foot on the SS *Independence* in the Bay of Naples, I boarded a plane in Portland, Oregon, to return to my homeland for the first time. In tow were thirteen of the most talented young wrestlers the state of Oregon had to offer, and one of them was from my own squad. I'd been elected by a vote of my peers as part of the Oregon Cultural Exchange Wrestling Program, set up by legendary coach Dale Thomas, to head up an all-star wrestling team that would spend one month in Italy.

Although born and raised into my preteen years in that beautiful country, I never knew of its splendors, and other than that fateful day in the city of Naples when I received my passport, I had never ventured outside the walls of the two small towns I knew best, Roccarainola and Cicciano. Now I'd be able to fully experience what lay outside.

When we arrived, the Italians put us up in a state-of-the-art

Olympic training facility in Livorno, and they'd bring in their best teams to dual with us. After the first few days, I realized they expected us to experience Italy from within the facility walls, and I knew these kids had come much too far to allow that to happen. I hopped a train to Rome by myself to meet with the head of FILA—the international governing body of wrestling. He knew more about soccer and volleyball than he did about wrestling, and we had trouble communicating in my Neapolitan and his standard Italian, but I eventually got it across to him that these kids needed to experience the culture. He agreed to give us enough money for the train, and I made a phone call to my Uncle Aniello, my mom's brother in Rocca, and explained what was happening.

It took him all of about thirty seconds to decide that his family—my family—would take in the entire team. The train ride to Naples with thirteen high-school wrestlers was an adventure in itself, but we made it. And unbelievably, the home I was born in was now my uncle's residence, and it remained unchanged, as did the small piazza I had played in as a child. The bundles of sticks like those Grandma Nappi had gathered when I hung from her skirt were still stacked on the flat roof of our brick oven, where the women continued to bake their hard-crusted bread. They were still doing laundry with a tub and washboard outside, an activity in which the athletes participated firsthand with their smelly gear.

They were also learning the custom of not eating a large American breakfast. One of my cousins mentioned to me that the wrestlers were asking for *pancetta e uova*, bacon and eggs, in the mornings. I had to explain to them, "Hey, they do things differently here, and you need to adapt. You're in their country and need to follow their rules." Espresso and biscotti in the mornings it was.

The Oregon All-Stars learning firsthand how to do laundry the old-fashioned way in the piazza of my hometown in Italy.

My friend Michele was still there, too, living in the same place, and when we met again after thirty years, the first words out of his mouth, of course, were, "*Ti ricordi quando hai ucciso l'uccello?*" Remember when you killed that bird?

"Yeah, that was crazy," I laughed, the memory of it fresher than I even knew.

My dad had joined us on the trip also; this would be a chance for him to reunite with friends and family. He was placed at the head of the table for every meal, and in our piazza he joined in the song and dance with his tambourine, partaking in his

Reunited with my cousin, Basilio, and best friend, Michele, at the top of the stairs my father climbed while I was making my debut into the world. The little girl in front is Nunzia, Basilio's daughter.

Our piazza in Italy. My dad is in the middle playing the tambourine. You can see the bundles of sticks on the roof of our brick oven like the ones Grandma Nappi used to collect with me in tow.

*My family in Rocca with my dad at the head of the table
during our trip to Italy with the Oregon All-Stars.*

favorite red wine and singing at the top of his lungs. He knew every occupant of both small towns. We couldn't get five feet down the road without stopping to have a full-on conversation when the passerby realized Aniello Russo was back in town. He'd always spout off after a glass or two of his beloved drink that someday he was going to retire in Italy.

At our next dual, which was to be held at a training facility in Naples, the family caravanned as a group to watch the match. They had become quite attached to the Oregon all-stars who were sharing their homes, and they filled the entire top row of the grandstands. Some strife arose when their fellow Italians realized these people had the audacity to be rooting for the Americans. My uncle talked his way out of a fight by explaining that these boys were guests in their homes, and his nephew was their coach. It all ended amicably.

A tournament in Naples with the Oregon All-Stars. My family caravanned to watch the wrestling, and they took up the entire top row of the stands. My uncle Aniello nearly got into a fight when the Italians took offense because my family was rooting for the Americans.

Our trip to Italy was an immersion into a different world for these athletes, but it was more than that. They became family. Leaving after our short month was heart-wrenching. The goodbyes were rough, and there wasn't a dry eye in sight, even amongst the athletes.

In a piazza in Florence with the Oregon All-Star team. A pigeon landed on my finger.

My Uncle Aniello would become an ambassador of sorts. Because of the great work he did during our trip, he became the guide for the following year's team. The team from Oregon, headed up by Greg Strobel, a three-time All-American from Oregon State University, encountered some struggles because of a conflict with the AAU—Amateur Athletic Union. The Italian teams were warned not to compete against the Oregon group, so the trip became more of a sightseeing tour, and Uncle Aniello became their tour guide.

He and Greg Strobel became fast friends as my uncle, even with his limited English, had a charismatic personality and could win over the masses like none other. He had always longed to come to America, so much so that his nickname in Italy was

Americaniello—the Italians have always been well-known for their nicknames. It would be Greg Strobel who helped arrange a visa so that my uncle could come visit the States.

He landed in Portland in 1980, fittingly, during one of the eruptions of Mount St. Helens. It didn't bother him in the least, as he was used to living in the shadow of Vesuvius. Uncle Aniello was able to visit his siblings in Portland, and it would be the first time he'd seen his brother Tony in forty years.

Since stepping off that ship as a young boy, to my dismay, I still haven't witnessed any trees blossoming with gold. Still, over the years, I've learned that, back when I was barefoot, working on our leased farmland and dirty from head to toe in my beloved countryside, or wracking my brain to learn something in school, my mother's words rang true: "You have to work hard. And if you do, good things will happen." And it was the sport of wrestling that helped guide me to this realization.

CHAPTER THIRTY

The Program

At the onset of my stint coaching the cultural exchange all-star team to Italy, I had nine years under my belt at a high school in Southeast Portland called Centennial. I was awarded the head wrestling coach position there in 1971 after a short time in Hillsboro coaching at the mid-high school. I was more than ready to start my own program and implement my own coaching ideas and strategies.

My wife and I found a wonderful home within walking distance of the school, and we now had a third child we named Trista. Three children in three years kept us more than busy, and I was also still working as a butcher during the summers at various grocery stores and on the weekends.

My garage had become an in-home butcher shop, and I cut mostly sides of beef, deer, and elk. My business was marketed solely by word of mouth from friends and family, and it helped supplement my teaching and coaching income.

When I started at Centennial, I worked with "athletes" who were unwilling to give up their smoke breaks, but I stayed the course and started implementing my coaching strategies anyway. I recruited wrestlers from every which side of that high school, and our numbers felt solid. Our first match was coming up, and I was pumped as were my coaches. My main assistant coach had devised a scouting and stats system where he would use a tape recorder so as not to have to write anything down, and he was excited about it.

We arrived at The Dalles High School, our opponent's gym for my first match as a varsity head coach. Once the introductions were done, the first two wrestlers ran out to the center of the mat to shake hands—the 98-pound weight class. The whistle blew, and our Centennial wrestler immediately took his opponent down, turned him to his back, and pinned him. The crowd went wild, and my coaching staff and I lost our minds. We were jumping up and down, ready to see the rest of the dual continue in this fashion.

My assistant coach pulled out his tape recorder and started excitedly dictating the match into it. We were thrilled and sat down for the beginning of the second match. It did not go our way, and unfortunately, our losing streak continued for the rest of that dual. My coaches' plan to speak into the tape recorder waned with each match as we got annihilated by The Dalles wrestling team.

I left there thinking maybe I was wrong about my goals and my mission to become a coach--I questioned everything.

The next morning I made a promise to myself on my way to school that I would *never* get beat by another team in that way again.

And I never did.

In my nine years at Centennial, we worked our way up to winning a district title and placing in the top five at the state level. And we weren't the only athletic program at Centennial doing well. They were a force in all sports, having won a recent state championship in football with coach Don McCarty. Centennial had a special camaraderie among its staff. Teachers, coaches, and administration alike supported one another. We were a unified group, and I had become an integral part of the Centennial community. I had no intention of going anywhere.

CENTENNIAL WRESTLING COACH Tony Russo and Eagle grapplers express obvious joy after watching teammate Tom Hewitt roll to a surprising 16-3 decision over Gresham's Ken Carter in Thursday Wilco League dual action. Centennial recorded victories in 10 of 13 matches to take a one-sided 48-20 win over the Gophers.

Cheering after a victory for one of our wrestlers while coaching for the Centennial Eagles.

One night at home, during dinner with my family, the phone

rang. It was a parent from Newberg High School named Victor Gerth. His booming voice came over the phone, "Hey there, Coach, we're tired of losing over here at Newberg, and we wanna get you out here!"

His words slapped me across the face, and the only response I had at the moment was a nervous chuckle.

He continued, "We've seen what you've done over at Centennial, and we remember our winning days here with your brother, Pete. Why don't you come have dinner on us? There's some people I'd like you to meet."

I told him I was happy where I was but agreed to meet him for dinner. In the meantime, out of curiosity, I called over to Newberg Schools and inquired about any job openings. There were none. In fact, the principal, Mr. Ray Simonsen, was adamant: "There are no teaching positions open in PE, Mr. Russo." His voice had a military finality to it.

I drove out to Newberg anyway, since I had agreed to meet with Mr. Gerth, and we met at J's Restaurant, a local diner. When I walked in, I saw a whole group of booster club parents. Mr. Gerth headed them up, and his rotund look perfectly matched his booming voice.

"Hey there, Coach, I'd like you to meet the boosters." He named them one by one, and we shook hands all around.

Dinner was served, and over burgers and fries, Mr. Gerth proceeded to ask me my philosophy on building a successful wrestling program. I started talking.

"Well, you start with a youth program for students in first through sixth grades. This is an integral part. And it needs to be something that becomes a part of the community." I saw the parents nodding their heads. I went on to talk about fundamentals, positive reinforcement, and keeping it fun. "Everybody's a winner. They all go home with a ribbon."

From the looks on their faces, I could tell I should continue, but before I could, one of them shouted out, "I've got hundreds of 'kid wrestling' T-shirts in the back of my store." He was the town pharmacist, and he explained that they had previously had a kids program, but the most recent coach dropped it.

"That's great," I exclaimed. "You can use those. You also need a club program for kids in fourth through eighth grade who want to get more experience. This is where we can start to develop championship mindsets."

I could tell they still liked what they were hearing, and one of them said, "We've got a great junior high school wrestling program here."

"That's perfect," I replied. "These are all opportunities for athletes to compete at different levels and to learn about the sport before they get to high school. We want them hungry when they get to high school, though, so we can't burn 'em out. Fun and encouragement is the key."

At this point, I began to understand that Mr. Gerth had brought me in for an "interview" with his cohorts. As the evening wound down, I mentioned that I had found out from Mr. Simonsen that no teaching positions were available in Newberg.

"Don't you worry about that," Gerth retorted.

Again, the only response I could think of was a nervous chuckle on my way out the door.

I returned home, ready to dig in and continue my work at Centennial, but the phone wouldn't stop ringing. Almost every night around dinner, to my wife's chagrin, booming on the other end was Mr. Gerth. My wife was beginning to question all this as she knew there were no positions open. Either way, Mr. Gerth was becoming a friend.

Then, one day, it was a different voice—Mr. Ray Simonsen, the principal at Newberg High School. "Mr. Russo," he said, "I'd like to bring you in for an interview."

It threw me as he had adamantly told me there were no open positions. I didn't question it and scheduled the interview.

When I walked into the main office at Newberg High School, Mr. Simonsen greeted me and led me into his office. He was tall and striking, wearing a freshly pressed suit, and he carried himself like a boss. All those around him knew it. He'd been an athlete in his own right during his high school and college years.

In his office, only one other person was present. His name was Dan Lever, and he had been the head football coach and my brother's assistant wrestling coach during his years at Newberg.

"You know," Simonsen said as I sat down, "we win a state title in wrestling about every five or six years."

"I hope it doesn't take that long," I replied.

He chuckled. "Well, we won one with your brother in '70, as you know. And we won a title in 1953 with Earl Gillis. Gillis brought the program back after the war. There was no wrestling here from 1941 to 1945 because all the athletes were enlisted."

Then Mr. Lever chimed in. "We also won a title in 1957 when Art Keith was coaching. We've got a strong tradition in the sport of wrestling, and we'd like to bring it back."

Simonsen started up again. "The boosters seemed to like your ideas on how to implement a successful program. Can you share some of that with us?"

"Yes, I can," I said, then paused for emphasis. "You need a kids program." I went over the same plan for a successful program that I had shared with the boosters during our dinner.

"We happen to agree with you, Mr. Russo," Simonsen stated when I finished.

"That's great," I said. "But you mentioned that you didn't have any teaching positions available."

Simonsen cleared his throat. "Well, some things have changed. We're starting an adaptive PE program for kids with special needs, and we're gonna need a teacher. You need five class periods to be considered full-time."

"That's great," I replied, but Simonsen interrupted again.

"For now, the position is only one class period per day," he said.

I knew I needed to make it clear that I could not leave my current position to coach wrestling in Newberg if there wasn't a full-time teaching spot open.

"I just need to say, I can't leave Centennial unless ..." I paused.

"We understand, Mr. Russo," Simonsen said. "I've thought about that. You'll teach one class of adaptive PE per day, and then you're gonna team teach with the other PE teachers for two classes per day—our classes are huge. That gets us three periods. Then, you're gonna monitor the cafeteria for two class periods, and that gets us up to five classes per day which is full-time."

"That sounds good," I replied, already thinking that I could use the time in the cafeteria to recruit wrestlers.

I went home from the interview and told my wife about the plan that was presented to me. The offer felt a little shaky, but I couldn't get over the idea of moving to a smaller town where wrestling already had a strong tradition and support.

My wife and I agreed to give it a go. She fell in love with a house in Newberg, and one of the boosters I met with for dinner worked for a trucking company. He called me and said, "I can bring over a truck." It seemed like the next thing I knew, he was pulling up to our home in Southeast Portland with a semi. We filled it with everything we owned and headed out of town.

Our new home sat on a large lot, but I hadn't scoped out my garden yet. We very quickly met one of our neighbors, Elaine Cole, an elderly woman who lived in a 1940s bungalow right next door, and her backyard was long and narrow and paralleled my yard. She only used about a quarter of it, which contained an old and very prolific apple tree. When I told her I was going to put in a garden, she said, "Why don't you use the back of my yard, and in return, you can make me an apple cobbler." I had no idea what an apple cobbler was, but I decided to figure it out because the back half of her yard was perfect for my garden.

She ended up being the very first schoolmarm in Newberg and had taught in a one-room schoolhouse. Over apple cobbler (I figured it out with help from my wife) Elaine told me story after story about her students. She seemed to know everyone in town, and I started realizing many buildings and streets were named after the people in her stories. By the end of summer, she had beaten me in rummy more than a dozen times. "You need to learn my version of the game," she'd tell me. I would laugh and tell her she was right. But I knew she was always going to beat me in rummy. We had become fast friends.

When the school year started, I found myself on a tour bus with the rest of the new teachers. As we drove around town, we learned that Newberg was the church and nut capital of the U.S.

I'm not sure how accurate those stats were, but it sure seemed like there was a church on every street corner, and as we continued to pass filbert orchards and farmland, I felt at home.

I began to realize that the camaraderie among the staff that I had at Centennial High School was nowhere to be found at Newberg. It hit me that I was hired a bit unconventionally and was not being well received by the existing staff.

I focused on the job at hand, building a successful wrestling program. That started with building my coaching staff. There was already an assistant coach, Jim Conway, but I needed a freshman coach, and I received a call from Marlin Grahn, the head coach at Portland State University. He said that he had a wrestler who had just graduated with a degree in education with a focus in biology, and he was champing at the bit to become a coach. Newberg happened to have a biology opening, and Dan Williamson was a perfect fit.

Between the coaching staff, the athletes, and the parent group, we had created our own world, and Newberg wrestling was becoming a cohesive and united community within the school and also within the town. Now I was ready to start winning competitions.

Just before our first dual, Mr. Simonsen called me into his office.

"Hello, Mr. Russo, take a seat," he said in his assertive tone. "Hey, I hate to break it to you, but you've got a wrestler who is ineligible for competition."

My mind was racing. *How could I have an ineligible wrestler this early in the season? Grades haven't even come out yet,* I thought.

"He's one of your freshmen," Simonsen continued.

I looked at him questioningly. Now I was even more confused. *How could one of my freshmen athletes be ineligible?*

"You're not gonna believe this, but last year's coach entered him in a high school tournament as an eighth grader. I guess he didn't think anyone would find out. But you know the OSAA (Oregon School Activities Association)—they found out."

"Who is it?" I asked.

When Mr. Simonsen said the name, I nearly fell off my seat. He was one of the best wrestlers on the team, freshman or not, and had an incredible career ahead of him. His dad was one of our biggest supporters; the one who brought his truck out to Portland for my family's move to Newberg, and the OSAA was threatening to take one year of eligibility away from this athlete for the stunt his coach had pulled. I knew Simonsen was just as dismayed as I was.

Simonsen filed a protest with the OSAA, and they went back and forth. It was not easy, but he came out the victor. That was a good sign for me; one, my administrator had gone to bat for a student-athlete, and two, he had gone to bat for me. I knew it meant there were good things to come for us in Newberg Wrestling.

And good things did come. My first season ended with the Newberg Tigers being crowned league champions. And although I wanted it faster, Simonsen had been right; it did take about five or six years to win a state title. And then they just kept coming. With all facets of my program now in place, we had depth. We won seven state titles within ten years.

My 1986 State Championship team. The Tigers of Newberg set a record with the most points scored to that date in a state tournament.

The juxtaposition of life is sometimes cruel, and circumstances for my sister did not become any better. During the high of winning my first state title, I lost my sister, her tiny body unable to withstand the years of self-inflicted punishment. She left behind five children, and they may never fully understand the sacrifices their mother made in our family's quest for a better life. It was a devastating loss for our family, and my mother never recovered from losing her daughter. In her mind, we could've done more.

My parents would both retire, after thirty years, from the same companies that had hired them in our first weeks of moving to Portland. They were loyal to their jobs, their family, and their friends. They were never looking to strike it rich—anything above what we'd had in Italy was worth a million dollars to them. Long before their retirement, they owned their home outright; it had been added on to and had become a neighborhood gem, the yard bursting with rhododendrons, roses, shrubs, fruit trees galore, and my father's bountiful garden.

My dad's garden in the backyard of our SE Portland home.
He's six feet tall, and his tomatoes are taller than he is.

To this day, when I see an umbrella with the ShedRain tag, I think of the piecework my mother did, the long hours we all put in helping her thread needles, and the essential role that work played in the hard-earned success we found in America.

Aunt Gladys and Uncle Tony, the people who saved me from my tumultuous days in New York, would eventually separate, and Aunt Gladys moved the kids across the country. Cousin

Joey ended up having a successful high school wrestling career at a New Jersey high school, and although he did not become a doctor, he came close—an optician, filling prescriptions for eyeglasses. We remain close friends to this day.

Throughout my time at Newberg, our state and national recognition brought with it many honors, such as Oregon Wrestling Coach of the Year, All Sports Coach of the Year, and Oregon Wrestling Classic Man of the Year, and during those years I was nominated for National Coach of the Year. But the honor that carries the most meaning is Newberg's national recognition in the category of most individual state champions.

The championships are outstanding, but the honor lies with every single competitor. Every time a wrestler goes into battle and steps off the mat, win or lose, and they've given everything they had, there is no loser. There are only gains.

In wrestling, as in life, recovery is key. You must recover from one battle and prepare for the next. It is never over. Respect is built around those battles. I have seen a crowd cheer for ten minutes for both competitors. Maybe only one hand was raised, but they had given their all and left everything on the mat, and this makes both individuals winners.

That is the beauty of the sport of wrestling: a team sport yet also an individual sport, and nobody knows better than those who have been in the arena—the gift to the individual from the sport of wrestling.

COACH TONY RUSSO

Coach Russo is celebrated as one of America's most successful high school wrestling coaches. With over 30 years of coaching experience—19 of which were at Newberg High School—he established a remarkable legacy. Under his guidance, the Newberg High School wrestling team achieved 7 Oregon State Championships and 17 District Championships, along with 7 Oregon Classic Championships.

Tony coached 92 district champions, 46 state placers, 24 state runners-up, and 22 state champions, with 5 of his wrestlers earning High School All-American recognition. His coaching record at Newberg stands impressively at 318 wins, 38 losses, and 1 tie. In 1986, he received the title of Oregon All-Sport Coach of the Year, followed by the Oregon Wrestling Coach of the Year award in both 1987 and 1991. In 1994 he was named the Oregon Wrestling Classic, Man of the Year. The nation took notice when he was nominated for National Coach of the Year in 1987 and *Amateur Wrestling News* ranked the Tigers of Newberg 2nd in the nation.

His significant contributions to wrestling were honored in 2003 with an induction into the National Wrestling Hall of Fame, where he received the Lifetime Service to Wrestling award. Tony Russo's inspiring coaching legacy is an enduring influence on high school wrestling in the state of Oregon and across the nation.

RECIPES

Looking back at the book to find the first time food was mentioned, I realized it was almost immediately. The first mention appears in the third sentence of the first paragraph: "The gathering was complete with thick, hard-crusted bread, salad made from tomato and onion fresh from the earth, and my family's drink of choice, red wine."

Food is a common thread throughout this story and plays a significant role. When I first arrived in the U.S., I couldn't get used to the smell or taste of American foods, as they were completely foreign to me. However, when my family arrived in the States, they brought many of our traditions from Italy.

In Italy, every day at 1:00 p.m., the entire town would shut down for lunch. That was our biggest meal of the day and also a time of connection with family. We wouldn't eat dinner until about 8:00 p.m., and it was mostly a light snack. Even when we didn't have much food, this was how it played out. And the amount of work that went into preparing food was immense—most times, it was an all-day affair, and if there was bread to be made, the day started before dawn.

When food was scarce, we would forage and get creative to elevate plain ingredients from our leased farmland, like boiled potatoes, beans, and greens of all varieties, which were usually mixed with pasta. Loaves of hard-crusted bread baked in our outdoor oven would be cut lengthwise and topped with chopped tomato, basil, and garlic, then drizzled with olive oil and sprinkled with salt (a meal in itself). These all made for nutritious and filling dishes.

Preserving foods became an art form. My mother jarred tomato sauce, along with eggplant and roasted peppers preserved in olive oil. She also dried the porcini mushrooms we hunted on Mount Hood. In Italy, we preserved meats as well—salamis, prosciutto, and sausage—and when I became a butcher, I was often given steaks and meat to take home that didn't quite make the cut for the butcher case. Of course, we always complemented everything with my dad's homemade red wine.

The following recipes have been made in our family for years and are some of my favorites. We continue to re-create them, sometimes adding a new twist here and there. I hope you enjoy them as much as I do!

TOMATO, POTATO, AND ONION SALAD

Serves 4-6

My family ate this dish while the midwife assisted in my birth at my home in Roccarainola, Italy, in 1940, and I have eaten it every summer and fall since. The dressing, made of olive oil, red wine vinegar, and oregano, elevates the flavors of the three basic ingredients.

Ingredients

6-8 medium to large tomatoes (any garden variety will work)

6-8 medium potatoes, any variety

2 medium or 1 large onion, any sweet variety

1 tablespoon dried oregano

1/2 cup red wine vinegar

1/3 cup Extra Virgin Olive Oil

Salt

Directions

To make the dressing, combine 1/2 cup red wine vinegar, 1/3 cup olive oil, and oregano. Salt to taste (about 1/2 teaspoon).

Boil the potatoes until barely fork tender, then chill immediately in an ice bath. You do not want to overcook them. Slice the potatoes into rounds.

Cut your tomatoes into wedges.

Slice your onions julienne style.

Toss tomatoes, potatoes, and onions in a large bowl. Pour the prepared dressing over the salad and toss again—the juices from the tomatoes will become part of the dressing.

You can serve this salad immediately or put it in the refrigerator and let the flavors meld for a few hours before serving. It's even better this way!

Notes:

You can make this salad based on what you are harvesting from your garden. If you don't have potatoes, make it with just the tomatoes and onions. If tomatoes are not in season, make it with potatoes and onions. Also, you can use any variety of potatoes, tomatoes, and onions. This salad is so versatile. One thing to note is that the oregano is the principal seasoning in this dish. Don't add basil (except for decorative purposes on top); you don't want anything to compete with your oregano. You may need to adjust the amount based on the type of oregano you use. To plan ahead, you can boil your potatoes in the evening and refrigerate them when they have cooled. You can then pull them out and assemble your salad quickly and easily the next day.

Lastly, this salad will not have the same flavor made with store-bought tomatoes. If you must use store-bought, purchase Romas, tomatoes on the vine, or even sweet cherry or grape tomatoes.

BRACIOLE

Serves 4-6

When my grandfather, Giuseppe Casoria, was able to raise a pig, we were all required to help with the butchering. Not one part was wasted; even the blood was preserved. My job was to cut larger pieces of meat into smaller ones to grind for sausages and salamis. This job assigned to me as a child foreshadowed my job as a journeyman butcher as an adult. During the times we had the shared pork, I always asked my mom to make braciole. She would use thinly sliced steaks or even the pig skin at times. In the States, she used beef, either flank steak or any thin steak she had.

Ingredients

4 thinly sliced steaks, pounded flat

1 cup breadcrumbs

1 cup Parmigiano cheese

Ingredients (continued)

Garlic, approximately 1 clove per steak
1 bunch Italian parsley
Tomato sauce
Salt and pepper

Directions

Mix breadcrumbs, cheese, parsley, and chopped garlic in a large bowl.

Make sure your steaks are thinly sliced and pounded flat.

Lay each steak out flat, and season each side with salt and pepper.

Top each steak with some of the breadcrumb mixture.

Roll your steaks and tie them with butcher string.

Brown each rolled steak on all sides in olive oil. Then, simmer them completely covered in your sauce for 1-3 hours, depending on the size of your steaks.

Remove from the sauce, untie, and slice into rounds. You should see a nice spiral of the breadcrumb mixture when sliced.

Top with more sauce and Parmigiano.

Enjoy!

Notes:

You can make a pasta side dish to use the rest of your sauce.

PASTA FAGIOLE

Serves 6-8

Pasta fagiole is a family specialty. My mother made it regularly. It is a delicious and nutritious meal and even better served with a piece of hard-crusted bread.

Ingredients

2 cans cannellini beans, approximately 14 ounces each

4-5 celery stalks, chopped

3-4 carrots, chopped

1 medium to large yellow onion, chopped

3-4 cloves garlic, finely chopped

2 cans cherry tomatoes, approximately 14 ounces each

1 tablespoon oregano, or to taste

Ingredients (continued)

1-pound package of any small-shaped pasta—Mista Corta (short mixed) is the official pasta used for pasta fagiole in Naples, but any will do.

Salt

Directions

Rinse the cannellini beans in a colander and set aside.

Sauté the chopped onions, celery, and carrots in Extra Virgin Olive Oil with a bit of salt.

Once they are cooked down, mix in the garlic. Once the garlic is fragrant, add the cannellini beans and heat through. Take the pan off the heat so as not to overcook.

Boil your desired pasta in salted water for about 2 minutes less than the package instructions. This will prevent it from overcooking.

Once done, transfer the pasta to the pan with the beans, celery, carrot, onion, and garlic mixture. Then, mix in the cherry tomatoes with juices, oregano, and some of the pasta water. Bring up the heat to get everything nice and hot, and add salt to taste.

Enjoy immediately!

Notes:

We usually eat this in a thick, hearty style, but you can make it as thick or "soupy" as desired with extra liquid.

RIGATONI—LIGHTLY SAUCED

Serves 6-8

The pasta was always the star of our dishes. It was never drowned in sauce and always al dente. Make sure to always salt your pasta water, and one trick for al dente pasta is to boil it for about 2 minutes less than the package suggests.

Ingredients

1 16-ounce package rigatoni (or any pasta you like)

1 onion

2-3 cloves garlic

Extra Virgin Olive Oil

1-2 quarts tomato passata (strained, puréed tomato sauce)

2-3 leaves basil

Salt

Parmigiano

Directions

Chop your onion and mince, or finely chop your garlic.

Cover the bottom of a sauté pan with olive oil.

Add your onions to the pan and add a dash of salt. Sauté until soft, then add your garlic.

Once your garlic is fragrant, add the tomato passata and 2 or 3 leaves of fresh basil to the onion and garlic mixture. Bring it up to a medium-hot simmer to get it hot and bubbly, and then turn your heat to low and simmer until the desired thickness is reached.

Once your sauce has reached the desired thickness, bring a large pot of water to a boil, making sure to salt your water.

Once boiling, add your pasta and cook for about 2 minutes less than the package instructs. The pasta will continue to cook when removed from the water, and this way, you'll end up with perfectly al dente pasta.

When done, remove the pasta from the water (do not rinse), place it directly into the sauce, and toss to coat. Then, remove the sauced rigatoni and place it in a large family-sized pasta serving bowl. If there is still sauce in your pan, you can keep it warm on the stove for those who would like to add a little more to their dish.

Top with Parmigiano and serve immediately. Enjoy!

MEATBALLS

Serves 6-8

The Italians never measured. They just dumped in a generous amount of all these ingredients. Also, they never used store-bought bread-crumbs. They used what they ate regularly, the loaf-style homemade or bakery bread. They would soak it in milk and then squeeze it out for the meatballs. Now, we freeze our day-old Italian bread in cubes and then use the food processor to grind them down for this recipe. You can add more or fewer of these ingredients to your liking. Lastly, this recipe is made with ground beef and pork, but you can also add ground veal to the mix.

Ingredients

1 pound ground beef

1 pound ground pork

2 large eggs

Ingredients (continued)

1 cup breadcrumbs

1 cup grated Parmigiano cheese

4 cloves finely chopped garlic

1 bunch fresh Italian parsley

3/4 to 1 cup milk

1/4 teaspoon salt

1/2 teaspoon ground black pepper

Directions

Mix your breadcrumbs, cheese, garlic, parsley, salt, and pepper. Then add your milk and let the breadcrumbs soak it up. Finally, mix in the 2 eggs and then add the meat. Combine all the ingredients and form into golf-ball-sized meatballs. You can roll yours bigger or smaller as desired. Align on a cookie sheet and bake in the oven at 400 degrees for 15 minutes or until done. You want them to be caramelized on the bottom and have some color on top.

Serve and enjoy!

CHILLED BROCCOLI SALAD

Serves 6-8

When this salad was prepared in Italy, it was simply made with boiled, then chilled broccoli, fresh lemon juice, garlic, and olive oil. Garnished with lemon slices, it made a simple yet striking presentation on the table. It wasn't until my family arrived in the U.S. that we started adding the olives and marinated peppers—those ingredients take this dish to another level. They add a depth of flavor and make for a beautiful color combination. This salad presents as a fabulous antipasto platter, and it is best when the flavors are given time to meld in the refrigerator.

Ingredients

3-5 bunches of broccoli

1 medium to large jar mixed olives

1 medium to large jar roasted red peppers

Ingredients (continued)

1 medium to large jar sweet cherry peppers, seeded and rinsed

Juice of 1-2 whole lemons

Extra Virgin Olive Oil

Salt

Directions

Cut off the hard bottom part of the stems, then boil the broccoli in salted water until just fork tender. Drain it in a colander with cold water to stop the cooking process.

Cut the broccoli lengthwise into long spears all the way down the stem. Arrange the broccoli in a deep-set platter. Squeeze the juice of 1 to 2 (depending on your taste) whole lemon(s) over the broccoli.

Layer your olives, roasted red peppers, and sweet cherry peppers (seeded and rinsed) on top of the broccoli. Be pretty generous with the juices from the jars, as these add to the flavor. Drizzle with Extra Virgin Olive Oil.

Leave the salad in layers; do not mix. Chill in the refrigerator overnight or for 4 to 8 hours to blend the flavors.

Use a large serving fork, making sure to get some of each layer onto your plate. Enjoy!

Notes

You can be as creative as you like with this salad and add more or less of each ingredient. This salad is vegan, but you could also add any variety of Italian salamis and cheeses.

PIZZAIOLA STEAK

Serves 4-6

This is one of my absolute favorites. It's basically steak cooked in pizza sauce. My mom would cook and slice up the steak, hollow out a mini loaf of her bread, and put the steak inside to make a sandwich. Of course, it was topped with Parmigiano cheese.

Ingredients

Steak, 1 per person you are serving (Depending on size, adjust the number. Use thinly sliced sirloin steak gently pounded down. You can also use strip loin, beef tenderloin, flank, or round steak.)

Extra Virgin Olive Oil

Garlic, approximately 4 cloves

Ingredients (continued)

1 whole onion, any variety

Oregano, about 1 tablespoon

White wine (optional)

Salt

1 large can of San Marzano tomatoes, or you can also use a high-quality store-bought or home-preserved tomato passata.

Directions

Gently pound the steaks until they are about 1/4" to 1/2" thick.

Season the steak with salt and pepper.

Add oil to your frying pan, and when hot, sear the steaks on both sides. Remove the steaks and set aside.

Sauté the onions until browned and softened. Once they are done, add the garlic and stir until fragrant.

Add approximately 1/4 cup white wine (this is optional but definitely adds to the flavor).

Add tomatoes crushed by hand and oregano and cook for 15-20 minutes—season with salt to taste.

Add the pan-fried steaks and juices to the tomato sauce and cook for about 15 minutes. Depending on your tastes, you can also cook it for longer.

Notes:

To use the extra sauce, you can serve a pasta side dish, or we like to serve this with the roasted rosemary potatoes.

ROASTED POTATOES WITH OLIVE OIL, ROSEMARY, AND SEA SALT

Serves 4-6

We often ate boiled potatoes, which were dressed in various ways or added to different dishes. This is a simple and delicious side dish to add to any meal and is much healthier than french fries served in a restaurant.

Ingredients

4-6 medium to large potatoes (russets work well, but you can use your favorite potato variety)

3-4 sprigs of rosemary

Extra Virgin Olive Oil

Sea salt

Directions

Preheat oven to 400 degrees.

Peel and cut your potatoes into wedges. You can cut them however you'd like, but this way, they turn out like nice, thick steak fries.

Coat them in olive oil, then strip your rosemary and toss it in. Sprinkle with a bit of sea salt to taste and toss.

Lay them out on a baking sheet with parchment (don't overcrowd) and bake at 400 degrees for 30-40 minutes. You can turn them over once they are golden brown on the bottom or turn the broiler on high and finish them off for about 10-15 minutes, watching closely.

Enjoy!

FOCACCIA BREAD

Serves 4-6

Ingredients

4-6 tablespoons Extra Virgin Olive Oil

2 1/4 teaspoons active dry yeast or 1/4 ounce packet

1 cup warm water

2 1/2 cups all-purpose bread flour

1 teaspoon fine sea salt

1 medium onion, sweet variety (optional)

Salt to taste

Directions

Combine the yeast, salt, and warm water in a large bowl. Let stand until the yeast is dissolved, about 5 minutes.

Add one tablespoon of olive oil and stir in.

Gradually add 2 1/2 cups flour, gently folding in with your hands until a ball is formed. Add more flour if necessary. The dough will be slightly sticky.

Coat dough with olive oil and place in an olive-oil-coated bowl for rising.

Cover and set aside to rise for 1-2 hours or until doubled in volume.

Optional: While your dough is rising, slice or chop your onion and sauté it in olive oil on low heat until caramelized.

Place parchment on a cookie sheet and brush the center generously with olive oil. This is where you'll place your dough.

Once the dough has risen, punch it down, and then, with your fingers, spread it out onto the oiled part of the parchment-covered cookie sheet, starting from the center and working your way out until it's about 1/2 inch thick. It will not reach the sides of the cookie sheet. Form whatever shape you'd like with the dough, and make sure the top is also coated in olive oil.

Cover with plastic wrap and set aside to rise again for an hour.

Once risen, press fingers into the dough to make deep dents, and then drizzle olive oil over the top.

Optional: Add caramelized onions or any topping you'd like.

Bake at 425 degrees for 25-30 minutes or until golden.

Remove from oven and enjoy!

AGLIO E OLIO *and* PASTA E PISELLI

My mom referred to the following two pasta dishes, Aglio e Olio and Pasta e Piselli, as *pasta bianco* or white spaghetti. Both are simple, delicious, and easy to make with just a few ingredients.

SPAGHETTI AGLIO E OLIO

Serves 6-8

Ingredients

1 pound dried spaghetti

1/2 cup Extra Virgin Olive Oil

6 cloves garlic, finely chopped, minced, or thinly sliced

Ingredients (continued)

1/2 teaspoon crushed red pepper flakes (adjust to taste)

1/4 teaspoon fine sea salt (adjust to taste)

Grated Parmigiano

Instructions

Add 1/2 cup olive oil to a cold sauté pan.

Finely chop, mince, or thinly slice your garlic, and then add it to the cold olive oil in your pan along with your red pepper flakes.

Turn the heat on medium-low to slowly extract the flavors from the garlic and red pepper flakes into the oil. Don't let the oil get too hot; remove it from the heat when the garlic is fragrant. Do not let it burn.

Cook the spaghetti in boiling salted water. Remove it about 2 minutes before the suggested time.

Add the spaghetti to the pan and toss it with the oil mixture. Turn the heat to medium-high and add approximately 1/4 cup of the starchy pasta water. Note: If enough water is transferred when you transfer the spaghetti to the oil mixture, you won't need to add as much water.

Bring your heat up to a hot simmer until the flavors meld and the water and olive oil are absorbed to your liking.

Sprinkle 1/4 teaspoon fine sea salt over your spaghetti and toss again. You can also add more red pepper flakes to taste.

Add grated Parmigiano cheese and serve immediately.

Enjoy!

PASTA E PISELLI

Serves 6-8

Ingredients

1 pound ditalini or other small-shaped pasta (small shells work great for this dish)

1/2 cup Extra Virgin Olive Oil

4-6 cloves garlic

1/4 teaspoon fine sea salt

1 package, approximately 10-16 ounces, frozen peas (or fresh!)

1 cup grated Parmigiano

Cracked black pepper

Instructions

Add 1/2 cup olive oil to a cold sauté pan.

Finely chop or mince your garlic, then add it to the cold olive oil in your pan.

Turn the heat on medium-low to slowly extract the garlic's flavor into the oil. Don't let the oil get too hot; remove it from heat when the garlic is fragrant.

Cook the ditalini in boiling salted water for 2 minutes less than the package directions.

Remove your pasta with a wire strainer or pasta spoon and add it to the garlic and olive oil with approximately 1/4 cup of starchy pasta water. Stir together. Note: If enough water is transferred when you transfer the ditalini to the oil mixture, you won't need to add as much water.

Add the peas and stir all ingredients together again.

Bring the heat up to a hot simmer until the water starts to absorb to your liking.

Add 3/4 cup grated Parmigiano and continue tossing, getting everything nice and hot.

Remove from heat, add another 1/4 cup of grated Parmigiano to the top, and add freshly cracked black pepper.

Add salt if needed, but be sure to taste because the Parmigiano is salty.

Serve immediately. Enjoy!

NOTE TO READER

Don't Cry in America is a result of years of extensive interviews with my father about his journey to America from Southern Italy, his incidental gateway into the sport of wrestling, and the hard-earned success he found that would eventually lead to his induction into the National Wrestling Hall of Fame.

Anyone who knows my father can attest to his motivational spirit and charismatic personality. He has always captured those around him with his animated way of telling a story. Thus, it made the most sense to write this book as a first-person narrative in my father's voice, starting at the beginning.

Regarding the Italian dialogue, the Russo family speaks Neapolitan. Although most of the dialogue has been written in standard Italian, there is some Neapolitan included as well.

All events contained herein are written as they were remembered by my father. Every attempt was made to accurately depict names, locations, dates, and other information pertinent to the story. In some instances, names have been changed. –Tonya Russo Hamilton

ACKNOWLEDGMENTS

Thank you to Caerus Kourt for your outstanding design work on both the cover and interior. Jane Ryder, I truly appreciate your wonderful sense of humor, valuable feedback, and ongoing support throughout this journey. To Amy Cecil Holm, thank you for your seamless editing and deep understanding of the narrative. Lastly, a heartfelt thank-you to Dr. Ilaria Serra for your inspiring words and the incredible dedication you demonstrate in highlighting the stories of Italian immigrants.

ABOUT THE AUTHORS

Antonio "Tony" Russo has been teaching and coaching in the state of Oregon for over thirty years. He was born in Roccarainola, Italy (a province of Naples), in 1940 and immigrated to the U.S. alone at the age of ten in 1951 with just the shirt on his back and salami and provolone cheese in his suitcase. Antonio graduated from David Douglas High School in Portland, and eventually, he went on to graduate from Arizona State University. Tony was presented with the National Wrestling Hall of Fame's Lifetime Service to Wrestling award in 2003.

Tonya Russo Hamilton is a teacher and author in the greater Portland area. She enjoys traveling and volunteering in her local community. Additionally, she serves on the Board of Directors at Italian Portland, a charitable nonprofit organization that provides Italian cultural programming, events, and opportunities in Portland and beyond.